Rahim Taghizadegan
Ronald Stöferle
Mark Valek
Heinz Blasnik

AUSTRIAN SCHOOL FOR INVESTORS

Austrian Investing between Inflation and Deflation

The Austrian School of Economics is as relevant as never before. The present work observes and describes the bubble economy of our days, analyzes the underlying monetary policy of the central banks and makes aware of possible investment philosophies.

It is also about historical recollection. The future is uncertain, unambiguous predictions cannot be provided. The Austrian School's perception helps us to see long-term patterns and opportunities that today are often hidden.

I wish all readers an exciting journey of discovery, especially those who have to deal with the task of sustainable and value-based investments. For the authors and their important work I hope for the well-deserved success and the widest possible audience of a bestseller.

H.S.H. Prince Philipp von und zu Liechtenstein,
Chairman LGT Group

mises.at
info@mises.at
© 2015 scholarium
Translation: Heinz Blasnik
Proofreading: Douglas Moser
Typesetting: Gerald Kalb
Cover design: Fanny Springer
Original title: Österreichische Schule für Anleger

ISBN: 978-3-902639-33-2

Table of Contents

Preface 9
Introduction 12
1. The Austrian School 17
    Subjectivism 23
    Marginalism 25
    Individualism 31
    Realism 37
2. The Illusion of Prosperity 41
3. Forecasts and Prophecies 59
4. The Monetary System 77
    What is Money? 77
    The Paper Money Era 96
    The Money Supply 100
5. Monetary Tectonics 107
    Inflation 107
    Deflation 111
    Tectonic Pressure Build-Up 113
6. Business Cycles 131
    Undistorted Production Structure 131
    Reorganization of the Production Structure 134
    Capital Structure 138
    Distorted Production Structure 141
    The Cantillon Effect 153
    The Skyscraper Index 156
7. Scenarios 165
    Hyperinflation versus Hyperdeflation 165
    Stagflation 173

    Financial Repression and Compulsory Levies............................178
    Special Drawing Rights as a Global Currency 182

8. Austrian Investment Philosophy 187
    The Morals of Saving 188
    Profit and Interest 194
    The Problem with Debt 207
    Hoarding 212
    Investing 220
    Consumption 227
    Endowment 232
    Speculation 237
    A Philosophical Portfolio 240

9. Austrian Investment Practice 245
    The Permanent Portfolio 251
    Precious Metals 257
    Stocks 280
    Analysis 292
    Bonds 305
    Mutual Funds 318
    Alternative Investments..325

Conclusion 347

Endnotes...354

Authors 364

Preface

What would Ludwig von Mises make of QE and ZIRP? Would Friedrich von Hayek be able to make sense of FOMC or ECB policy statements? What would these giants of the Austrian School and their cohorts think of hedge funds, ETFs, mutual funds and the array of other assorted investment vehicles? Would precious metals fit into an Austrian template superimposed on the present day investment world? How will the spread of government into all aspects of the private sector be ultimately resolved? The answers, in some cases obvious and in other cases complex, require an understanding of Austrian economic thought which is all too absent in modern investment discourse or media commentary.

What passes for economic wisdom in the casino like financial markets of the 21st century emanates from the conceptually flawed drumbeat of Keynesian analysis reconstituted into senseless quantitative aggregations of historical data extrapolated into future outcomes. The prevalence of economic illiteracy evident in the constant eruptions of supposedly learned PhDs infects both public policy and investment thinking alike. These deeply rooted afflictions distort valuations and investment flows and suggest there is an inherent unsustainability for the complacent status quo.

Analysis grounded in Austrian thinking has been remarkably accurate in separating illusion from reality. It provides a sensible, highly accessible big picture of view of what exists and what is likely to happen as a result. That is because it portrays economic activity and likely developments as the product of individual behavior, a common sense and practical framework. It does not employ abstract groups or forces that are somehow quantified and correlated by unintelligible formulas, a methodology that succeeds only in explaining the artificial reality that it has created.

The challenge for the modern reader is first to become acquainted with the basic precepts of Austrian economics. These are well explained in the following pages. For many the exercise will seem like learning a new language, a testament to the corruption of thought and perception that is evident in the mainstream financial media and educational system. Whatever the struggle, the result will be clarity of thinking and a removal of confusion.

The Austrian analytical framework is not a prescription for short term investment success or even a pathway to building a fortune. There is no such magic here. However, it does provide a foundation for sanity in the midst of mass delusion. It is grounded in ethical behavior, common sense, and sober reflection. The Austrian investment approach eschews leverage, promotions, and fads. It is likely to steer one away from disastrous investment outcomes through a balanced approach to wealth preservation. In short, the Austrian methodology is based on reality, not fancy, and its application in daily practice will provide an investor with favorable odds to achieve financial well-being.

This book is the result of extensive research. It is a compilation of wisdom from many sources filtered by Austrian economic thought. It is a highly relevant contribution to a complex world that cannot be understood in simplistic terms. It covers a broad range of topics ranging from macro to micro economics, from history to current events, from theoretical to practical, and from general to anecdotal.

The financial markets of today are dominated by hyper active high frequency trading guided by trend following quantitative algorithms. Original thought is replaced by artificial intelligence. Market prices are manipulated and gamed by institutional and political interests. Valuations are inflated by the zero interest rate policies of all central banks for whom it is dogma to drive up the prices of paper assets to

Preface

influence the behavior of individuals and corporations to achieve their announced goals of full employment, moderate inflation, and financial market stability. Financial wealth has become an illusion that has little resemblance to real wealth. Financial wealth is dependent on the functionality of a matrix that must be navigated according to its unique rules that are often at odds with common sense. For those who fear that the functionality of this matrix is unsustainable, The Austrian School for Investors offers a path to the kind of critical thinking that will provide sustainability for its practitioners long after the demise of the artifice of paper wealth.

John Hathaway, Senior Portfolio Manager of Tocqueville Gold Fund

Introduction

Confusion and uncertainty with regard to investing have rarely been as pronounced as they are today. On the one hand, we are living in an era in which wealth can seemingly grow to incredible heights. On the other hand, there are always rumors of crisis – a dark premonition that security prices could collapse at any moment, and the savings of a lifetime could be decimated overnight. Although official data show only moderate inflation, in some cases even deflation, many people feel that their currency is continually losing value. Most of them suspect that they should give a bit more thought to preserving the value of their savings, but are faced with contradictory advice. Trust in "experts" is declining, whether they are economists, bankers or politicians. If someone dispenses investment advice, he wants to make money from it – just as everyone seems eager to make money from retail investors.

It is difficult for investors to do the right thing, but incredibly easy to make a mistake. The current economic environment seems like a game with marked cards, with the odds of winning systematically stacked against the multitude of small players. One gets the impression that it is all a giant rip-off.

This book does not introduce a new investment fad, it is not an advertisement for a new investment product and not an ideological program. It aims to make knowledge that is highly useful in dealing with the questions of our time but has been unjustly forgotten, available to the average investor. It is based on the research of an economic school of thought that has only in recent years slowly been rediscovered by the broader public, because it was once again proved to be prophetic. In the history of ideas, this tradition is known as the "Austrian School" or the "Viennese School of Economics". Engaging with the Austrian

Introduction

scholars of yesteryear is tantamount to being inoculated against all sorts of illusions. The Austrian school makes clear why the so-called "orthodox" perspective on the economy, savings and investment borders on irresponsibility. While the Austrian School definitely offers a kind of therapy, it is not a ready-made miracle cure, but rather a thorough program in disillusionment helping to activate one's own mind.

Why should investors of today study an old and possibly outdated theory of economics? Is that not tantamount to a waste of time, or even misleading? Does it provide a crystal ball, or a secret recipe for higher returns? Indeed, there is some evidence for both and the evidence is astonishing and seemingly paradoxical. This is because the Austrian School, like no other school of economic thought, categorically rules out that theoretical forecasts can be made based on past data. Most adherents of the Austrian School regard the models of modern economics that claim to represent expert forecasts as the work of quacks, unless the models simply serve as illustrations or mental tools. Moreover, most theoreticians are not good investors, something that also applies, and sometimes to an even greater extent (if for a good reason), to representatives of the Austrian School. Nevertheless – and this may actually be quite surprising – several of the greatest forecasters of their time were adherents of the Austrian School. Their foresight often proved downright spine-chilling.

In terms of practical application, Austrian theory has also left its mark. Two of today's most famous investors are testament to this: Warren Buffet's father was strongly influenced by the Austrian School and passed important insights to his son. George Soros' longtime partner and most important analyst Jim Rogers is also an Austrian School adherent. Benjamin Graham, Buffet's teacher and mentor, developed a methodology that shows astonishing parallels to the Austrian School's ideas, although Graham actually was not aware of it. Lastly, the Austrian School originated when its founder Carl Menger, who worked as an economic journalist, came to realize by observing activity on the stock exchange in great detail that classical economics was unable to explain the real world.

Introduction

High returns can never be obtained – at least in the long term – without exposure to commensurately high risk. The only long-term path to high returns consists of sustainable capital accumulation through entrepreneurship. The theories of capital and entrepreneurship are the greatest strengths of the Austrian approach. However, this approach cannot be employed without first embarking on the difficult road to disillusionment. The Austrian School is utterly useless for "system dorks" – i.e., those who blindly follow majority opinion and are constrained by the exigencies of the present. This is also the reason why the school is not more widely known; its insights are generally considered uncomfortable.

To begin with, the practice of Austrian investing requires theory: *theoría* was the term used by the ancient Greeks for what they considered the highest form of practice, namely critical reflection. It is no coincidence that the terms "crisis" and "criticism" have the same etymological root. Times of crisis as a rule exert a positive effect on the ability to reflect. The Austrian School was established and has matured amidst the most severe crises of the 19th and 20th centuries. Austrian economists were the world's leading crisis experts: they had a close-up view of stock market bubbles, recessions and severe depressions, hyper-inflation episodes, economic and political decline, dramatic geopolitical upheaval and two world wars.

Times during which the monetary system was impaired were always times when monetary theory made great strides, as Friedrich Hayek remarked.[1] In times of crisis, the enduring value of the Austrian School comes to the fore. It is no great feat to make money during a boom – it practically self-multiplies. Good investors differentiate themselves from bad ones in times of crisis. The most famous recent example of an investor who succeeds in times of crisis is probably Nassim Taleb, who is clearly influenced by the Austrian School. His long-term partner and even more successful investor, Mark Spitznagel, has written a book on "Austrian" investing as well.[2] A book that, although penned by a practitioner, is far more theoretical and philosophical in its approach to the topic than this book.

Introduction

The necessary process of reflection demands nothing less than a radical rejection of conventional investor perspectives. Anyone who has decided to read this book in the hope of being able to jump on a new trend or to be provided with a few tips and tricks to make a fast buck is going to be disappointed. Although the typical speculator will certainly not be left entirely empty-handed, this book will pull the rug out from under today's dominant illusions and that may prove painful. This book came into being at the academy *scholarium* in Vienna (scholarium.at), where the authors met. Rahim Taghizadegan is one of the last representatives of the Austrian School of Economics in Vienna and is an interdisciplinary theoretician; Ronald P. Stöferle and Mark J. Valek are two professional investors who have founded an investment fund in Liechtenstein, which incorporates the insights of the Austrian School in its investment strategy. This combination of theory and practice led to many fruitful debates at the *scholarium*, followed by joint courses and finally this book. A number of people from the scientific staff at the institute have lent a helping hand in its creation, Raphael Schaad, Johannes Leitner and Andreas M. Kramer in particular. Michael Schmidt assisted us with the topic of value investing, and Harald Steinbichler on the treatment of the 'distressed bonds' asset class. We want to express our sincere thanks to all of them.

This book is to date the most comprehensive attempt at a critical examination of today's investment universe from the perspective of the Austrian School and deriving conclusions for investors from it. To this end, we frequently move back and forth between theory and current practice. The difficulty of connecting these two worlds will become clear to the reader as the book progresses: the relationship between taking the time for slow and deliberate reflection and the pressure and urgency that characterize investing in financial markets under distorted and volatile circumstances.

1. The Austrian School

Ever since news of crises began to dominate the headlines of the financial press a number of years ago, the reputation of economists has suffered grave damage. After all, the dynamics that have dictated events since then were a complete surprise for most economists and economic journalists. Willem Buiter, professor at the London School of Economics and former chief economist of the European Bank for Reconstruction and Development, concluded after the crisis that the research approach of mainstream economists had at best consisted of "self-referential, inward-looking distractions":

> Research tended to be motivated by the internal logic, intellectual sunk capital and esthetic puzzles of established research programs rather than by a powerful desire to understand how the economy works – let alone how the economy works during times of stress and financial instability. So the economics profession was caught unprepared when the crisis struck.[3]

The loss of reputation resulting from this was necessary and unfortunately did not go far enough: the majority of economists continues to mislead in an attempt to defend the little prestige of their presumed science that remains. Although most people suspect that the forecasts and models of economists are largely unrealistic pseudo-science, they have not yet drawn the correct conclusions.

On the other hand, as an economist, one must deplore the loss of reputation, as the views of a small group of economists were actually quite accurate, and a realistic science of economics is urgently needed, especially today. One of the few economic schools whose adherents were not revealed as an incompetent bunch, is teaching such a – in the

1. The Austrian School

words of its founder – causal-realistic economic science: the so-called Austrian School. It was not named after today's Republic of Austria, but owes its name to the fact that once upon a time, many of Europe's leading economic scientists were based in Vienna and attained international renown with their accomplishments. At the time, economics was one of several still young scientific disciplines that experienced significant progress. Unfortunately, today's mainstream economics has actually regressed in many respects relative to the insights discovered at the time.

What makes the Austrian School special? It came into being in an environment that seems distant to us on the one hand, but also quite close on the other. The Vienna of yesteryear represented the most prominent divide between the old order and modernity. As a result, an especially focused and critical view of modernity emerged. It is no coincidence that almost all fields of modern science were strongly influenced in Vienna. For a brief period in history, Vienna was the global center of science and culture. The Austrian School of Economics was born during this period and took its place amongst many other Viennese schools of thought, among which there are three different schools of psychology, a school of logic and epistemology (the Vienna Circle), of music, ethics, ethology, medicine and quantum physics, etc.

The modern era was an age of ideologies. The social and economic sciences in particular did not remain unaffected by this. As a result, Austrian School adherents attempted to study economic phenomena in a value-free manner. Of course they did not always succeed in completely ignoring their own values; that would not have been sensible anyway. The most important proponents of the Austrian School were all "classical liberals". At the time, this meant that they supported individual liberty and were keeping a wary eye on the trend toward totalitarianism. Classical liberalism was essentially dying out at the time – one can rightly call Ludwig von Mises the last great representative of classical liberalism in Europe.

1. The Austrian School

This fundamental liberal attitude prevented the usurpation of the school by the two big totalitarian tendencies of the time: national socialism and international socialism. However, it also led to the marginalization of the Austrian School and ultimately forced most of its adherents to emigrate. This was a catastrophe for the scientists concerned, but a boon for the science: Austrian economics as a result remained a movement far removed from power and critical of power.

Economics is the supreme scientific discipline of modern government. As a consequence, it is also the most corrupted of all scientific disciplines. Paid work for economists exists wherever there is an effort to plan and control. Once upon a time, it was the Soviet Union that employed the largest number of economists. Today, it is the central banks, and the US Federal Reserve System (Fed) first and foremost among them; currently between 200 and 300 graduate macro-economists work for the board of governors of the Fed, not including numerous posts for assistants. Every year, the board of governors distributes hundreds of millions of dollars in subsidies to economists, so an estimated 500 economists are working full-time for the Fed's 'agenda' in addition externally. A press report on the topic concludes:

> One critical way the Fed exerts control on academic economists is through its relationships with the field's gatekeepers. For instance, at the Journal of Monetary Economics, a must-publish venue for rising economists, more than half of the editorial board members are currently on the Fed payroll -- and the rest have been in the past. [In short: the entire profession of economists has been bought off by the Fed.][4]

The Austrian School of Economics is largely free of the prostitution for influence and income that is so typical for modern-day economists. If the tradition had survived in Vienna without interruption to this day, it may well have been completely subsumed in the mainstream as a result of these incentives.

Today, the Austrian School is often accused of being dogmatic and ideological. And to an extent, this accusation is perhaps not entirely

1. The Austrian School

unjustified, but it is only partially deplorable. The ideologically tinged reception in the US and the preponderance of old texts and dead thinkers may well make the flowering of a once again living and relevant science from the seed that has been preserved more difficult. However, the preservation would not have succeeded otherwise: dogma can protect against errors, and ideology against wrongful usurpation. In a world characterized by exaggerated short-termism that slavishly follows day-to-day events, engagement with the Austrian School is akin to time travel: it brings a perspective into our world that has become alien to us, and which offers fantastical possibilities for insight.

The present can never be understood in isolation. The Austrian School provides the necessary context to better understand our times, but it is not at all antiquated: most of its insights are timeless, some were so revolutionary a century ago that they still feel fresh today, while the remainder are maturing and growing as new knowledge is gathered. Today, there barely exists a tradition that is better suited to bidding farewell to *Zeitgeist* illusions.

It is for this reason that the Austrian School is especially valuable to investors, although its value may not be immediately apparent. The school that solved the so-called paradox of value, challenges investors initially with another paradox: investors who utilize the insights of the Austrian School will 'normally' earn lower returns. This is due to a degree of self-constraint on the one hand, which weighs short-term material aspects against longer-term ethical ones and due to the fact that what is considered "normality" is anything but normal on the other hand.

Austrian School adherents observe the madness soberly. This perspective is typical for Vienna. In the Vienna of the long-perished old world, one used to speak of the "cheerful apocalypse". An anecdote from a joint Austrian-Prussian battle in WW I illustrates this perspective well. A Prussian officer reported: "The situation is serious, but it is not hopeless." An Austrian commander retorted: "The situation is hopeless, but it is not serious." This paradoxical fundamental attitude

1. The Austrian School

influenced the Austrian School and clearly differentiated it from other economic traditions.

Not only the big wars changed the world, there has also been an economic transformation taking place over the past few centuries that is unique in history. This transformation goes well beyond the industrial revolution. It is a monetary revolution, which initially promoted rapid and massive industrialization, but later had a de-industrializing effect. Every investor who wants to understand the present and the future needs to learn about this monetary revolution, which we will explain further in chapter two.

The transformation of the world, especially of Western societies and economies, led to polarization from the very beginning. Only very few sober observers remained; most were either attracted or repelled. And even those who were initially repelled, were soon helped onto the bandwagon. In the tide of the times, they believed they were swimming backward for a while, but that was only the undertow. The ship of the Austrian School soon ran aground, broken into small pieces and dispersed, regarded as sunk and no longer heeded as time went on. Economists who swam along and wrestled with modernity parted ways: some saw the flood as rapid progress, only in need of a little steering. These mainstream economists regard the situation as serious only when their steering attempts are periodically unmasked as illusions, but do not see its hopelessness. Others, so-called "heterodox" economists, suspect the entire economy of being driven by ideology and regard all economic activity as hopeless unless it is submitted to their supervision and their rules. They take themselves far too seriously in this, as they could probably not even run a Viennese sausage stand, and depend on the very money flows that are part of the monetary flood of modern times for their own livelihood.

By contrast, the remaining and "beached" Austrian School adherents have retained their grip on reality: they see the hopelessness of trying to steer the economy, however, they do not take the modern-day situation overly seriously, neither as a fulfillment of utopian dreams, nor as

1. The Austrian School

a conspiracy of ideological enemies. History has not yet ended, and we do not live in the best of all worlds. The monetary revolution nourished a lot of entrepreneurship and with that also human beings quite well, at least in terms of calories. Many profited, some were even well aware of it all and occasionally conspired with varying degrees of success; much more important though was that the masses had the impression of being on the winning side. Financially, this was and certainly remains the case, but the financial perspective falls far short in a time of money multiplication. Amazing towers were erected on the rotten pillars of excessive money supply growth, the height of which is not dissimilar to that of the Tower of Babel. We in the West are enjoying the view from the upper floors; however, we could easily have the rug pulled out from under us.

The perspective of the Austrian School thus offers a paradoxical look at the present: free of ideological grudges against the development of the economy and human beings, against the creation of fortunes and continual change, against the citizen and economic actor, but sober and disillusioned regarding the present day hope that things will simply continue as they have in the past. Modern economics has seemingly developed a new alchemy, but it is not gold that glitters so temptingly. Between the anti-capitalist mentality and financial euphoria, the dominant currents of our time, the sober outlook of Austrian economists is timelessly important and valuable. It is the economics of moderation, set apart from extremes.

So what does the Austrian School consist of? To begin with, it entails a number of methodological approaches to the economy. There are essentially four pillars – central to "Austrian investing" as well – which the research program of the Austrian School rests on. They can be traced back to Carl Menger, the school's founder. Menger was born in 1840 in Neu-Sandez in Galicia (today Nowy Sącz in Poland). In Vienna he founded the newspaper *Wiener Tagblatt* and ultimately worked for the *Wiener Zeitung*, a government-owned newspaper that survives to this day. In 1871, his work *Principles of Economics* was first published and represents the founding document of the Austrian School – a revolution in economics.

Subjectivism

The Austrian School differentiated itself from then existing economic traditions especially in terms of one important insight, and hence owes its origin to this insight: the subjective theory of value. This does not refer to subjectivism in terms of moral values, but rather the insight that human beings are subjects with the ability to learn and make choices freely. Economic values and prices are neither determined by the past, nor by unchanging physical qualities, but result from the subjective appraisal of an uncertain future. This is why looking at the ubiquitous charts of price trends can be quite misleading. They merely represent a graphical illustration of past decisions, which tells us little about the future. At best they serve in helping to understand the present a little better, which is why numerous illustrations can also be found in this book.

Economics is crucially different from the natural sciences precisely because the object of its investigations is at the same time an acting *subject*. While economics is concerned with material effects, its basis is the mind. This is what makes this field both very exciting and quite difficult. The subject, acting man, is at the center of the Austrian School's teachings, his actions are the main object of observation. By means of this subjectivist approach, the Austrian School avoids a cardinal mistake of bad economics: the misguided "objectivization" and equalization of human action, which shows no respect for human diversity and can easily degenerate into a manic desire for control.

Subjectivism helps to avert an investment mistake that is at the top of the list of potential mistakes: extrapolation of past events into the future. We easily fall prey to this temptation due to the sobering uncertainty of the future. However, present value is not the result of yesterday's costs, but the consequence of today's expectations with respect to tomorrow's wants and possibilities. A second investment mistake is closely related to this one: namely the confusion between price and value. Value in the economic sense is the basis of human decisions: namely, the subjective appraisal of the usefulness of available means for the attainment of our ends. Prices on the other hand are specific, already consummated exchange ratios lying in the past, which reflect our choices in interaction with the choices of others. Prices do influence our future value-related expectations, however, they are always located somewhere below or above them. Prices express what we have to surrender in exchange, not what we are getting. The difference between value and price is our subjective, psychic profit. If we were not expecting such a profit, we would not engage in exchanges with strangers.

Today most people are far too fixated on prices. This too is a consequence of the monetary revolution, which we will take a closer look at later. It is, however, also a consequence of the fact that most people are "price takers", not price makers, as they are in most instances small cogs in a large structure. For the typical consumer, prices appear as hard data of the economy to which he must adjust. In reality, prices are the documentation of past exchanges as well as offers for future exchanges. The typical consumer today is completely dependent on these offers, as he has no other basis of existence than the wage he receives (the height of which represents the current offer for cooperation). The perspective of the Austrian School is an incentive to emancipate oneself from the dictate of prices and orient one's economic actions toward values. Values are subjective, i.e., they originate from our individual reflection regarding our goals and the recognition of suitable means. Prices serve to put our values into context with the wants of other people, and help us with estimating whether our goals are really worth the costs they entail. If not, we must either change our goals or search for different means.

For investors this orientation toward value means a break from the typical fixation on prices, from keeping an eye on security prices every day. Value-oriented investors *create* prices instead of being swept along by them. The daily price is an offer for the sale or purchase of an investment asset. The difference between these two prices, the bid and offer price, or spread, is an indication of market liquidity, and thus more relevant than the height of the price itself. The current price is only important insofar as it represents an open invitation to reflect on value. As a rule, the value of an investment asset reflects its expected return, as this is the reason one invests: to transform income into wealth, in order to be able to transform wealth back into income again.

With respect to the investment of capital, the Austrian School therefore leads to the basic principles of so-called value investing. While this term was only coined at a later stage in the US, "value-oriented investment" is an important part of the "Austrian" perspective. However, it is only a part; contrary to modern-day value investing it is complemented by a further, sober analysis of markets and especially market distortions.

Marginalism

The Austrian School was able to explain the phenomenon of the different valuation of goods by supplementing the subjectivist perspective with another important insight: the theory of marginal utility. The term defines the insight that economic changes always happen "at the margin": at the point where actual actions occur, based on concrete choices with regard to relevant units of goods. This perspective leads to a more dynamic contemplation of the economy. In neoclassical economics, this approach was clad in mathematical formalism, however, this has resulted in losing sight of the essence of marginalism: marginal action – the suspense-filled area of human action, where changes occur. This is where the effects of incentives are unfolding, which explain a great many things, and even allow for modest forecasts.

Similar to marginalism, incentives also found their way into neoclassical economics, but acting man is reduced to a being primarily driven by materialistic concerns. The Austrian School has no need of this limitation: incentives work because no one person is the same, and some of them are always "on the edge", about to change their concrete behavior.

1. The Austrian School

It is not the general utility of a good that is relevant to its value, but the marginal utility of a concrete unit of a good, which we may either give up or gain. Besides Menger, Heinrich Gossen already described something akin to this (Gossen's law of satiation): "The intensity of one and the same enjoyment declines while we continue without interruption with indulging in the enjoyment, until satiation is reached" (first law of Gossen). Thus the increasing consumption of a good leads to a successively declining marginal utility. An analogy from agriculture: it is possible to raise the productivity of soil with the help of fertilizer. However, if one exaggerates, over-fertilization results, and every additional unit of fertilizer is no longer useful, the soil is destroyed.

However, it is best to regard Gossen's law of satiation only as a mental stepping stone for understanding the concept of marginal utility. The essence of marginal utility lies in the *service* an additional unit that is added to a homogeneous supply of a good is able to render. It is not the good itself, but the goal that can be attained by using it that is the decisive factor. Thus, a person may use the first ten gallons of a supply of water for drinking, which he regards as the most highly valued, most urgent use. The next ten gallons may be used for washing, the next ten for watering the plants in the garden, and so forth, with each employment of additional units lower on the value scale of the individual concerned than the preceding ones. The theorem of marginal utility represents a law of economics that is universally and time-invariantly valid; moreover, it does not require "empirical proof" - its validity is evident by reflection and reasoning alone. There exist no exceptions to the law of marginal utility. At the time of writing, a very common mistake could still be found in the Wikipedia entry on marginal utility. It is asserted in this entry that there *are* actually exceptions, and that the marginal utility of additional units of the same good can actually increase in certain circumstances. As an example illustrating such a supposed "exception", Wikipedia states:

> Bed sheets, which up to some number may only provide warmth, but after that point may be useful to allow one to effect an escape by being tied together into a rope.[5]

This is actually incorrect – and it should be obvious why that is the case. The difference between a bed sheet that is providing warmth and ten bed sheets that can be tied together to form a rope, is that the ten bed sheets that have been tied together are actually a *different good*. They are no longer bed sheets; they are a rope. So in this case, one can apply the law of marginal utility to the good "bed sheet" and the services it renders (such as providing warmth) on the one hand, and the good "bed sheets forming a rope" and the services it renders (such as offering a means of escape) on the other hand. It is not legitimate to assert that the marginal utility of additional units of bed sheets has somehow increased. Murray Rothbard explains this principle as follows:

> For example, it is erroneous to argue as follows: eggs are the good in question. It is possible that a man needs four eggs to bake a cake. In that case, the second egg may be used for a less urgent use than the first egg, and the third egg for a less urgent use than the second. However, since the fourth egg allows a cake to be produced that would not otherwise be available, the marginal utility of the fourth egg is greater than that of the third egg. This argument neglects the fact that a "good" is not the physical material, but any material whatever of which the units will constitute an equally serviceable supply. Since the fourth egg is not equally serviceable and interchangeable with the first egg, the two eggs are not units of the same supply, and therefore the law of marginal utility does not apply to this case at all. To treat eggs in this case as homogeneous units of one good, it would be necessary to consider each set of four eggs as a unit.[6]

As an aside, the above is a good example demonstrating another important Austrian insight, that has unfortunately become controversial in modern times as economists have increasingly promoted empiricism in economic science, in a failed attempt to make economics more akin to physics. Namely, economic laws are arrived at by deductive reasoning. The validity of an economic theorem can only be proved or disproved by the application of logical thinking. In this instance, deductive reasoning allows us to prove that Wikipedia is promoting an erroneous interpretation of the law of marginal utility.

1. The Austrian School

Marginal utility thus declines in dependence of how much of a good we already possess. The first conclusion for investors is thinking in terms of portfolio: investment decisions should not be taken according to an "all or nothing" scheme, but should rather represent an attempt at optimization with respect to one's personal goals using the available means. Investment is a step-by-step process, not a one-off decision. Blanket decisions often prove fatal. The marginal approach consists of trying to find incremental, specific improvements. Investment positions are altered in small, but steady steps. Marginalism has of course nothing to do with speculating on margin by employing credit leverage. The Austrian school's perspective is rather akin to an ongoing margin call, a continual critical examination of one's coverage.

From the subjectivist perspective, one could also speak of a kind of "coverage" if the marginal utility of investment assets remains above their price. "Uncovered" are those investments where the price stands above their value. In times of inflated prices, the "Austrian" investor thus eschews most popular investment assets – and thus misses out on speculative gains, while being safe from speculative losses. In rally phases, "Austrian" investors are often ridiculed, in recessions they are often censured as crisis profiteers. A marginalist approach, however, tends to dampen strong fluctuations, so that the "Austrians" are more likely to be ignored. This is actually an advantage; good investors should not seek publicity.

The law of marginal utility can be applied to numerous areas of finance, inter alia to debt. Figure 1.1 shows the increase in US gross domestic product per dollar of additional debt and illustrates impressively that we are in the so-called "Keynesian endgame" – which means that the policy of Keynesian "stimulus" for the economy no longer has an effect. It can clearly be seen that ever more debt is buying less and less growth. In short, the marginal returns per unit of additional debt are continually declining. While an increase in debt was still associated with a large effect on output in the 1960s, it has nowadays become almost impossible to boost economic output by increasing debt. Additional stimulus programs achieve only anemic economic growth. If the doses of debt should not be escalated further, resp. should debt growth even cease entirely, the withdrawal symptoms would likely be extremely painful.

Diminishing Returns from debt financing by decade 1950 – 2014			
Date Range	Change of debt, USD bn.	Change of GDP, USD bn.	Debt/GDP
1950 - 1960	33.6	243.1	0.14
1960 - 1970	90.4	497.4	0.18
1970 - 1980	528.1	1,612.3	0.33
1980 - 1990	2,297.3	3,025.5	0.76
1990 - 2000	2,422.4	4,002.9	0.51
2000 - 2010	7,900.1	4,758.1	1.66
2010 - 2014	4,265.7	2,454.5	1.74

Figure 1.1: Clearly declining marginal utility of additional units of debt (Sources: Federal Reserve St. Louis, Incrementum AG)

Numerous studies confirm the declining marginal utility of additional units of debt. According to Paul Vreymans, the correlation between GDP growth and the expansion of the money supply currently stands at 0.1102.[7] This is statistically *de facto* no longer a significant magnitude. Vreymans notes that the effect is confined to the first quarter after the application of stimulus. This positive short-term stimulus effect however quickly evaporates, and in subsequent months it even seems to have a counter-productive impact. A number of empirical studies by Harvard economics professor Robert J. Barro have shown that the so-called "fiscal multiplier" from government spending is actually negative in most cases - it ultimately crowds out so much private investment that the effect on economic output is net negative. Austrian economists reject the "multiplier" concept entirely, but it is refreshing that at least some mainstream economists are beginning to realize that the Keynesian shibboleths on the topic are flawed.

The marginalist perspective also leads to a better understanding of costs: in the economic sense, costs not only refer to actually required expenses, but also to the inevitable opposite side of choices. Every choice means a renunciation of alternatives. Our actions thus leave an entire chain of renounced options behind and are constrained by them. Perfect decisions are impossible, as the future is uncertain. We are all blindly groping, also and perhaps especially the "experts", this uncertain future, which is why we should act step-by-step and look to mistakes as an opportunity to learn something, if they cannot be avoided. Every investment strategy will be littered with mistakes, missed opportunities, too expensive purchases and too cheap sales, underestimated risks and overestimated returns. Good investment strategies reflect an awareness of these mistakes and will strive to minimize their effects, while bad investment strategies are characterized by an overestimation of one's abilities and will be fully exposed to the effects of mistakes.

The desire to avoid uncertainty can actually lead to the worst investment mistakes. On the one hand, we cling to the past: economists speak in this context of our inability to let go of sunk costs. Investors hang on to assets the value of which is in rapidl decline, in order not to have to admit their mistakes. The "Austrian" investor, on the other hand, expects that there will be mistakes and remains calm. Psychologist Erich Fromm gets right to the heart of the problem:

> Not to move forward, to stay where we are, to regress, in other words to rely on what we have, is very tempting, for what we have, we know; we can hold onto it, feel secure in it. We fear, and consequently avoid, taking a step into the unknown, the uncertain; for, indeed, while the step may not appear risky to us after we have taken it, before we take that step the new aspects beyond it appear very risky, and hence frightening. Only the old, the tried, is safe; or so it seems. Every new step contains the danger of failure, and that is one of the reasons people are so afraid of freedom.[8]

Due to uncertainty and because the accumulation of wealth as a rule is a gradual process, the hoarding of assets is inescapable. The higher the uncertainty, the greater our liquid means must be. Profitable investments will not be possible in every environment and in every conceivable magnitude, we must therefore bridge time gaps and specific levels.

The other economic traditions disdain hoarding as unproductive and damaging. Only the Austrian School appreciates it as a necessary consequence of reality. Liquidity is an unavoidable requirement in an uncertain world, in which no one knows the future and trust is not always justified.

Liquidity is essentially a function of a good's marketability. The concept was introduced by Carl Menger, who recognized that the marginal utility of different goods tends to decline at varying rates. A strong decline in marginal utility and thus very low marketability occurs in goods that are only useful to a small circle of customers. A strong decrement in marginal utility means that the second, third, fourth and subsequent units of a good are worth considerably less than the first unit. The less its marginal utility declines, the higher a good's marketability. As Antal Fekete showed, high marketability is expressed by a smaller increase in spreads in the face of a rising supply.[9] Money has the highest marketability of all goods.

However, "money" is not a fixed magnitude, it is not something that can be fixed once and forever by decree. Friedrich A. Hayek describes the "Austrian" approach to money well, by pointing out that the term should actually be an adjective, and not a noun.[10] "Moneyness" is a feature, which different goods possess to varying degrees. Throughout history, various alternatives have turned out to be more "money-like" than money imposed by government decree, which of course obtains an artificial increase in marketability due to legal tender laws and coercive taxation.

Individualism

The methodological individualism of the Austrian School Hand works hand in hand with the marginalist perspective. This is not a normative individualism, which praises isolation; on the contrary, the economy

1. The Austrian School

is regarded as a social process. "Methodological" refers to the fact that it must be possible to ultimately explain every economic phenomenon with the actions of individual, real human beings. Collective magnitudes like "the people" or "the race" cannot act, and thus are inadequate or erroneous when used as ultimate explanations. When different people have similar goals or are employing similar means, this is not altered by a national border that happens to lie between them by chance.

This does not mean that social, ethnic or coercively created attachments have no influence on human wants and goals, but it is precisely these wants and goals that are the ultimate reason for action. Social structures can develop dynamics of their own, but we cannot understand these dynamics without observing the people acting within them. Especially historical narratives tend to lead economists astray: peoples and states are often portrayed therein as though they had their own will. That may be admissible in a poetic or metaphorical sense, but analytically it is inadequate. Austrian economists are therefore not impressed by big words, which are often used in place of a deeper understanding: "the State", "demand", "the economy"…

The individualism of the Austrian School leads to great skepticism toward mass phenomena. As respectable as individual man is, he often acts dreadfully as part of a crowd. Peer pressure and group-think can often already be detected even in small groups.

In large, anonymous crowds, which are connected by mass media, man is ultimately often acting like a "system dork" (we already mentioned him): he simply runs in the same direction as everybody else. This leads to rapid self-reinforcement. Since everybody has become a potential financial speculator in the wake of the modern monetary revolution, mass phenomena have also become a feature of the capital markets. While speculation normally has a balancing effect that keeps financial markets liquid and dampens fluctuations, mass speculation amplifies volatility. Normally, markets will tend to self-correct and the lemmings and fools are relieved of their funds, which flow toward those with cooler and clearer heads. However, today's monetary flows tend to artificially feed mass-speculation during booms.

Of course, all action is speculative – the Austrian School therefore appreciates speculation as well. The individualist perspective, however, shows that speculation can only lead to profits if specific individuals are able to see what others have overlooked. Their profits are the reward for having appraised the future better. Whenever an individual has bought low and sold high, there must have been another individual who sold too cheaply and another who bought at too high a price. Systematic and general speculative gains are only possible in an artificial boom, which transforms the financial markets into a Ponzi scheme. In this case, the few with early access to newly created money are followed by harrowed chasers, more of whom are constantly recruited by the trickling down of continually newly created fiduciary media.

The "Austrian" investor is always a rather marginal phenomenon, and thus predestined for counter-cyclical investing. The crowd drives prices up, which as a result soon exceed underlying values. After the monetary revolution, the world has transitioned into an age of the masses. Masses in the sociological sense are not merely a large number of people. They are a phenomenon in their own right: human beings in relationships of dependency, which are strongly connected with each other. Wilhelm Roepke, the eminent economic sociologist of the Austrian School and the most important fount of inspiration for former German chancellor Ludwig Erhard, describes the modern-day masses as follows:

> The inhabitants of a large apartment house are complete strangers to each other and meet perhaps for the first time in the air raid shelter, but on the other hand, they have the closest anonymous relations with the totality of their fellow men, relations of an external and mechanical kind, as buyers and sellers, as members of crowds jostling each other, as voters, as radio listeners and visitors to the motion pictures, sharing the same acoustic or optic impressions with millions of others, as tax payers, as recipients of pensions and public assistance, as members of health insurance societies and this or that centrally organized association.[11]

1. The Austrian School

If one wants to avoid the destructive flood of the modern bubble economy, one must look at the crowd as a contrary indicator: a guide as to what should be avoided, or what should be bought respectively. Marketability unfortunately requires the participation of the masses, therefore no investor can ignore the crowd. The economy is a social process, and choosing life as a hermit cannot be an economic, but at best an anti-economic decision, if the dangers emanating from misguided people become too great. In a mass society, it is however crucial to avoid the beaten tracks. This is what makes the Austrian School of Economics so difficult: when everybody is talking about something and it receives universal praise, there is already something very wrong with it. Decisions that are held to be correct by the masses, are almost always coming too late in the game, and for this reason alone can already be wrong for the individual. After all, timing, the selection of the correct point in time, is essential in an environment of financial bubbles exhibiting high volatility. A decision that is correct at all times does not exist.

In precisely which market sectors a bubble will form cannot be predicted, it can only be suspected on the basis of counter-cyclical indicators. When a bubble finally bursts, we can always find numerous defects upon looking closely; but even if things had held together in one place, another breaking point would have given way. Bubbles that can be observed in all types of asset classes and beyond, have a structure akin to Ponzi schemes. In a Ponzi scheme, no real capital is formed, but "returns" are generated by new entrants. The system is simple: every person who takes part in the Ponzi scheme needs to find people who are even greater fools than he is. While the extent of such foolishness is often underestimated, it is still finite. At the base of Ponzi pyramid, things are getting tight. Find ten people who are greater fools than you are! This is not an easy task for everybody. Could those ten find another ten each? When does the game begin to stall?

This mechanism was recognized by US president John F. Kennedy's father. An important indicator for investors can be derived from his observations, which could be called the "shoeshine boy phenomenon": Joseph Kennedy was in the process of getting his shoes cleaned, when the shoeshine boy suddenly surprised him with "sure-fire" investment recommendations. The very next day he sold all his stocks – just in time. His idea was that shoeshine boys are at the very bottom of the pyramid. They would hardly be able to find someone to sell their stocks to.

One must refrain from misconstruing this line of argument: it is not so much about the purchase of stocks, but about the flooding of society with the illusion of a quick buck. Since this illusion has no real foundation, it displays a Ponzi structure. The banker believes the president of the central bank. The manager believes his banker. The employee believes his manager. The unemployed man believes the employee. Who believes the unemployed man? As soon as an investment recommendation has made its way to the title pages of the mass media, it needs to be avoided. As soon as trends appear in our Facebook stream, they are close to ending. For the "Austrian investor", mass media are only useful as contrary indicators that show the current state of sentiment. If the masses are pessimistic on the prospects of an asset class, it is a sign that one will be able to find items that are priced below their value within it, while optimism by the masses is a sign that prices are excessive.

Of course, the task is not simply to always do the opposite of the crowd. What is crucial are individual value scales, and at times they may coincidentally be congruent with whatever is being hyped. Occasionally, the herd will stampede in the right direction. If one has not managed to get ahead of the herd, one needs to stoically pick up whatever crumbs are left over. In practice, the Austrian School instructs its followers to look farther than the herd. Unfortunately, "Austrians" do not possess a crystal ball. Precisely because of individualism, and because mass phenomena are also the result of the actions of individuals, quantitative forecasts are not possible in economics. Predictions by "experts" that display numbers beyond the decimal point can be safely ignored – or even better, be used as contrary indicators.

It may be difficult for us to believe in human liberty in a mass society. Markets appear merely as an expression of "animal spirits". However,

1. The Austrian School

the fact that people tend to display animal-like traits in a crowd tells us nothing about the extent and the length of time for which these instincts will prevail. The psychologization of market processes does not help an investor. In a worst case, one believes oneself to be superior to the masses, believes in some expert's advice, and jumps on yet another mass trend.

The Austrian School is sober enough to not merely regard the crowd as "the others". We are all "system idiots" to some extent, whether we want to be or not; we can at best gradually and occasionally reduce our idiot status. Whoever reduces his fellow human beings to merely representing the "masses", creates this as his reality. Even when inflamed crowds were braying for their lives, Jewish representatives of the Austrian School like Ludwig von Mises never for a moment ceased to uphold individual liberty as an ideal. Only free human beings can bear responsibility.

The "system idiot" of the present age flees from taking responsibility and thereby undermines his own liberty. The bulk of investment literature serves this need: the need to delegate responsibility for difficult decisions to gurus, which can be used as an excuse if anything goes wrong. Contrary to the illusion of risk-free returns, the present time is one of the historically most difficult for investing. For the vast majority of people, losses of value are inevitable. No matter how much they may read about the Austrian School, the mistakes of the past cannot be unmade by even the wisest person. Much is already gained by becoming aware of this loss of value and facing up to reality. It is the only way to minimize the damage. Of course one is always tempted by the more grandiose promises made elsewhere. The Austrian School thus remains a program for a minority. With respect to macroeconomics, this is of course bitter and quite a pity, on the micro-economic level – with respect to the individual investor – it offers however a small ray of hope that one will be able to avoid the beaten tracks.

Realism

Carl Menger himself referred to his method as "causal-realistic". The Austrian School wants to describe reality, it is its only yardstick. It is averse to unrealistic assumptions and models favoring simplified or formalized descriptions. The Austrian School is therefore in the Aristotelian tradition, which, while it respects the non-material, does not lose its grounding by falling for fanciful idealism. Even if reality is uncomfortable, if it is regarded as politically incorrect to openly talk about it, if prophets, who – depending on their target audience – offer simpler or more complicated explanations, enjoy great popularity, the only purpose of good economics remains to better understand the reality of human action and economic activity.

However, in order to fully grasp this reality, it is hardly sufficient to merely be an economist. If one looks closely at the interests, writings and seminars of Austrian economists, what stands out is an impressive interdisciplinary approach, which can hardly be found anymore in today's highly specialized academic world. Although it was once in conflict with the historicist school, the Austrian school also has a strong focus on history: real human action is given more weight than any theoretical assumptions. The theoretical systems developed by Austrian economists always had the goal to improve the intelligibility of history. As a result, the theory is in constant development: it has to be measured against reality, even though the gathering of statistical data is entirely inadequate as a source of theory.

A major insight of the Austrian School consists of the consideration of relative rather than absolute prices. We are all too easily misled by high nominal prices and systematically underestimate the debasement of currencies. The focus on prices in terms of paper currencies leads to a false perspective, which regards rising stock prices as indicators of good economic progress and buy signals. Following this logic, Zimbabwe's stock market would have been the strongest in the world in the last decade. In reality, rising stock prices merely signify a decline in the currency's purchasing power, as expressed by the share prices of listed companies. The average income earner thus is forced to work ever more in order to be able to afford a share in the means of production. If we were all speculating in potatoes, we would gaze at rising potato prices in joyful anticipation – however, their prices would likewise merely indicate a decline rather than an increase in general welfare in real terms.

Stock prices can rise for two reasons. Firstly, if a majority of market participants alters its expectations of future corporate returns and is anticipating an increase in earnings. If one recognizes this positive corporate trend before others do, one's own investment gains in value – at least on paper. These higher prices reflect the purchase offers of others who have recognized their previous error. However, nowadays the majority of price increases is due to investors trying to flee from monetary debasement.

Realism means to return the focus with respect to economic values to real benefits for real people. Valuations that are solely based on finding greater fools who will pay even more lack a realistic long-term foundation. Accounting method abuse has led to book values becoming virtual chimeras. Debt can only represent a real asset if it is backed by capital that is able to create value in the long term. Behind the better part of today's credit claims, no such capital can be found, they require either more debt issuance or new taxes to be serviced. The bubble in debt securities is going hand in hand with dramatic long-term currency debasement. People's money has been gradually replaced with currencies that are "backed" with nothing but debt.

The extent to which people underestimate this spiral of devaluation is quite astonishing. It is the biggest open secret in economic history. Open, because all historians are aware of it, because it is sufficiently well documented and astonishingly universal. In almost every culture, the guardians of the currency have abused their position. Since the modern monetary revolution, this abuse is however even less obvious, as currencies no longer have a real foundation and have become arbitrarily elastic. Thus the dilution and debasement of debt-based currencies, which is referred to as "inflation" by economists, is a secret for most people: they feel constant pressure as a result of the devaluation, but they are unaware of its causes and are looking in the wrong direction.

The indispensable counterpart of this artificial inflation is deflation. Economic realism is the attempt to stay grounded in the face of the wavelike movement between bubbles in asset prices and their bursting. In this sense, the goal is to understand the real basis of price trends. Realism also means sobriety, so as not to allow oneself to get carried away by the bubble economy. Inflationary eras are always times of grandiose promises, utopian scenarios, impatient greed, overconfident wishful thinking and stubborn hubris. The realist is seen as a spoil sport in such times, someone who asks critical questions and stoically endures mockery.

The realism of the Austrian School is not least the historically based insight that most investors simply tend to overlook the greatest threats to their wealth. It is not price declines, bad timing, a wrong portfolio composition or excessive risk that have led to the greatest losses of wealth. The generations before us, similar to those preceding them, have not lost their savings merely on account of investment mistakes. The greatest threat to private wealth throughout history has always been institutionalized violence, the incarnation of which we have referred to as "the State" only over the past few centuries. This observation is not grounded in an abiding, ideological enmity against the state, but in the thorough study of history. Not even the best investment advice will help those refusing to face this reality. Especially the last century offers bitter lessons in this respect. The State as a rule reacts to devaluation pressure, which is an inevitable consequence of the debt-based bubble economy, by instituting financial repression. Understanding the incentives behind this and the relevant dynamics accompanying it is essential for every investor.

2. The Illusion of Prosperity

The typical European or US investor believes himself to be living in an era of historically unprecedented levels of prosperity. In such a privileged situation, the main purpose of investment is to increase returns, to make even more money from an already large amount of money. Investors wish for price increases in order to build up a large fortune that is supposed to deliver security and independence. However, is this evaluation correct? Are we really living in an era of unprecedented wealth that only needs to be secured and increased?

The level of material wealth certainly appears to be high. The era without hunger and massive infant mortality in our latitudes is a relatively young one. Only in the 19th century did modern prosperity begin to quickly extend to the masses. The destruction of the world wars led to the most bitter impoverishment, which was once again overcome in a relatively short period of time. The fast swing from riches to poverty and poverty to riches within a single generation has significantly influenced our view of prosperity. This view neglects the long-term foundation of prosperity and is instead focused on short-term symptoms.

In the 19th century, the global division of labor developed on a large scale. There was a strong yearning for economic growth, as the modern age had in the context of absolutism, the enforcement of centralized government authority, initially resulted in a devastating regression in peoples' living standards. The Austrian School was founded at this time, which is why its proponents focused on the preconditions for economic growth and on individual liberty. Both in the economic miracle of the 19th century, which expressed itself in the form of rapid industrialization in Austria, as well as in the German-Austrian economic miracle after World War II, too much attention was paid to material prosperity. In

2. The Illusion of Prosperity

the course of this, its intellectual basis was overlooked. Although even the Austrian School was perhaps too focused on material well-being, it was this school of thought that recognized economics as primarily an intellectual endeavor. Ludwig von Mises wrote:

> Production is not something physical, natural, and external; it is a spiritual and intellectual phenomenon. Its essential requisites are not human labor and external natural forces and things, but the decision of the mind to use these factors as means for the attainment of ends. What produces the product is not toil and trouble in themselves, but the fact that the toilers are guided by reason.[12]

The post-war economic miracle was not only shaped significantly by Wilhelm Roepke, but at the same time found its most fervent warner in his person. Roepke worked together with Mises in Geneva, who introduced him to the Austrian School of Economics. Later, Ludwig Erhard would smuggle Roepke's writings into Germany. Roepke warned of the proletarianization and "stable-feeding" of human beings, who would become dependent on consumption without being in control of their own livelihood. The same mistake had already been made in the 19th century and had led to the catastrophe of the next century: due to impatience, economic "growth" had been artificially boosted, and the social and moral framework became overstretched. The same impatience subsequently provoked a backlash in the form of the ideological rejection of economic freedom. The problems of growth were all blamed on entrepreneurs and "capitalists", who are of course, to paraphrase Mises, always the promoters of economic change.

Entrepreneurship, long-distance trade, corporations, stock exchanges and so forth, were not an invention of the 19th century that had been pushed through against the peoples' will. Nevertheless, these institutions at the time appeared to unfold such unusual and powerful momentum, that "capitalism" became a derogatory term. The background of this momentum is largely not understood, or misunderstood to this day. The Austrian School specifically contributed greatly to a

2. The Illusion of Prosperity

better understanding of this episode in economic history, and with it also to the understanding of the present era.

This requires a brief look at the 18th century. This was the century in which the banking system merged with the State. Up until then, government financing was dependent on taxes (theft), plunder (war), seignorage (the gain from minting coins, often in concert with monetary debasement) and credit. However, the first three methods of financing tended to undermine the latter, as the risk in lending to an institution that was based on violence always appeared too high – not only to most people, but also to other States. A private person making money from government loans will inspire a desire to engage in theft, just as a State that profits from loans to another State, inspires covetousness that can lead to war. In the age of Absolutism (16th to 18th century), the cancer-like growth of central governments demanded ever more funding. However, the costs of war, taxation and monetary debasement most of the time exceeded their long-term returns. All three of these coercive types of revenue lead to the disappearance of mobile wealth: over borders, into holes, and into consumption. The traditional methods of reducing the scarcity of money for government led to an increase in the scarcity of money in the economy, and in the long term therefore resulted in a drying up of the State's revenue sources as well.

In 1694, England showed a possible way out of this dilemma: the establishment of the Bank of England was one of the first systematic attempts to cover the government's debt requirements with "capitalistic" means. The entire 18th century was then characterized by a process of development that was necessary to transform this innovation into durable institutions and orient the entire economic process toward them. This innovation can be seen as a kind of new alchemy, and it puts all previous experiments by the alchemy of old in the shade. One may call it a "monetary revolution", the importance of which for the modern economy is widely overlooked or underestimated.

The alchemical formula has an infinite number of variations, but at its core it exhibits the following pattern: government debt securities are

2. The Illusion of Prosperity

commingled with private sector ones, and serve as the foundation upon which a pyramid of fiduciary media is erected. The State thus solved the dilemma of financing, by usurping institutions private merchants had built and using them for its own purposes.

Initially, private sector economic activity does not dry up as a result, but is even given a shot in the arm due to the expansion of fiduciary media – at least in the short term. According to Ludwig von Mises, fiduciary media are bank claims that serve as a substitute for money, but are not fully covered by money with respect to their maturity and liquidity. The expansion of fiduciary media should thus rapidly increase the risk that the issuing banks will become insolvent. The modern alchemy, however, is based on granting privileges to the banks in exchange for their help in financing the State, putting them above the laws that were previously governing the conduct of merchants.

The monetary revolution was a stroke of genius delivered in installments. The most entrepreneurial elements of society, who would otherwise represent a danger to the State's claim to power, were so to speak essentially bought off with imaginary values. The first big experiment involving the inclusion of private initiative in the expansion of fiduciary media on the basis of mass speculation was conducted by Scottish economist John Law in France. At this time, the term "millionaire" was invented, which to this day is the proverbial characteristic of the supposedly "capitalistic" tale of investment success possible for everyone – at least until it is replaced by the term "billionaire". A great many zeroes are the fetish of the new financial regime.

France was especially receptive to the monetary revolution; it is no coincidence that it is closely intertwined with the political revolution that shook the country at the end of the 18th century and would change the world. Both the monetary and political revolution spilled over from England to France and unfolded their full effects only on the continent. After the French Revolution, the first great experiment in paper currency in Europe was attempted – inspired by Law's speculative bubble – with the issuance of *assignats*. Property confiscated from the church

2. The Illusion of Prosperity

was employed as the "backing" of these financial claims. Of course this was on the one hand not in keeping with commercial collateralization requirements, and on the other hand, the supply of fiduciary media was subject to government whim and naturally was rapidly increased. While this made it possible to finance the government, society and the economy suffered such grave damage that the Napoleonic era soon followed. Expansions of fiduciary media and the associated debt spirals most often end with the ascension of tyrants. The *tyrannis* was already regarded as a drastic method of debt repudiation in antiquity.

The modern character of the monetary revolution was all too visible in France. While the madness of Law's speculative bubble was still confined to specific social classes, all of society was now gripped by fundamental change, which put economic activity on a new, if very rickety, foundation. Andrew D. White describes the consequences of this revolution very vividly:

> Out of the inflation of prices grew a speculating class; and, in the complete uncertainty as to the future, all business became a game of chance, and all business men, gamblers. In city centers came a quick growth of stock-jobbers and speculators; and these set a debasing fashion in business which spread to the remotest parts of the country. Instead of satisfaction with legitimate profits, came a passion for inordinate gains. Then, too, as values became more and more uncertain, there was no longer any motive for care or economy, but every motive for immediate expenditure and present enjoyment. So came upon the nation the obliteration of thrift. In this mania for yielding to present enjoyment rather than providing for future comfort were the seeds of new growths of wretchedness: luxury, senseless and extravagant, set in: this, too, spread as a fashion. To feed it, there came cheating in the nation at large and corruption among officials and persons holding trusts. While men set such fashions in private and official business, women set fashions of extravagance in dress and living that added to the incentives to corruption. Faith in moral considerations, or even in good impulses, yielded to general distrust.[13]

2. The Illusion of Prosperity

One problem of the revolutionary monetary experiment in France was that the only sector of the economy it stimulated directly was the real estate business. In order to perfect the monetary revolution, it was necessary to broaden it to encompass the biggest part of the economy – industry and commerce, which produce and distribute movable goods. This stage of the revolution was also first realized in France. The foundation of the modern economic order was laid with the founding of the so-called *crédit-mobilier* banks. Although this order is often called "capitalism" - in the derogatory sense of the term that became fashionable as the negative effects on society became noticeable – this is leading one down a completely wrong track. The people behind these measures were in reality intellectual pioneers of socialism, who were dreaming of a centralized economy under the dictates of industrialists and engineers. Friedrich A. Hayek explains the background in terms of the history of ideas:

> [T]he founders of modern socialism also did much to give Continental capitalism its peculiar form; "monopoly capitalism," or "finance capitalism," growing up through the intimate connection between banking and industry [...], the rapid development of joint-stock enterprises and the large railway combines are largely Saint-Simonian creations. The history of this is mainly one of the Credit Mobilier type of bank, the kind of combined deposit and investment institution which was first created by the brothers Pereire in France and then imitated under their personal influence or by other Saint-Simonians almost all over the European Continent. [...] And it cannot be denied that they succeeded in changing the economic structure of the Continental countries into something quite different from the English type of competitive capitalism.[14]

Of course, in the end neither industrialists nor engineers or technocrats rule, but always bureaucrats. In centralized structures based on violent coercion, there is always adverse selection. Only those who are unable to serve their fellow human beings are eager to rule over them. Ludwig von Mises expressed this fact with great clarity:

2. The Illusion of Prosperity

> Every half-wit can use a whip and force other people to obey. But it requires brains and diligence to serve the public. Only a few people succeed in producing shoes better and cheaper than their competitors. The inefficient expert will always aim at bureaucratic supremacy. He is fully aware of the fact that he cannot succeed within a competitive system. For him all-round bureaucratization is a refuge. Equipped with the power of an office he will enforce his rulings with the aid of the police. [...] He who is unfit to serve his fellow citizens wants to rule them.[15]

The count of Saint-Simon was one of the most important intellectual pioneers of socialism, even though Marx later disavowed him. This is understandable, after all, Saint-Simon created a religious cult, while Marx was a rather cold analytical person. Nevertheless, the Soviets later hailed him as a leading figure, and Friedrich Engels lauded him as well. The brothers Pereire were bankers and followers of Saint-Simon, whose slogan they made into their guiding principle: "From each according to his abilities, to each according to his needs". The Pereirian *crédit-mobilier* bank was established in 1852, the year in which Charles Louis Napoleon Bonaparte was crowned emperor of France, with his support, in order to finance his claim to power and his economic policies. Napoleon III was influenced by Utopian socialism as well and wanted to radically industrialize France. The redesign of Paris by prefect Haussmann was performed on his initiative and was partially financed by the Pereire brothers. This was accompanied by a real estate bubble.

A similar boom, luckily of lesser extent, took place in the context of the construction of Vienna's *Ringstrasse* a few decades later. The decisive point is the combination of government and private initiative: the government shows the way, enforces its wishes against all opposition, covers the required cascade of debt and spurs it on, while banks and entrepreneurs are making profits – which are the greater the closer they are to the government. This boost to economic activity of course eventually trickles down bit by bit through the entire population, but it produces massive distortions.

2. The Illusion of Prosperity

The increase in economic activity in turn feeds the State. The *crédit-mobilier* bank was also used to finance wars, especially the Crimean War (1853-1856). In 1867, the bank collapsed, ruining itself as a result of speculation in Austrian government bonds, but the monetary revolution had been completed. Since then, only detailed aspects of the financial system have been fine-tuned further. It became clear that a privileged central bank in possession of an absolute currency monopoly was required, which would be able to act as a lender of last resort extending liquidity to banks. Otherwise only very few banks would survive the business cycles they themselves help to set in to motion.

The modern economic system was erected on this foundation of government and private debt, privileges and currency monopolies. Earlier financial systems had been confined to employing what had been saved in the past and was made available in the present. Contrary to precious metals, which were formerly used as money, debt can be multiplied almost without limit, as it makes it possible to tap into future income. Although this was also possible prior to the monetary revolution by the extension of trade credit, it was confined to liquid, respectively productive investments. Government privileges made increasingly "creative" accounting practices possible.

The consequences of the monetary revolution were perceived especially vividly in Vienna. It started with a lag there, but all the more forcefully. The damage only became obvious after the old order had collapsed as a result of World War I. But even before that time the gratifying growth in prosperity went hand in hand with the devastating dynamics of a bubble economy. The "*Gruenderzeit*" crash was a first hint that economic growth would not be sustainable. Without the war, however, it may still have been possible to put the economy on a more realistic foundation and to mitigate the urge to amass debt. The basic preconditions for this existed. In his autobiographical work about "*The World of Yesterday*" in the Austria of yesteryear, Stefan Zweig describes the apparent stability that made the sudden collapse all the more painful:

2. The Illusion of Prosperity

When I attempt to find a simple formula for the period in which I grew up, prior to the First World War, I hope that I convey its fullness by calling it the Golden Age of Security. Everything in our almost thousand-year-old Austrian Monarchy seemed based on permanency, and the State itself was the chief guarantor of this stability. [...] Our currency, the Austrian crown, circulated in bright gold pieces, an assurance of its immutability. Everyone knew how much he possessed or what he was entitled to, what was permitted and what forbidden. Everything had its norm, its definite measure and weight. He who had a fortune could accurately compute his annual interest. An official or an officer, for example, could confidently look up in the calendar the year when he would be advanced in grade, or when he would be pensioned. Each family had its fixed budget and knew how much could be spent for rent and food, for vacations and entertainment [...]. Whoever owned a house looked upon it as a secure domicile for his children and grandchildren; estates and businesses were handed down from generation to generation. When the babe was still in its cradle, its first mite was put in its little bank, or deposited in the savings bank, as a "reserve" for the future. In this vast empire everything stood firmly and immovably in its appointed place, and at its head was the aged emperor; and were he to die, one knew [...] another would come to take his place, and nothing would change in the well-regulated order. No one thought of wars, of revolutions, or revolts. All that was radical, all violence, seemed impossible in an age of reason. This feeling of security was the most eagerly sought-after possession of millions, the common ideal of life.[16]

In the course of the ideological counter-reaction to the consequences of the monetary revolution, all aspects and institutions of the economy have come under general suspicion: money, interest, credit, banks, stock exchanges, speculation, entrepreneurship, capital, and so forth. The Austrian School of Economics attempted to break through this ideologization and false moralizing. Economic science should initially be understood as value-free, before one presumed to make any judgments. The Austrian School not only became an alternative to economic enmity as a result of ignorance, but also to the euphoria which sees the "best of all worlds" in the current financial system. Only the

2. The Illusion of Prosperity

"Austrian" perspective reveals that modern-day prosperity is a pyramid built on sand. As an achievement, this pyramid is remarkable, after all it is testament to human creativity and ingenuity. However, the construction activities in connection with this pyramid are further and further removed from actual human needs, and thus represent a waste of human potential. It is increasingly a world of calories without nutritional value, stories without comfort, information without knowledge, contacts without friendship, politics without community, creation without beauty, activities lacking sense. On the basis of a growing spiral of debt, only quantitative, but not qualitative growth can thrive.

Modern-day prosperity must therefore be questioned in several respects from the perspective of the Austrian School. This is not because prosperity is somehow considered bad. "Austrian" economists are certainly not romanticizing poverty, as many have experienced poverty first hand. They are not moralizing "growth critics", nor worriers about "economic ethics", nor ideologists, who want to see their plans implemented from above to replace peoples' individual plans. They neither allow the promises nor the condemnation of modernity to carry them away. In troubling times, cool heads are needed.

From a sober perspective, prosperity is dubious when it lacks a long-term foundation. Consumption is nothing bad either, but is an expression of human life. However, one of the most devastating economic errors is the confusion between the return on capital and capital consumption. There is quite a difference between milking a cow and slaughtering it before it had a chance to calve. The high level of consumption in our latitudes these days is partially based on a large endowment with capital – alas, only partially. Without the rapid enlargement of our economic sphere in recent decades towards Asia, on the one hand as a result of the collapse of the Soviet system, on the other hand due to the belated trend of catching up there with the monetary and industrial revolution, we would have been forced to drastically reduce our consumption a long time ago. Under a policy of credit expansion, this as a rule expresses itself in rising prices.

2. The Illusion of Prosperity

The end of the economic miracle was therefore somewhat delayed. However, this delay increasingly requires one not to look at things too closely. With respect to cheaper alternatives of lower quality, we close one eye, while our trading partners in Asia are closing both eyes and are still allowing themselves to be fobbed off with the illusory value of our currencies. In the euro area, there is still some industry, while the US dollar is mainly "backed" by military might. This industry was built with the intellectual capital of pre-war Europe and the diligence of post-war Europe. However, its continued existence is under threat: namely by a distortion of the capital structure, and the consequent effect of capital consumption.

The distortion of the economy's capital structure is a result of the monetary revolution. It has created the typical pattern of business cycles, characterized by alternating periods of distortion and rectification. As long as periods of growth go hand in hand with credit expansion, growth no longer directly follows the expected wants of consumers, but is driven by distorted price and interest rate signals. The consequence is an overstretching of the economy's structure in certain areas, and a thinning out in others. Correction periods are inevitable and strike people when unprepared. The corrections are so painful, because they reveal the misdirection of human decisions. Not only investment and entrepreneurial decisions are revealed as erroneous, but also the education and career decisions of the young, the investment decisions of the old, and the consumption and savings decisions of others. Erroneous in this context means: not sustainably in line with subjective needs and real conditions.

Generally, an illusion of prosperity results: an overestimation of one's own wealth and of the state of prosperity in the economy at large. Due to nominal prices that have been blown up as a result of credit expansion, people believe themselves to be richer than they really are, entrepreneurs deem themselves more clever than they are, workers more productive than they are, investors more skillful than they are – and of course politicians as more savvy than they are.

2. The Illusion of Prosperity

This results in continuous hidden capital consumption. According to the Austrian School, capital is composed of much more than mere monetary values. Capital consumption is reflected in a lack of reserves, in too high profit disbursements, bonuses and wage increases, in excessive risk taking amid decreasing liquidity, in a declining propensity to save, in profligacy, in a throw-away and entitlement mentality, in careless treatment of co-workers and fellow citizens in general, a hectic short-termism, overwork, a lack of health consciousness, pragmatism instead of integrity, and bluffing instead of substance. The monetary revolution has far-reaching moral consequences, which are concurrently a symptom and the backdrop to economic decline.

The "Austrian" perspective does not call the material level of consumption into question, least of all economic activity and consumption as such. It merely offers a widely ignored and forgotten criticism of the modern-day "prosperity" which we have become used to. The problem is that it comes at a price: the dissolution of its own long-term foundation, an increasing focus on the short-term (respectively a lack of "sustainability" to use a fashionable term) and a decline in quality consciousness.

Austrian School economists like Mises and Hayek analyzed the concatenation between the financial system, business cycles and economic distortions and warned of the destruction of the capital structure in favor of a phantom economy, the production process of which has lost touch with actual human wants. This distortion is then supposed – as Joseph Schumpeter disparagingly wrote – to be compensated for by psychological advertising techniques, this is to say manipulated selling pressure, and political slogans. Advertising and politics ever more blatantly demand more consumption. Wilhelm Roepke also warned of the consequences of an illusory prosperity for society, which confuses passive, debt-financed consumerism with wealth. The acquisition of wealth is an active process. It describes our potential as free human beings to attain the goals we set out to achieve. Thus, Mises always writes of human goals which economic activity serves, never about cravings, "growth" or the gross domestic product.

2. The Illusion of Prosperity

Leopold Kohr, another important figure in the Austrian tradition, warned of merely taking the abundance of goods as a yardstick by which to measure prosperity. The question is always: which goods? One must consider that in the artificial growth set into motion by the monetary revolution, an abundance of growth goods was created. These growth goods only became a necessity to the extent they have due to the accompanying distortions. For instance, the car is as such an ingenious entrepreneurial solution to the human goal of individual mobility. However, it only becomes a necessity as a mass product because work places and residences have grown ever farther apart as cities expanded – like points on a balloon that is filled up with air. And as a mass-product, it produces traffic jams, which demand the growth of road networks, which once again increase traffic and lead to even more traffic jams. The ideologue sees these changes and begins to hate roads and cars.

Ecologism is a result of the destruction of nature due to the bubble economy, but as an ideology it feeds new bubbles. The Austrian School does not despise human beings while praising a deserted natural landscape. It only points soberly to the fact that it is a logical consequence of the monetary revolution that nature was pushed back in favor of artificial structures to an extent that no longer reflects human preferences.

Preferences in this context designate goals revealed by human action, not mere expressions of opinions. The latter are subject to excessive fluctuations and have little connection with reality. "Talk is cheap" as the saying goes, only action involves real costs. Markets, prices and interest rates are instruments that serve to coordinate the actions of countless different human individuals. If these institutions of the division of labor are distorted, coordination is impeded. This is probably the most ingenious and at the same time most disastrous aspect of the monetary revolution: it feeds the economic activities of the private sector with frustration and drives more and more people into the embrace of the State. The State must then distribute wealth among its growing number of dependents and minions, a wealth it is unable to generate itself. As a result, the symbiosis between state and industry is not viable

2. The Illusion of Prosperity

in the long run. At some point real wealth begins to decline, as production is no longer able to keep up with consumption.

Leopold Kohr warns of relying on statistics. After all, the prosperity illusion is mainly an illusion of numbers. More general indicators provide better insight into the decline in real prosperity. For instance, prior to the emancipation of women, a husband's salary was as a rule sufficient to support a family. Could it be that the emancipation of women is simply a necessary consequence of the economic trend that has resulted in the typical net salary no longer being enough by a long shot to provide a good life for a family with children?

This lengthy introduction is important, as it stands the typical investor perspective on its head. Since the monetary revolution, the increase in the value of various asset classes is no longer solely the result of entrepreneurial ingenuity and superior knowledge, but is primarily a consequence of economic bubbles. If a hitherto ignored asset class suddenly has the wind in its sails, it perhaps indicates a hunch on the part of some investors, but more likely it is a symptom of the group-think of most other investors. Profitable investment opportunities become gradually scarcer in the course of a bubble. Bloated financial means hurtle around the globe to pick up even the last crumbs. Thus the "Austrian" investor, Jim Rogers, explained why he liquidated his investments in emerging markets in 2007, just as they became a favorite of investment gurus. The main reason for the price increases was no longer the expectation of real wealth creation, but rather the following phenomenon:

> There were twenty thousand MBAs flying around the world, looking for the new hot market. So I sold Botswana, after eighteen years of great gains.[17]

Low interest rates and the inflationary policy of the Fed known as quantitative easing have led to a vast bloating of the stream of fiduciary media in the past several years. Almost every "economic miracle" of the past decade, from Turkey to Brazil, is a consequence of the opening up

2. The Illusion of Prosperity

of new markets to floods of money in a panicky search for yield, and the consequent domestic expansion of fiduciary media.

A corollary of the prosperity illusion is the illusion of investors. Just as managers claim that rising prices in their companies' shares are due to their own efforts, the bubble economy also produces stock market gurus. In both cases, the so-called halo effect is at work. This effect was discovered by US psychologist Edward Thorndyke: officers would ascribe the highest intelligence and the best leadership qualities to soldiers exhibiting the best body posture. Certain traits – in the economy especially recent success – form a "halo", an aura, which all sorts of things are read into.

This mistake most often happens in the evaluation of companies: as soon as a company has drawn attention to itself due to short-term success, this success is explained by its supposedly superior characteristics. Managers suddenly find themselves on the title pages of news magazines, and their foibles serve as the basis of new management styles and fashions, which feed an entire industry of consultants, authors and lecturers. However, any longer-term observation of successful companies is quite sobering: easy come, easy go. In his analysis of the halo effect, Phil Rosenzweig also examines the list of successes of Collins and Porras, who – as so often happens in management literature – chose a group of companies based on their recent success in order to analyze their best practices. However, these turned out to be completely arbitrary:

> In the ten years from 1991 to 2000, only six out of sixteen Visionary companies kept pace with the S&P 500; the other ten did even match the market. You would have been better off investing randomly than putting your money on Collins and Porras's Visionary companies. [...] For the five years after the study ended, only five companies improved their profitability while eleven declined, with one unchanged. [...] More likely, the very things Collins and Porras claimed to be drivers of enduring performance — strong culture, commitment to excellence, and more — were attributions based on performance. [...] Lasting business success, it turns out, is largely a delusion. [...] Guess how many

2. The Illusion of Prosperity

companies on the S&P 500 in 1957 were still on the S&P 500 in 1997, forty years later? Only 74. The other 426 were gone — nudged aside by other companies, or acquired, or bankrupt. And of the 74 survivors, guess how many outperformed the S&P 500 over that time period? Only 12 out of 74. The other 62 survived, yes, but they did thrive. [...] The dominant pattern is not stability or endurance, but the "perennial gale of creative destruction" that Schumpeter talks about. It's entirely normal and very predictable that companies fall back after outstanding performance.[18]

Due to the prosperity illusion, most investment recommendations are dubious. The first step for investors must consist of repudiating illusions and taking the time for in-depth reflection: what if most assumptions regarding wealth management are wrong?

We are often tempted to think in terms of false alternatives. Shortly before the beginning of WW I, which he sought to forestall by all means, the brilliant Austrian School economist and banker Felix Somary made the following investment recommendation to his much more famous colleague Gustav Cassel during a stay in Switzerland:

[Cassel]: "Where would you prefer to invest wealth nowadays, in Berlin or London?"

[Somary]: "If my plan should fail, in neither. They would ruin each other."

[Cassel]: "And where would you invest?"

[Somary]: "In the United States, or here."

"Here?" Cassel asked, astonished. "I'm visiting this place for many years already, but I have never regarded this small Alpine country as anything but a summer vacation place."[19]

2. The Illusion of Prosperity

Somary was one of the first people who realized that the then poor agricultural country of Switzerland would become Europe's new financial center. He was also one of the few to intuit the breakout and magnitude of World War I. A few days before the war began, he converted the bank deposits and stock market investments of his clients into gold, which was ridiculed as a "barbaric relic", and stored it in Switzerland and Norway.

The aim of this book is to put alternatives on the table. Which scenario eventuates in the end, history will show us. The only thing that is certain is that the end of the prosperity illusion is coming. In a best case, real wealth creation will once again flourish after the prosperity illusion ends and bitter impoverishment will be held at bay. This is unfortunately not the most likely outcome. However, instead of dabbling in prophecies, we want to try to better understand the talent for prediction, if it indeed exists.

3. Forecasts and Prophecies

In February 2007, the vice president of one of the most respected German language business news agencies described the mood among economists and business journalists as follows:

> Certainly there are growth and inflation risks [...]. Ultimately though, the US economy is currently regarded as being largely in balance – in short, it is the best of all worlds.[20]

Near the end of 2007, the contrast became obvious to all: there had only been very few warning voices, and they were proved right. Representatives of the Austrian School were particularly prominent among them. Especially in the US media, a number of proponents of this tradition – such as Peter Schiff – in the months and years leading up to the US mortgage debt crisis, participated in heated debates with mainstream economists and journalists, who were wedded to the fairy tale of the "best of all worlds". Although a few people from other economic schools were also issuing words of warning, these were primarily "heterodox" economists who rejected capitalism for ideological reasons and predicted its imminent demise with Marxian certitude.

Does engagement with the Austrian School of Economics provide one with a special prophetic talent? Anyone who studies the history of its adherents closely, is likely to be astonished and will tend to acknowledge that such a talent appears to exist. It begins with the School's founder Carl Menger and continues to the present day. Ludwig von Mises described Menger's foresight as follows:

> "His keen intellect had recognized in which direction Austria, Europe, and the world were pointed; he saw this greatest and highest of all

3. Forecasts and Prophecies

civilizations rushing toward the abyss. He had anticipated the atrocities with which we are faced today [...]. He realized that his fight was futile and hopeless, and became filled with a dark pessimism that exhausted his strength. He passed this pessimism on to his student and friend, Rudolf, successor to the throne. The crown prince took his own life because of despair over the future of his empire and that of European civilization, not because of a woman. [...]

According to my grandfather, as told to me around 1910, Carl Menger had made the following remarks: The policies being pursued by the European powers will lead to a terrible war ending with gruesome revolutions, the extinction of European culture and destruction of prosperity for people of all nations. In anticipation of these inevitable events, all that can be recommended are investments in gold hoards and the securities of the two Scandinavian countries Menger's savings, in fact, were invested in Swedish securities. One who so clearly foresees disaster and the destruction of everything he deems valuable before his fortieth year cannot avoid pessimism and depression. [...] This same pessimism consumed all sharp-sighted Austrians. The tragic privilege attached to being Austrian was the opportunity it afforded to recognize fate."[21]

Are the "Austrians" time and again proved correct because they are especially pessimistic? This would misconstrue the characteristic of the Viennese mentality described further above: a kind of fun-loving sobriety. The proponents of the Austrian School do not close their eyes, even if they do not like what they see. Menger's pupil and assistant Felix Somary, whose prophetic talent was already mentioned, wrote in his memoirs:

> The great catastrophes of our time have not surprised me. As I rejected both of the most extreme political ideologies, Nationalism and Communism, I was able to evaluate things more calmly than the people around me.[22]

Somary was later called the "Raven of Zurich". He aroused a lot of attention when Germany's former minister of finance, Count Lutz

3. Forecasts and Prophecies

Schwerin von Krosigk, documented a conversation with Somary in his book '*It Happened in Germany*':

> In the spring of 1931 the Swiss banker Somary, who had made a name for himself as an economic theorist as well, visited the ministry of finance in Berlin. When asked how long the global economic crisis would last, he replied that three events had to happen before one could even think of a recovery: the banking sectors in Vienna and Berlin would have to be restructured by a crisis, the British Pound had to be untied from gold, and the matches manufactory of Swedish entrepreneur Ivar Kreuger had to collapse. In the early summer of 1931, the banks crashed, later in the summer, the pound was devalued. When Somary was again in Berlin in the spring of 1932, he was received with the question, whether one really still had to wait for the third event. Somary did not take anything back, but rather affirmed that the Kreuger Group would shortly reach the end of the road. Four weeks later, Kreuger shot himself in Paris.[23]

Somary describes the effect of these fulfilled prophecies as follows:

> The prediction, leaked by official bodies, upon eventuating created a certain reputation for me, a strange reputation, and many regarded me with superstitious dread. Some were interested in how I could have foreseen the precise sequence of these events. Anyone who feels the dynamics of a crisis or a revolution in himself, has a clear view of coming events. Forecasting is not a matter for mathematicians or statisticians, and especially not for schoolmasters.[24]

Even though they have a reputation as interpreters of bad omens, the evaluations of Austrians are neither characterized by excessive optimism nor by excessive pessimism. For the liberal (in the classical sense) Ludwig von Mises, the failure of communism was good news, because he recognized much earlier than others what terrible suffering it would produce. He foresaw its end based solely on his economic analysis, wishful ideological thinking played no role in it. This sober approach helped him and other adherents of the Austrian School to maintain

3. Forecasts and Prophecies

cordial relations with the leading socialists of the day. Menger's favorite pupil Richard Schueller was even a good friend of Leon Trotsky.

Mises, Somary and Schueller played a much underestimated role in world history due to their prophetic talents. Felix Somary, who was blessed with almost clairvoyant abilities, was tirelessly active with diplomatic efforts behind the scenes in an attempt to forestall World War I. He almost succeeded. Those who think this is an exaggeration should read his memoirs.

Among the many things Richard Schueller and Ludwig von Mises deserve credit for was rescuing Vienna from an almost certain famine. The people of Vienna, many of whom would not have survived without the secret missions of Schueller and Mises, rewarded their rescuers with ingratitude, by completely erasing their names from memory. If one studies the actions of these three "Austrians" closely, another conclusion can be drawn: a sovereign Austrian state would probably not have existed after the world wars without the efforts of Somary, Schueller and Mises.

Apart from an unerring geopolitical and historical intuition, the economic forecasts of past "Austrians" are also quite impressive. The Great Depression was predicted by several economists of the Austrian School: in Austria, Ludwig von Mises recognized the problem when it was still in an early stage of its development, and told his colleagues in 1924 that the then largest Austrian bank, Creditanstalt, would ultimately become insolvent. Friedrich August von Hayek published several articles in early 1929, in which he predicted the collapse of the US economic expansion. Felix Somary uttered numerous warnings in the late 1920s. In the US, the economists Benjamin Anderson and E.C. Harwood warned that the monetary policy of the Federal Reserve would lead to a crisis. However, as was Somary, they were widely ignored. The breakdown of the Bretton Woods system and the subsequent rise in the price of gold was correctly predicted by several economists of the Austrian School, including Murray Rothbard and Henry Hazlitt.

3. Forecasts and Prophecies

However, even the forecasts of many modern-day "Austrians" are often astonishingly correct: the dotcom bubble and its eventual demise was forecast by numerous proponents of the Austrian School. In October 1999, Sean Corrigan remarked that an enormous bubble had formed and predicted it would burst. He compared the situation with that of the late summer of 1987, the Japanese bubble of the late 1980s and the "roaring 20s" in the United States. In March 2000, Christopher Mayer pointed out that all the ingredients of a major bubble – the fundamental basis (i.e. a technological revolution), the financial basis (i.e. an expansion in the supply of money and credit) and the psychological basis (i.e. the willingness to ignore traditional valuation yardsticks) seemed to be present in the bull market and also predicted that it would end in a crash.

After the dotcom bubble burst, a number of economists predicted the real estate bubble of the 2000s, which led to the "Great Recession" of 2008. In 2002, Robert Blumen characterized the activities of the state-supported mortgage banks Fannie Mae and Freddie Mac as representing growing systemic risk and predicted that they were eventually going to be bailed out. Sean Corrigan pointed to the booming real estate business amid a great many bankruptcies and noted that real estate bubbles tend to burst several years after stock market bubbles, and that mortgage debt securities could suffer an even worse fate than stocks – together with their owners.

Mark Thornton wrote in 2004 that rising interest rates (initiated by the Fed) would trigger a reversal in the housing market, and would unmask the fallacies of the new paradigm. The discovery of past misallocations would ultimately end with the forced nationalization of Fannie Mae and Freddie Mac. Later, he analyzed the effects on the construction industry, the labor market and the rescue of banks in great detail and forecast a deep recession.

In 2005, after observing the real estate mania in Las Vegas, Doug French remarked that "condominiums are the last sector that is buoyed by a boom, and the first that collapses in a bust" and concluded that

3. Forecasts and Prophecies

the end of the boom had to be close. Gary North warned already at an early stage of the dangers of variable rate mortgage loans.

Investor Peter Schiff became famous due to a number of appearances on television (mainly in 2006 and 2007), in which he stood in opposition to a multitude of financial experts and predicted that a huge downturn lay dead ahead. For several years, Schiff had stridently warned of excessive real estate speculation, the boom in mortgage credit, and the coming rescue operations. Banker and economist, Kurt Richebächer, who published a newsletter for investors, also correctly evaluated the situation before he passed away in 2007.

In the German-speaking regions, Roland Baader in particular deserves mentioning, as he warned in his writings on the stock market bubble, the financial and debt crisis, as well as the euro. The story of soccer star Oliver Kahn has become famous; he was inspired to sell his stocks due to Baader's economic analysis, and pointed to Baader's book *Geld, Gott und Gottspieler* (*Money, God and People Playing God*) in a talk show on television. One may be tempted to regard the critique of the euro as ideologically motivated, but it reflects the skepticism of the Austrian School with respect to all forms of centralization.

The precision of the critique reveals its theoretical foundation, especially in the case of Wilhelm Roepke. Roepke already warned of a European currency union in 1965, as its proper precondition was the integration of "the entire economic, credit, financial, and social policy" of the countries involved. He predicted that one would eventually agree on "a minor commitment to monetary discipline rather than a rigorous one".[25]

Should the school of thought that has described and predicted the current dynamics better than others be assumed to be in possession of the better crystal ball?

In reality, the Austrian School is actually characterized by its modest approach to forecasting. Those who now decide to engage more closely

3. Forecasts and Prophecies

with the Austrian School because they are looking for simple ways of forecasting the future will soon be disappointed. Austrians are in fact convinced that the future is uncertain, as it is solely created by human action. They regard the mathematical models that are usually offered as forecasting tools as pseudo-science. The figures of these "forecasts" are really an alibi for cowardice. Their market value consists mainly of providing politicians, managers and bankers with pseudo-scientific excuses to avoid making decisions. A study of 6,500 forecasts by "economic experts" showed that they were on average congruent with reality in 48% of the cases. This means: it is safer to flip a coin than to follow the forecasts of an economic expert.[26]

The more publicity and media fame these "experts" garner, the more their forecasts will tend to diverge from reality. The stock market recommendations of gurus work rather like pyramid schemes: the recommendations themselves cause prices to rise.

There is only one group whose forecasts are even worse than those of "economic experts" and that dominate the mass media to an even greater extent, those of politicians. Even if they require a pseudo-scientific fig leaf, forecasts have only one function for them: to provide cover for their own decisions and provide statistical support for the implementation of specific policies. Let us for instance take a look at the political forecasts in the context of the stimulus effect of recent inflationary policies enacted in the US, which are euphemistically referred to as "quantitative easing". These contain forecasts about how, after the inflation, a controlled decrease in the newly created money substitutes should be performed. However, as we will show later, without reflation it would become immediately apparent that the stimulus had no sustainable effect.

3. Forecasts and Prophecies

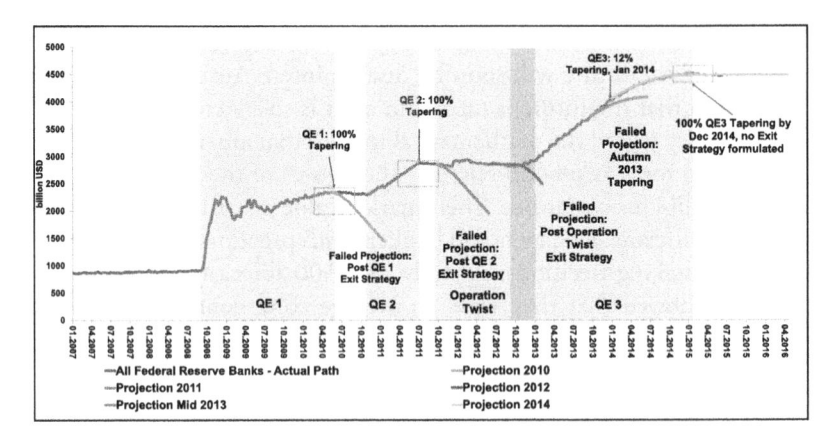

Figure 3.1: Fed balance sheet vs. expectations
(Sources: Federal Reserve St. Louis, Incrementum AG)

How can one explain the prophetic talent of "Austrians" compared to that of other economists and politicians? With respect to an evaluation of the geopolitical situation, which in our highly politicized times is unfortunately often more important than economic analysis, several factors are coming to bear: for one thing, the attempt to eschew ideology and perform a "value neutral" analysis. Proponents of the Austrian School were of course also characterized by strong values and principles, as well as a nigh chivalrous determination and integrity. "Value neutral" only means that one is not closing one's eyes to things one does not like, and does not emphasize or see solely what one especially likes or what one especially detests. Especially in times of electronic networking, tunnel vision often predominates, with people egging each other on toward either excessive optimism, or excessive pessimism or an apathetic search for distractions.

Due to their personalities alone, all the great adherents of the Austrian School were counter-cyclical in their outlook: they stood out from the masses, and stoically endured being ignored, ridiculed and persecuted. However, their status as outsiders was not the only noteworthy feature. These world-class scientists were not exactly lone crackpots.

3. Forecasts and Prophecies

What is remarkable is that their strength of character allowed them to endure falling from the greatest heights on one day, and rising from the greatest depths the next. These changing tides made them unreceptive to mass phenomena like hypes. In the course of their lives, the great representatives of this School went from the status of the most important thinkers and doers of their time, who wrote history and acted eye-to-eye with famous state leaders, to that of enemies of the State, subjects of ridicule falling into obscurity – and back again.

Another major factor behind their forecasting talent was undoubtedly their universal education. All the great adherents of the Austrian School excelled as linguistically gifted universal scholars with vast libraries who, aside from economics, not only had mastery of numerous scientific disciplines, but partly inspired and revolutionized them.

Their common economic perspective was probably only the third most important factor that can explain their geopolitical perceptiveness. Especially helpful in this respect is probably the analysis of incentives. The Austrian School treats men as human beings, and not as super-humans, nor as automata. Pondering the usefulness of alternative courses available to acting men is an excellent method of seeing things one might otherwise overlook. While studying the Austrian School is no doubt helpful in this regard, it is merely complementary in the attempt to understand the world and its dynamic processes.

What about practical investment decisions? Most adherents of the Austrian School managed their private wealth with considerable success, which did not prevent them from often ending up penniless. As their biographies reveal, politics can destroy all economic success. Ludwig von Mises warned his future spouse before their marriage:

> If you want a rich man, don't marry me. I am not interested in earning money. I am writing about money, but I will never have much of my own.[27]

3. Forecasts and Prophecies

Good economists are rarely good speculators. Much more dangerous is, however, the popular notion that a good speculator has to be a good economist. This is just as absurd a fallacy as the idea that the greatest swashbuckler must be an expert on martial law. Similar to "top managers", "top speculators" are often nothing but a myth. Almost all investment gurus are only right during certain periods and stay mum about periods in which they were consistently wrong.

Speculation is largely a question of timing, and decisions regarding proper timing are a rather intuitive affair. One can be the most talented man with respect to clothing, be the best couturier who ever lived, and still be no better than others in foreseeing the exact form and timing of a new fashion trend. Conversely, someone who knows absolutely nothing about fashion could by sheer coincidence act in line with the trend setters.

However, it is quite possible that the conscious manipulation of trends is already a predominant factor these days. Attempts to control the economy are increasing as well. With that, the character of speculation changes: in a politicized environment, a good speculator has an especially good ear for the scheming of politicians or even enjoys good political connections. This is true of most famous speculators, especially the number one: Warren Buffett. A large proportion of his wealth comes from taxpayer funds. Rolfe Winkler summarized this for Reuters as follows:

> Were it not for government bailouts, for which Buffett lobbied hard, many of his company's stock holdings would have been wiped out. Berkshire Hathaway, in which Buffett owns 27 percent, according to a recent proxy filing, has more than $26 billion invested in eight financial companies that have received bailout money. [...] The federal deposit insurance corporation (FDIC) backs more than $130 billion of their debt.[28]

Useful knowledge is nowadays often of the type that provides one with influence and ability to have an impact: powerful friends, well-heeled

3. Forecasts and Prophecies

clients, and a multitude of imitators. This form of "practice" is however corrupting. Corruption means "breaking". We either break ourselves because of it, as no amount of money in the world can outweigh the emptiness that a bad conscience, envy and hate bring about. Not without good reason did Austrian psychologist Viktor Frankl refer to conscience as the "organ of meaning". If we are not breaking ourselves due to our corruption, then society will ultimately break apart because of it. In turn, no amount of money in the world can replace a destroyed society, since one cannot eat money. Locking oneself in a bunker with one's money is not a good investment strategy.

Knowledge that is mainly concerned with "usefulness" is therefore often tainted. It is either out-of-date or too close to the spirit of the times. Some of the worst investment mistakes happen due to overestimating such knowledge. The corruption of mainstream economics discussed above is partially explained by this. Friedrich A. Hayek describes this corruption as follows:

> Not only are there no glittering prizes, no Nobel prizes and – I should have said till recently – no fortunes and no peerages [Hayek alludes to Keynes here], for the economist. But even to look for them, to aim at praise or public recognition, is almost certain to spoil your intellectual honesty in this field. [...] The reason why I think that too deliberate striving for immediate usefulness is so likely to corrupt the intellectual integrity of the economist, is that immediate usefulness depends almost entirely on influence, and influence is gained most easily by concessions to popular prejudice and adherence to existing political groups. [...] [An economist] above everything must have the courage to be unpopular.[29]

Leaving political influence aside, speculation, just as commerce, is however primarily a craft. Good traders have an intuition for prices, for "correct" and "incorrect" prices, prices that work, prices that can be obtained, when one must wait, when one can bid more. And most importantly: when to let go of purchases so as to avoid growing losses. It would be absurd to believe that a trader's experience can be completely replaced by algorithms. With respect to a "perfect investment

3. Forecasts and Prophecies

strategy", the sober assessment of Robert Soros, the son of one of the greatest "investment gurus", is quite revealing:

> My father will sit down and give you theories to explain why he does this or that. But I remember seeing it as a kid and thinking, Jesus Christ, at least half of this is bullshit. I mean, you know the reason he changes his position on the market or whatever is because his back starts killing him. It has nothing to do with reason. He literally goes into a spasm, and it's this early warning sign. [...] And he is living in a constant state of not exactly denial, but rationalization of his emotional state. And it's very funny.[30]

However, Soros, who similar to Buffett must be counted among today's politically connected investors, has every reason to present this intuition as some sort of secret economic knowledge, so as to boost the credibility of his economic policy recommendations. Adherents of the Austrian School are as a rule more honest and more modest in this respect. Felix Somary was one of the most successful investors of the Austrian School. His son relates a similar interpretation as that of Soros' son, however, while the latter is overwhelmed by his father's hypocrisy, the former is overwhelmed by his father's honesty:

> Upon my question how he could see coming events with such clarity, he replied: "I feel what is coming in my bones; it is not solely a matter of knowledge. It does announce itself in the head, but in the marrow of my bones."[31]

Somary took a pass on higher returns if he regarded them as amoral or unnecessary. Economists of the Austrian School look at money as an important means, however, not as a goal or an end in itself. Somary's son describes his father's investment strategy thus:

> With his keen sense for evaluating historic events, he regarded his profession as a priestly office: the preservation of cultural and financial values, in order to be able to afford the freedom to pursue more important efforts, especially the freedom to confront those in power. To lose

money due to inattentiveness, or speculation on credit, he regarded as unforgivable; to speak of billions, as unrealistic. He quietly held the view: money should be anointed by the spirit, the blossoming of the spirit should be made possible by money.[32]

No amount of studies can make up for a lack of intuition, including the study of the Austrian School. An artisan may gain a deeper understanding of his own work, gain self-confidence, and perhaps occasionally a good idea by the study of the history of art, but it can never replace talent and craftsmanship. Books as a medium stand in the great occidental tradition of *theoria*, but practical books about economic topics are as a rule of little value.

This is so because economy means change. Entrepreneurial success means doing something different than has been done hitherto. It is similar with investment success: it requires seeing things others do not see. This ability to see is primarily a talent, secondly down to practice, and only thirdly accessible to rational conception. Many banks prefer not to hire academics for their trading operations, as they think too much and do not have enough intuition.

The greatest danger for every theory is to no longer be *theoria*, curious, purposeless examination, but "a theory" - this is to say, an attempt at explanation through which one tries to adjust the world. The Austrian School is mainly an immunization strategy against both too little and too much "knowledge": against illusion and hubris. F. A. Hayek in particular was critical of the pretense of knowledge, the error to believe that one can immediately explain everything rationally and remove all inconsistencies from the world. These inconsistencies are of special importance: for the scientist, the philosopher, the entrepreneur and the investor. Hayek warns:

> We flatter ourselves undeservedly if we represent human civilization as entirely the product of conscious reason or as the product of human design, or when we assume that it is necessarily in our power deliberately

3. Forecasts and Prophecies

> to re-create or to maintain what we have built without knowing what we were doing. [...]
>
> Many of the greatest things man has achieved are not the result of consciously directed thought, and still less the product of a deliberately co-ordinated effort of many individuals, but of a process in which the individual plays a part which he can never fully understand.[33]

The successful "Austrian" investor Mark Spitznagel regards a recommendation of his "practically-oriented" teacher Everett Klipp confirmed by the Austrian School. When Spitznagel asked Klipp for advice as to what he should study in order to make a career in investment, Klipp opined:

> Anything that won't make you think you know too much.[34]

In the context of the topic of investing, all attention is focused on successful speculators. Due to the halo effect, we tend to believe they are in possession of superior knowledge, and crave a few crumbs of their wisdom. This knowledge in essence appears to concern proper timing, which makes a better view of the future so decisive. This is, however, a grave misunderstanding, as this book will make clear.

First, the bad news: Austrian School economists are on average no better than others with respect to the timing of good buying or selling decisions. Their success is as a rule based on avoiding mistakes and picking investment classes independent of their popularity. From a historical perspective, this has sometimes resulted in instances of astonishingly precise timing, but it has little to do with being better at recognizing favorable price points due to a secret method.

"Austrian" investor Jim Rogers openly admits that he is especially bad at predicting the moment when other investors suddenly become aware of their mistakes. He describes the problem of timing with the following anecdote: in 1970, he expected a sharp market correction. He picked six companies that seemed to have especially large correction

3. Forecasts and Prophecies

potential and sold their shares short. However, their prices initially rose and Rogers was forced to close out his positions, losing everything he had bet on the trade. Nevertheless, he was subsequently proved right:

> Within the next two or three years, every one of those six companies I had shorted went bankrupt, and I was a genius. Which put me in mind of the saying "If you're so smart, then why are you rich?"
>
> This was a perfect example of being smart and not being rich. I had been so smart I went broke. I did not know what the markets were capable of.
>
> On Wall Street there is no truer adage, I learned, than the one attributed erroneously to John Maynard Keynes: "Markets can remain irrational longer than you can remain solvent."[35]

The big question every Austrian School economist is asked today is: when is the big crisis going to happen? What is meant by this is a bursting of bubbles, which leads to such dramatic losses in asset prices that even the mass media will be full of crisis talk. However, waiting for a crisis makes no sense. The point in time when large market breaks happen cannot be foreseen with certainty by anyone; some may be able to intuit them, but this is something we only ever know in hindsight.

Nassim Taleb speaks of "black swans",[36] remote events, which no-one can foresee and which therefore surprise everyone. His main thesis is that due to emotional deficiencies, people's cognitive abilities are susceptible to underestimating the role of randomness in almost all financial and economic circumstances. These deficiencies are mainly the result of prejudices, which tempt people to overestimate their forecasting abilities. What appears to be investment acumen, is often nothing but sheer luck. A financial loss can be the result of rare events – i.e. "black swans" - which are considered unforeseeable. Taleb's warning regarding exaggerated confidence is inspired by Scottish philosopher David Hume, who wrote:

3. Forecasts and Prophecies

> No number of observations of white swans can allow the inference that all swans are white, but the observation of a single black swan is sufficient to refute that conclusion.[37]

In Taleb's opinion, economists are susceptible to erroneous assessments, as soon as they ascribe excessive precision to statistical methods. He provides inter alia two major reasons for this. First of all, they often fall prey to the fallacious assumption that extensive amounts of historical observations permit conclusions about the future, and secondly, that future events are subject to a bell-shaped probability distribution. In other words: they do not assume that past correlations may be subject to randomness as well.

In many respects, especially in his critical assessment of mainstream economists, who are proponents of the "religion of efficient markets", Taleb sounds like an Austrian School adherent. The economists he criticizes are misguided because they start from the erroneous hypothesis that human action is perfectly rational and mathematically "optimal". However, a crisis is not an unforeseeable, sudden event from the perspective of the Austrian School. The correction in prices would be sudden, due to self-reinforcement effects, but it would not be unforeseen. Taleb's former colleague Mark Spitznagel therefore corrects him by saying:

> The real black swan problem of stock market busts is not about a remote event that is considered unforeseeable, but rather a foreseeable event that is considered remote [...].[38]

While the assumption that the correction is temporally remote delays its occurrence, it also increases the potential danger of losses when it eventually does occur. What is important is the realization that the crisis is already here, and is not something that has yet to happen. The term crisis, similar to the term critique, come from the Greek term *krinein*, which means "to part with", or "to separate". At present, we are living in such a crisis period, which separates illusion from fiction and requires uncomfortable decisions.

3. Forecasts and Prophecies

Much that people in our latitudes regard as perfectly natural these days is built on sand and is not sustainable. Of course this is only bad news for those who are surprised by the crisis or unable to part with their comforting illusions. The ignorant become even more impatient and restless in times of crisis; they cry for the practical and useful and detest all that is theoretical or fundamental. Their error is significant. Especially in times of upheaval, a new type of practice is needed, a different form of action, which demands a calm contemplation of what is important first. Without contemplation, without knowing what is fundamental and important, no sensible actions and decisions can be taken.

"Austrian" investor James Grant describes the modest role of good economic theory in the daily routine of the concrete decisions made by a professional investor as follows:

> What we do is look for extremes in markets: very undervalued or very overvalued. Austrian theory has certainly given us an edge. When you have a theory to work from, you avoid the problem that comes with stumbling around in the dark over chairs and night stands. At least you can begin to visualize in the dark, which is where we all work. The future is always unlit. But with a body of theory, you can anticipate where the structures might lie. It allows you to step out of the way every once in a while.[39]

4. The Monetary System

What is Money?

We have been talking about a monetary revolution in the previous chapters, but let us begin by answering what money is all about. From a strict perspective of the Austrian School, we can no longer label the circulating banknotes and deposits of today money. The euro is therefore not a monetary unit, but the name for a fiduciary medium – we can speak of a "currency" as opposed to money. A currency rests on confidence in the State and the banking system and loses its value if this confidence is lost. That may sound like sophistry, but its importance seems obvious in light of historical experience. All economic activity has been a race between people who were searching for a money to transfer and store their economic energy, and those who abused the monetary standards that evolved or were created.

Adherents of the Austrian School emphasize that exchange is not only the primary function of money, but also its origin. Carl Menger regarded money as a "social phenomenon" that was one of the "unintended results of social movement".[40] "The economic interest of the economic individuals, therefore, with increased knowledge of their individual interests, without any agreement, without legislative compulsion, even without any consideration of public interest, leads them to turn over their wares for more marketable ones" […] "which our predecessors called *Geld*".[41] The conclusion to be drawn from this brings Menger into sharp opposition with his mainly *etatiste* expert colleagues, who rationalize the unlimited right of the State to intervene in monetary matters by asserting that money is a creation of the State. Menger by contrast states:

> Money is not an invention of the state. It is not the product of a legislative act. Even the sanction of political authority is a notion alien to the concept of money. Certain commodities came to be money quite naturally, as the result of economic relationships that were independent of the power of the state.[42]

The "Austrians" thus assume that money is a result of voluntary actions. Certain commodities, which are valuable to people without a government decree, prove to have greater marketability. That there is definitely a close connection to their character as goods is suggested by the multitude of commodities that have been used as preferred media of exchange in a variety of cultures, ranging from seashells to salt to tea and even dried tiger tongues.

The additional monetary demand, this is to say the demand for the commodity for the purpose of indirect exchange, leads to an increase in its value, which deviates from the previous industrial demand. Industrial demand is based on a good's direct use-value. Exchange value can easily reach a multiple of use value. Friedrich von Wieser defines exchange value as the "anticipated use value of the things which can be obtained for it".[43] Ludwig von Mises explains the process as follows:

> When individuals began to acquire objects, not for consumption, but to be used as media of exchange, they valued them according to the objective exchange-value with which the market already credited them by reason of their 'industrial' usefulness, and only as an additional consideration on account of the possibility of using them as media of exchange.[44]

The explanation of money's exchange value on the basis of its earlier use value is called the "regression theorem" by Austrian economists. Before Mises came up with the regression theorem, the explanation for the demand for money was circular: why is money demanded? Because it possesses purchasing power, because one can buy things with it. Why though does it possess purchasing power? Because there is a demand for it. Mises resolved this circular reasoning by going back in time: people purchase goods and commodities as well as money at certain prices, because they recall the successful exchanges of yesterday. On occasion of these exchanges, they in turn found prices that were determined by the exchanges of the previous day, and so forth. At the end of the temporal regression is the moment when the money commodity was solely exchanged based on its use value, and thus was valued in the market according to the subjective evaluations of its marginal utility. When the money commodity begins to gain acceptance as a medium of indirect exchange, market participants therefore already know which and how many goods can be exchanged for it.

The highest exchange value is accorded to the commodities with the highest marketability; the ones that are most likely to meet with the approval of potential exchange partners and the exchange of which is also practicable. This practicability appears to be a characteristic of especially the kinds of commodities that enjoy a special value as money commodities as well. William Stanley Jevons enumerated the characteristics of money commodities, which are listed in decreasing importance:[45]

1. utility and value
2. portability
3. indestructibility
4. homogeneity
5. divisibility
6. stability of value
7. cognizability

However, not even metal coins are recognized as possessing the characteristics of commodities by a great many people. Hardly anyone exercises a demand for coins in order to use the metal they contain. However, this objection is irrelevant. First of all, it is the very essence of money that its monetary demand far exceeds its industrial demand. Secondly, the commodity character is not a physical characteristic that

4. The Monetary System

is accessible in terms of direct and immediate usefulness. Final consumers have little use for the tradable form of a great many goods. A pallet of trading units used in the wholesale trade is almost as far removed from potential consumption as a coin is from silverware. Carl Menger states the following to this:

> For no "commodities" as such serve a consumption purpose, and least of all in the forms in which they are traded (i.e. in the form of ingots and bales, and in cases, packages, etc.). To be consumed a good must cease to be a "commodity" and relinquish the form in which it has been traded (i.e. it must be melted down, divided, unpacked, etc.). The coin and the ingot are the most common forms in which the precious metals are traded, and the fact that these forms must be abandoned before the precious metals can be brought into consumption is therefore nothing that justifies doubting their commodity-character.[46]

Thirdly, the origin of money from commodities must be viewed as a historical process, not as a snapshot in time. Convincing circumstantial evidence for this consists of the fact that many of the names of currencies that are still in use today were originally measures of weight. There is plenty of evidence of weighing in connection with payments. Even the bible speaks of money that "has its full weight". Currency names that cannot be traced to measures of weight often have some other connection to a commodity, such as the Indian rupee, which is derived from the word for livestock.

Even if the exchange thesis should not be historically tenable, modern experience still argues in its favor. In societies of the past, indirect exchange may not have had sufficient significance; however, if money were to originate in a society with a well-developed division of labor, it could very well emerge directly from the need to facilitate exchanges. This is shown by events of the recent past: after wars and currency collapses, cigarettes quite often became a medium of exchange. After World War II, there were even still a few advertisements that quoted prices in terms of cigarettes. In this case, we are looking at a consumer good that is quite useful as a medium of exchange in line with the criteria of Jevon's list. Cigarettes also often serve as a medium of exchange in jails, along with razor blades in negligent institutions and drugs, resp. syringes in the most negligent ones. In German-speaking regions, butter, rye and flour sometimes served as mediums of exchange after wars and crises. Loans and participatory interests were also fixed in terms of commodities at this time. In the Mediterranean region, people fell back on olive oil after World War II, which had already possessed the function of money there in antiquity.

Precious metals, however, have rarely emerged anew as mediums of exchange in modern times, probably because they are not available to the general public, and do not attract direct demand for consumption purposes. After all, wars were also always periods of expropriation, during which the population was as a rule relieved of its gold in exchange for iron or paper.

An alternative thesis regarding the origin of money as a medium of exchange regards money primarily as a means for the accumulation of wealth. The most obvious commodities for accumulating wealth appear to have been those that are useful such as clothing or jewelry. Rings are mentioned in numerous cultures as goods that were employed in wealth accumulation. In India, the close connection between jewelry and wealth has been preserved to this day. When the rupee was still a metallic money, Indians would regularly carry their savings to a blacksmith, in order to melt the coins down and rework them into bracelets. A similar dual function once appears to have been fulfilled by devotional jewelry made from precious metals as well. As a result, temples were the first banking houses. Precious metals, which were used for ornamental purposes, were concurrently employed as stores of value. In emergencies, ornaments and bells would be melted down again.

This wealth accumulation function is curiously overlooked in most disquisitions on money. This is paradoxical, after all there are strong arguments for this not only being an important, but possibly even the historically most important function of money. There are several reasons for this neglect. On the one hand, hoarding is often perceived negatively, and things that are scorned are often ignored. The enmity towards hoarding can probably be ascribed to negative historical experiences with the accumulation of goods like livestock and slaves, and on the other hand to the moral taint associated with a purely quantitative fixation on growth. Another reason for wealth accumulation being overlooked consists of the fact that this function does not define money, but at best appears to be one of its subsidiary attributes. While numerous goods are useful for wealth accumulation, they would never be described with the term money, due to their lack of divisibility and mobility, such as real estate, pageantries, obelisks, steles, etc. Similarly, most jewelry, apart from that made from precious metals, is not considered money due to its lack of homogeneity.

It is therefore understandable that money's function as a medium of exchange is the preferred definition. This is, however, not an obstacle to acknowledging the historical primacy of wealth accumulation. After all, there exists plenty of historical evidence for it. For instance, African tribal chiefs were hoarding ivory long before it became a medium of exchange due to the demand of European merchants. Carl Menger himself conceded that "accumulation [...] by its nature is older than the appearance of the exchange of goods and money".[47] He employed the German term "Thesaurierung" to describe the function of wealth accumulation. On the other hand, Menger contends that it is precisely their function as media of exchange that makes specific commodities useful for the accumulation of wealth. Thus these two functions are in a reciprocal relationship:

> With the increase in the division of labor and the growing dependence of individual economies on the market, exchange commodities especially gain in importance for the purpose of wealth accumulation, among them however particularly the media of exchange. [...] Conversely, the special usefulness of a commodity for wealth accumulation and, as a consequence thereof, the widespread employment of the same for the above purpose, is one of the most important reasons for its increased marketability, and hence its usefulness as a medium of exchange.[48]

What is Money?

Commodities that are used as money exhibit a relatively slow rate of decline in their marginal utility. The law of declining marginal utility states that as the supply of a good at one's disposal increases, the utility of the last unit added to the stock of the good tends to steadily decrease. To put it differently: monetary commodities appear to be the kinds of goods one can hardly get enough of. Established money in a materialistic culture indeed appears to exhibit an almost (but not quite) stable utility. This was already observed by Xenophon in ancient Greece in the context of the monetary metal used at the time:

> [...] but of silver no one ever yet possessed so much that he was forced to cry "enough." On the contrary, if ever anybody does become possessed of an immoderate amount he finds as much pleasure in digging a hole in the ground and hoarding it as in the actual employment of it. And from a wider point of view: when a state is prosperous there is nothing which people so much desire as silver. The men want money to expend on beautiful armour and fine horses, and houses, and sumptuous paraphernalia of all sorts. The women betake themselves to expensive apparel and ornaments of gold. Or when states are sick, either through barrenness of corn and other fruits, or through war, the demand for current coin is even more imperative (whilst the ground lies unproductive), to pay for necessaries or military aid.[49]

Due to the less pronounced decline in their marginal utility, money commodities are hoarded to a greater extent than other goods. This results in the accumulation of relatively large inventories. In economics, the relationship between these inventories and production is referred to as the stock-to-flow ratio. Precious metals have even today the highest stock-to-flow ratio of all commodities. This is the result of thousands of years of hoarding. It is interesting that precisely this fact has an economic effect that increases their usefulness as money: commodities with high inventories are less sensitive to changes in production and due to the price stability this confers are more useful as measures of value. Jevons already recognized this characteristic of precious metals:

4. The Monetary System

> Its value too remains very stable for periods of fifty or a hundred years, because a vast stock of the metal is kept in the form of plate, watches, jewelry, and ornaments of various kinds, in addition to money, so that a variation in the supply for a few years cannot make any appreciable change in the total stock.[50]

Antal Fekete differentiates between a monetary commodity's usefulness for hoarding, on which its usefulness for wealth accumulation depends, and its marketability, on which its usefulness as a medium of exchange depends.[51] In his interpretation of the history of money he even states that these distinguishable characteristics were often expressed by the employment of two different goods as money: one commodity is used as a medium of exchange, which especially enables transfers through space, and another is used as a hoarding money, which enables especially transfers through time. Prior to the employment of precious metals as money, cattle served most often in the former and salt in the latter function.

The connection between money and debt appears to be especially close in our time. This has led to the increasingly popular view that debt itself is the essence of money. Debt relationships have probably existed since the dawn of civilization. That the provision of a service and receipt of consideration for it do not always coincide is almost a necessity of economic activity through time. However, is money indeed primarily a debt claim?

Some slices of historical evidence appear to affirm this; these are however exceptions, which should actually be regarded as "economic maladies", i.e. misguided developments, which represent a long-term threat to the existence of the societies concerned. If debt becomes the central focus of economic activity, there is on the one hand a disciplining incentive effect observable, but economic activity then begins to serve the associated constraints rather than human needs: people no longer work in order to live, but live in order to work. We will take a closer look at the dynamics of debt later. In order to gain a timeless understanding of the phenomenon of money, it is better to separate it from

What is Money?

the phenomenon of debt. As we will also show, today's "money" is as a rule created by credit expansion. This has resulted in the "Debitism" school of thought defining money as a debt medium, and interpreting the history of money as a history of debt relationships. In its analysis of the contemporary monetary system, Debitism is in large parts accurate, however, its historical analysis must be regarded as too one-sided.

Today's attempts to interpret money generally and primarily as a fiduciary medium is in most cases subject to a confusion between different types of money. Mises differentiated between commodity money, fiat money and credit money:

> We may give the name of commodity money to that sort of money that is at the same time a commercial commodity; and that of fiat money to money that comprises things with a special legal qualification. A third category may be called credit money, this being that sort of money which constitutes a claim against any physical or legal person. But these claims must not be both payable on demand and absolutely secure; if they were, there could be no difference between their value and that of the sum of money to which they referred, and they could not be subjected to an independent process of valuation on the part of those who dealt with them. In some way or other the maturity of these claims must be postponed to some future time.[52]

Since today's paper money offers no enforceable legal claim, it does not represent credit money, but fiat money. It is of course a special form of fiat money, which is created by an act of credit expansion. Hence the confusion. There have been repeated attempts to legitimize fiat money as credit money. Credit money requires a money or a good that exists independently of it as a reference. After the French Revolution, claims to expropriated real estate were used to create a kind of pseudo-mortgage money, the assignat, which ultimately ended up as a fiat money anyway. One cannot speak of credit money when the claim is too vague or not actionable, resp. not legally enforceable. Government fiat money is often interpreted as a claim to "national wealth". This is pure rhetoric and has no basis in reality.

From these types of money Mises differentiates payment orders, which he does not regard as money. A payment order is a kind of receipt for services rendered, which represents a claim to some sort of consideration. Without a reference value this attribution is however arbitrary, and can hardly be handled outside of a command economy. Payment orders would be the equivalent of bearer certificates, which confer a claim to dividends in kind. This may be doable within a company, such as an agricultural enterprise: every year such bearer certificates, which are denominated as a percentage share, could be exchanged for a share in the harvest. The greater the variety of goods however, the more difficult this would become. Applied to an entire economy, the feasibility of such a scheme is hardly imaginable. Moreover, the return is so uncertain, that such bearer certificates would always have the character of a lottery. They could not possibly serve as a measure of value. As Mises explains:

> If, with the same number of hours of labor, the income of the society in a given year was only half as big as in the previous year, then the value of each receipt would likewise be halved. The case of money is different. A decrease of 50 per cent in the real social income would certainly involve a reduction in the purchasing power of money. But this reduction in the value of money need not bear any direct relation to the decrease in the size of the income. It might accidentally happen that the purchasing power of money was exactly halved also; but it need not happen so. This difference is of fundamental importance. In fact, the exchange-value of money is determined in a totally different way from that of a certificate or warrant. Titles like these are not susceptible of an independent process of valuation at all.[53]

While a money substitute in the form of such payment certificates is theoretically thinkable, it can neither be observed in reality, nor is it plausible as a practical matter. Company-issued certificates would never be useful as a general medium of exchange, while certificates referring to a national economy are unrealistic. Most arguments in favor of a payment order money as well as credit money are more or less plausible "what if" stories, which are incongruent with actual history. There is, however, evidence that credit is an age-old phenomenon, which may often well have preceded exchange. If there is no generally accepted medium of exchange, direct exchange can be made easier by "chalking up" debts, which is conceivable even without a writing system. Whether debt comes first, which can later be repaid with a medium of exchange, or a medium of exchange comes first that makes the standardization of debt possible, is actually a rather irrelevant question.

The theory that regards debt as the origin of money, often assumes the State to be the actual originator of money as a debt standard. This would make money, contrary to the "Austrian" perspective, a creature of the state. The interpretation of money as a sign of sovereignty is an approach that has received ideological cover since the romantic school of economics and empirical cover with the paper money experiments of modern times.

The great importance of demands for tribute for the valuation of money commodities is not in question. The demand for coercive payments in the form of a specific commodity, a monopolized means of payment, indeed allows one to explain the value of such state-issued money. Georg Holzbaumer speaks of the "tax foundation" of currencies that are forced on people by usurpers.[54] The state theory of money was also proposed in exaggerated form by Georg Friedrich Knapp. Knapp's writings were well received at the time of their publication and continue to shape the debate to this day. Especially John Maynard Keynes was strongly influenced by Knapp. Today money is undoubtedly a government undertaking everywhere, however, the present cannot be evaluated without understanding the social and economic phenomenon money, which preceded its usurpation by the State.

Knapp's theory, which does not regard money's value, but its validity purely as a state-issued decree, is referred to as Chartalism in the literature. In the 19th and 20th centuries, the dispute between Chartalism and its supposed opposite, metallism, rumbled on. Chartalism regards money as a mere token, the carrier of which is of secondary importance, which therefore may have no substance at all. Metallism by contrast

4. The Monetary System

sees the value of money solely embodied in its metallic value. Money in its original sense is thus regarded as a fixed unit of precious metal. This dispute was unfortunately not especially fruitful, as normative, historical and economic perspectives were jumbled up.

From an economic perspective, money in the form of an insubstantial token can at best serve as a medium of exchange, whereby it is hardly plausible that people would accept an insubstantial token, which is not a direct claim on a good, en lieu of payment without coercion. Historically, there exist however numerous hints as to the token character of money, not least because every money commodity becomes increasingly remote from its mere commodity character due to monetary demand. Most metallists are well aware of the fact that monetary demand can exceed industrial demand by far and become the main criterion of value. Nevertheless, it is understandable from historical experience, why the token character is perceived to be so important: once a money commodity has become a generally accepted medium of exchange, it appears only as a token of value to the average user in everyday life. The direct connection to the metal content, by measuring and melting, disappears. As a result, Chartalists can point to a supposedly long intellectual tradition. Plato already referred to money as a symbol, with metal merely functioning as a guarantor.

However, the countless hints in the literature regarding the importance of minting coins for the purpose of fixing values are different from the pointed ideological emphasis in modern Chartalism. In most cases, merely the definition of a specific aspect is in focus, namely the legal one: the State's definition of a specific money commodity as the preferred commodity for taxation and tribute and as the means for discharging debts. This aspect, in the sense of a historical observation, as well as the token character of money, by no means has to be in contradiction with the perspective that most money originated from precious metals. Metallism and Chartalism are therefore imaginary contradictions, similar to most modern-day ideologies. In line with the Historicist School, which was predominantly metallistic, Austrian School adherents are also most often regarded as proponents of metallism.

What is Money?

The School's founder, Carl Menger, strongly contested Knapp's theory at any rate. Of course he did not deny that there is heavy government intervention in monetary affairs. He only wanted to make perfectly clear that money already existed as a social phenomenon without coercion and government decrees. It was therefore fruitless from an economic perspective to include the State in its very definition. He resolves the confusion surrounding Chartalism and metallism as follows:

> The best guarantee of the full weight and assured fineness of coins can, in the nature of the case, be given by the government itself, since it is known to and recognized by everyone and has the power to prevent and punish crimes against the coinage. Governments have therefore usually accepted the obligation of stamping the coins necessary for trade. But they have so often and so greatly misused their power, that economizing individuals eventually almost forgot the fact that a coin is nothing but a piece of precious metal of fixed fineness and weight, for which fineness and full weight the honesty and rectitude of the mint constitute a guarantee. Doubts even arose as to whether money is a commodity at all. Indeed, it was finally declared to be something entirely imaginary resting solely on human convenience. The fact that governments treated money as if it actually had been merely the product of the convenience of men in general and of their legislative whims in particular contributed therefore in no small degree to furthering errors about the nature of money.[55]

It is however correct, as the Chartalists suggest, that the growth of the State and its demands have greatly propagated the use of money. The close connection between money and demands for tribute has persisted up until our age. Every collector of compulsory levies is faced by the problems of measuring, transporting and storing valuable goods.

Undoubtedly each of the factors mentioned above is relevant to the phenomenon of money. The debate over which factor preceded the others is of historical rather than of economic importance. Irrespective of the historical sequence, the question of defining money is important. The most prevalent definition of money is tied to its function as a medium

4. The Monetary System

of exchange, and this is quite sensible. Even if other factors should prove ultimately more important in practice, they are less useful for the purpose of defining money. What is required for a useful definition are the characteristics that represent the sole and distinguishing features of money. Numerous commodities can serve as a means to save, as a unit of account, as a means to pay tribute or debt, without necessarily being money. Money is ultimately what we regard as a means of payment because counterparties will accept it in exchange. We would not refer to commodities that may be useful as a means for the accumulation of wealth or serve as units of account as money, if it were not possible to use them for payment. If a commodity is not yet generally accepted as a medium of exchange, we may strictly speaking only state that it *might* be useful as money, but not that it already *is* money.

The essential characteristic of money is indirect exchange. In contrast to direct exchange, trust in one's counterparty no longer plays such a dominant role anymore. This trust is now largely transferred to a medium. It is not surprising that when dealing with issues of trust, state and religion often play an important role, in the worst case by replacing well-founded trust with blind faith.

However, it is not enough to consider only money's exchange function. There are other factors that help to distinguish good from bad money. A certain type of money could fulfill one function well, but the others either not at all, or badly. Thus the transition from commodity money to fiat money has perhaps simplified its function as a medium of exchange, however it has made the function as a means of saving and a measure of value more difficult, as money has become more susceptible to interventions and money supply expansion. One must be careful with the phrase "measure of value" in the context of money though, regardless of what type of money one considers. Since the value of money is itself subject to the forces of supply and demand and the associated subjective value judgments of acting men, its value can never be constant. This fact incidentally renders all attempts to calculate "price indexes" such as CPI, which purport to measure the mythical "general price level" moot. Mises already remarked that every housewife probably knows more about the continual decline in the purchasing power of state-issued money than the statistics offices of the government. However, a money that has originated in the market will as a rule rarely experience large short-term fluctuations in its exchange value. It will therefore be useful for the purpose of economic calculation, and in this narrow sense may be regarded as a "measure of value". The differentiation between the different functions of money could well serve as a model for an actual separation of these functions by employing different goods or auxiliary means. Thus money could easily serve well as a medium of exchange because it is generally accepted, but still be a very inferior means of saving due the steady downtrend in its value. This is the situation we are faced with today.

In summary: money is defined most clearly as the generally accepted medium of exchange, even though the term "generally accepted" still leaves a lot of room for clarification. Often other functions are connected with it as well. While it is not necessary, it is advantageous if money is able to fulfill these other major functions as well. The historical question whether exchange, debt or coercion stood at the beginning of money, is secondary. There exists some evidence for all these forms of money origination. It is, however, beyond doubt that commodities can attain a monetary function without debt relationships and without coercion. As Ludwig von Mises notes in Human Action:

> A medium of exchange which is commonly used as such is called money. The notion of money is vague, as its definition refers to the vague term "commonly used." There are borderline cases in which it cannot be decided whether a medium of exchange is or is not "commonly" used and should be called money. But this vagueness in the denotation of money in no way affects the exactitude and precision required by praxeological theory. For all that is to be predicated of money is valid for every medium of exchange.[56]

What then is today's money? To a minor extent it consists of uncovered paper fiat money, which has been put into and is kept in circulation by coercion, and which has developed out of partially backed receipts for

4. The Monetary System

commodity money and the existence of which can thus be explained with the aid of the regression theorem. To a much larger extent, it consists of certificates and fiduciary media referring to this fiat money. It is a coercive money, in the form of central bank-issued notes and where applicable coins and deposits, insofar as they are legal tender. In most countries of the world, the creation of money follows a similar procedure. We want to call this special category of coercion-supported fiat money *currency*, in line with today's linguistic usage. However, as the definitional aspect of money, namely voluntary exchange between individuals, is thereby undermined, we should refrain from referring to this arrangement as "money". It is a replacement for money, which cannot replace money in the long run though. The respective leading currencies which are employed as this inadequate replacement standard mainly correspond to military superiority and do not represent a superior quality of money.

In present times, we can observe what is to some extent a desperate attempt to find alternatives to currencies. The entire problem of investing consists of this at its core. Since no sound money is available, even hoarding becomes a matter of speculation. Thus alternatives are sought for every function of sound money: the exchange function, the saving function, the measure of value function (keeping in mind the limitations of the latter discussed above).

In order to better understand this problem in modern times and evaluate possible future developments, it is important to once again take a closer look at the dynamics which lead to the creation of money. Candidates for money, actual monies and replacement monies differ from each other in their demand structure. As we have seen, the demand for money consists essentially of monetary and industrial demand. This basic segmentation can however be subjected to a finer gradation. Industrial demand is demand for a commodity for the purpose of using it as a direct means to achieve a goal. These goals can however be one's own, voluntarily chosen ones, or be the result of coercion (such as tax payments). Monetary demand in turn has even three aspects: firstly, the already mentioned aspect of marketability, which equates to a demand for additional exchange possibilities.

Secondly, a demand for facilitating exchange. Certain means of payment turn out to be more practicable than others for this purpose. Often this practicability comes at the detriment of use value though. Thus, digital transfers are more practicable than the transfer of banknotes, banknotes in turn are more practicable than coins. Due to the demand for the facilitation of exchanges, money substitutes such as delivery notes and bills of exchange have developed, which initially go hand in hand with a decrease in marketability (additional trust issues, introductory difficulties, learning barriers regarding their use).

The third type of monetary demand is demand for speculative purposes. Every commodity that stands on the threshold of being accepted as a general medium of exchange experiences a bubble-like development: due to additional monetary demand, its value rises by multiples. Since some market participants are able to forecast this to varying degrees, speculative demand ensues, this is to say a demand which anticipates this future increase in value.

Based on these five types of demand, potential means of payment can be differentiated. In figure , the following cases are examined by way of example:

1. A commodity – this has only use value, at most a small speculative demand, should some market participants anticipate an increase in its marketability.

2. A proto-commodity money – this implies that it is realized step by step that a commodity is becoming more marketable, however, use as a medium of exchange has not yet become widespread, or there are no markets yet, resp. only direct exchange. In this case, people already demand the commodity to an extent that exceeds their own needs for direct use.

4. The Monetary System

3. A commodity money – in this case, the most marketable commodity opens up new possibilities for exchange. Marketability often correlates with the facilitation of exchange due to specific physical characteristics of the commodity, as described above. People increasingly demand this commodity in order to make trading with others easier. It is a general medium of exchange and hence money.

4. A commodity money certificate can replace a commodity money partly or to a great extent, if the demand for facilitating exchanges increases due to trading volume. Direct use thus increasingly moves into the background. This is why commodity monies can be easily replaced with fiat money, if one succeeds in resolving the problem of trust – which in the short term often requires deceit.

5. Proto-fiat money designates the possibility that even with only very little industrial demand (willingness to pay out of curiosity, or due to esthetic or non-material appreciation of the idea, identification with a group/religion, etc.), monetary demand is strong enough to create a new means of payment. A current example for this is Bitcoin, which we will later discuss in more detail. Origination of a token money without preceding industrial demand is unlikely due to the problem of trust.

6. A fiat money can however emerge from a proto-fiat money, if speculative demand is proved correct insofar as the proto-fiat money ultimately provides a simplification of exchange compared to alternative means of payment, and allows new markets to be opened. In that event, industrial demand may eventually become entirely unimportant. If speculative demand is, however, never replaced by the two other types of monetary demand, it represents a speculative bubble. In addition, this has the characteristics of a pyramid scheme, if not even a reasonable basis to assume simplification of exchange or marketability exists, but the focus is only the prospect of rising prices.

What is Money?

7. State-imposed fiat money – historically, this money has as a rule emerged from a commodity money by means of deception. In theory, it could also emerge from a proto-fiat money, the industrial demand for which is artificially supported by compulsory levies. It would, however, only be used as a general medium of exchange if a simplification of exchange seems possible (useful form, denomination, etc.).

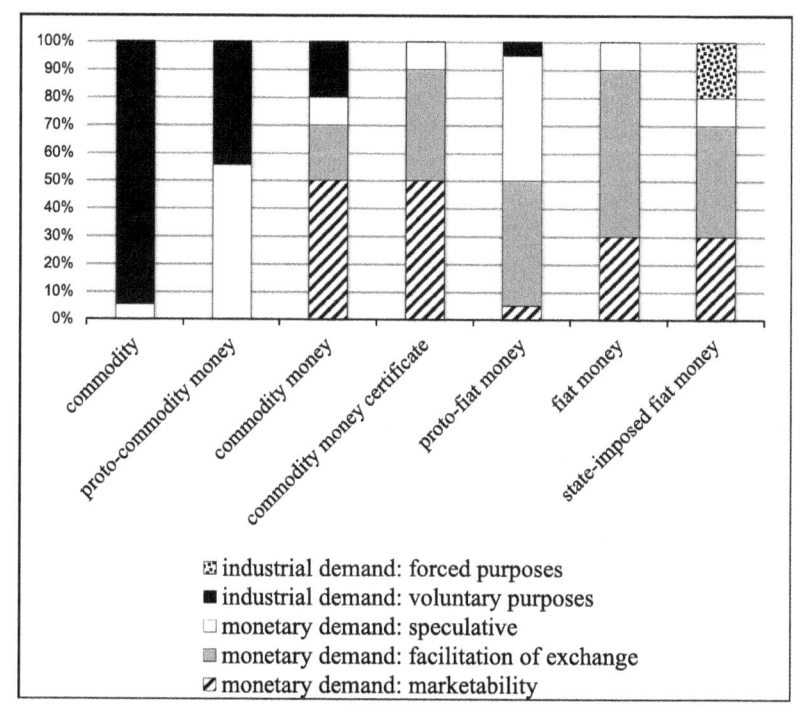

Figure 4.1: The road from commodity money to fiat money

4. The Monetary System

The Paper Money Era

For the past several years, the media have time and again reported about an "economic crisis". Most of the time the term is mentioned in connection with a number of different phenomena, such as high unemployment rates, high public deficits, zero interest rate policies, etc. The "financial market crisis" of the autumn of 2008 is still pointed to as the reason for these crisis symptoms. In the course of this ongoing crisis, thousands of interviews have been given, countless scientific papers published and countless political decisions taken. What is, however, far too rarely questioned is whether the reasons for the current crisis are endogenous or exogenous. Exogenous shocks as a matter of principle come from outside the economic and currency system. Among these are for example crop failures due to bad weather, the destruction of productive capital due to natural catastrophes, and so forth. Endogenous problems by contrast can be attributed to system-intrinsic instability.

If one wants to identify the core of today's systemic crisis, it is imperative to consider the currency policy related events of August 15 1971, when president Nixon ended the Bretton Woods agreement with the words:

> The dollar will be worth as much tomorrow as it is today. The effect of this measure is the stabilization of the dollar.[57]

In the course of the past century, the global currency regime was revised every few decades. In this context, the years 1914, 1933 and 1971 are of special historical importance. Today's currency regime developed gradually, from a classical gold standard (until 1914), to a gold exchange standard, and subsequently to a pure paper money system (fiat money). The restriction that central banks could only expand their balance sheets and with it the monetary base in a certain relation to their gold reserve has been relaxed one step at a time. On August 15 1971, the dollar's final tie to gold was finally cut by Richard Nixon.

The US dollar had ascended to the status of global reserve currency in the framework of the post war order, thus this step had global consequences. Ultimately, the decoupling from gold was a logical consequence of the fact that the US had abused its privilege of creating currency, which led to a crisis of confidence in the US dollar. Many countries – with France at the forefront – were increasingly suspicious that the US would not keep its promise that the dollar would "remain as good as gold". The fear that this "exorbitant privilege" would be abused was to come true. The US war policy of the 1960s as well as a massive increase in public welfare spending were partly financed by uncovered money supply expansion, i.e., monetary inflation. Repatriation of the gold reserves that had been stored mainly in the US after World War II began in the 1960s. After the final repudiation of the gold exchange standard, the door had been opened to additional extensive monetization of government debt. This led to a significant devaluation of the US dollar versus gold and crude oil, as well as relative to other currencies. The strong rise in oil prices during the 1970s was a direct consequence of the new monetary order. OPEC stated the following in a communiqué after Nixon had cut the dollar's tie to gold:

> Our member nations will take all the necessary steps and/or negotiate with oil companies, in order to find ways and means to counter adverse effects on the real income of member nations which may result from the international monetary developments of August 15 1971.[58]

Price inflation increased dramatically in the following decade. The transition also had severe effects on capital markets and the real returns of investors. Due to the monetary and subsequent price inflation of the 1970s, the decade turned out to produce well below average returns for bonds and stocks, whereas commodities and precious metals rallied. Between 1979 and 1980, the young fiat currency US dollar suffered a serious confidence crisis. As a result of ongoing price inflation, flight from the dollar ensued. Only a radical change in monetary policy under new Fed chairman Paul Volcker managed to defuse the looming dollar crisis. As a consequence of the dramatic interest rate hikes enacted

4. The Monetary System

by Volcker, the economy suffered the most severe recession since the Great Depression.

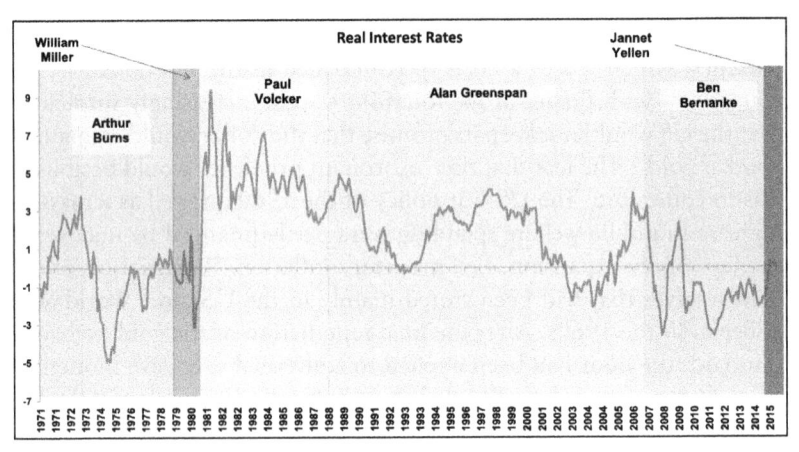

Figure 4.2: Real interest rates after Bretton Woods
(Source: Federal Reserve St. Louis)

A further consequence of the new monetary order was the transformation of gold from a risk-free (and thus free of fluctuations) investment asset into a volatile, "risky" asset. Ever since, one takes on currency risk if one exchanges currencies for gold. This perception of risk and the often cited "high volatility of gold" irritates risk-averse investors. Moreover, the short to medium-term fluctuations of paper currencies relative to gold often cloud the long term, sober perspective of gold as a store of value. In an environment of negative real interest rates, the term risk needs to be redefined though, as nominally "safe" investments can produce losses. However, this does not mean that asset classes that exhibit low volatility are risk-free or relatively safe.

Since the founding of the Federal Reserve System in 1913, the US dollar has lost more than 95% of its purchasing power, and 82% since the end of the Bretton Woods system in 1971 alone. Government debt has increased by a factor of 44 since then. The "closing of the gold window" on August 16, 1971, by Richard Nixon was a *de facto* declaration of default by the US: within 20 months, the US dollar lost almost 40% relative to the German mark. The devaluation relative to gold was even more dramatic. In 1971, one still received approximately 25 ounces for $1,000, 10 years later this had shrunk to just two ounces. The gradual erosion of purchasing power since 1971 can be illustrated with numerous comparisons. Figure 4.3 shows how many units of gold one would have received for one unit of the respective currencies. It can be clearly seen that the purchasing power of fiat currencies in terms of gold is continually declining. The loss of purchasing power of the dollar, the British pound and the euro stands at roughly 98% since 1971. It is especially noteworthy that the Swiss franc, which was the last currency to abandon gold cover, clearly exhibits relative strength, as it has lost "only" 90% of its purchasing power since 1971. The abandonment of gold cover was among other things a major precondition for the pretense of the prosperity illusion, as the continual loss of value of paper currencies makes objective measurement of prices extremely difficult.

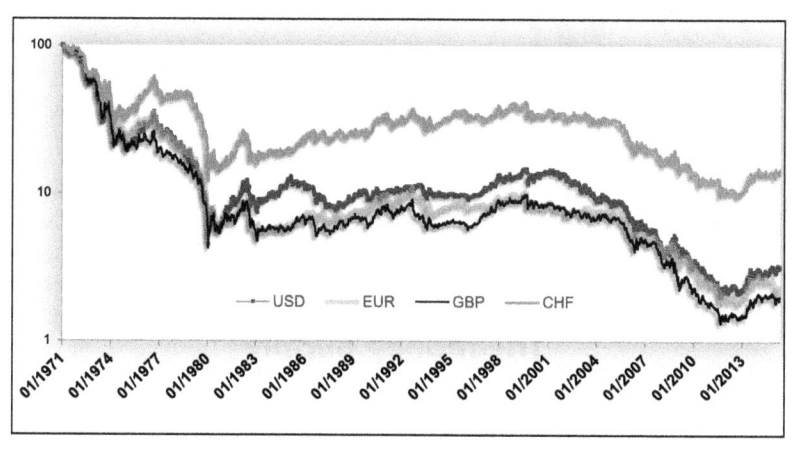

Figure 4.3. How many units of gold can be bought with one unit of currency (logarithmic scale, indexed to 100) (Source: Incrementum AG)

It is quite astonishing that the dollar still exists as a currency after such a large loss in purchasing power and that confidence has not yet completely evaporated. How the history of the Fed and the dollar will evolve can, apart from the precise timing, be forecast with considerable certainty. The concept of a reserve currency is by no means new, thus from a historic perspective alone, the demise of the global reserve currency dollar is likely. Why should its fate be different from that of the British pound or the Dutch guilder that preceded it? History has yet to show though how long it will take until it leaves the stage.

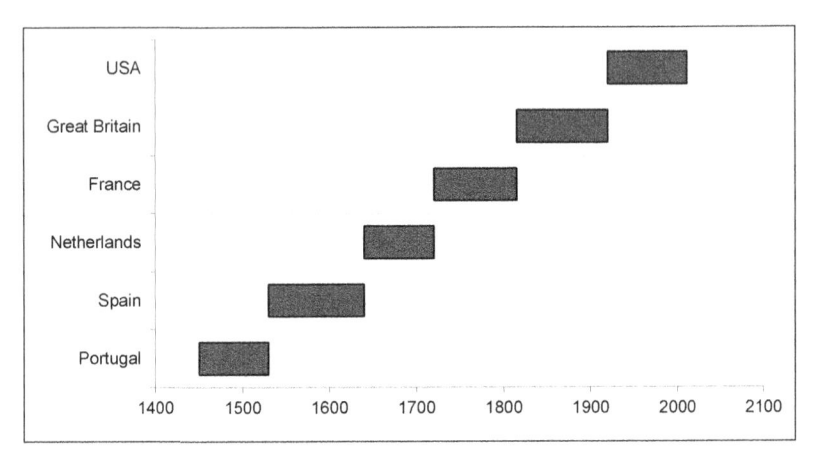

Figure 4.4: Global reserve currencies since the 15th century
(Sources: JP Morgan/Eye on the Market, Hong Kong Monetary Authority, Erste Group Research)

The Money Supply

After this theoretical review of the beginning of the global paper money era, it is important to examine the money supply more extensively as well in order to gain a deeper understanding of inflation and deflation. What does the "money supply" actually consist of? In order to answer this question, a brief look at a few special aspects of Austrian monetary theory will be helpful.

Adherents of the Austrian School have developed a calculation method for monetary aggregates that differs from official monetary aggregates (such as M2) in a number of important points. The method can be traced back to Ludwig von Mises, who first attained recognition as a monetary theorist with the publication of his 1912 work *"The Theory of Money and Credit"*. A critical component of his work was revealing the precise errors that British economists of the Currency School had committed in the 19th century. The Currency School successfully pushed through the adoption of the so-called Peel Act in 1844, which was supposed to banish business cycles once and for all, by strictly limiting the issuance of banknotes. If banknotes were not backed by specie, their issuance was not permitted. Contrary to the Currency School's expectations, business cycles failed to end. Mises explained this phenomenon, by providing a proper definition of money. Murray N. Rothbard summarizes Mises' definition of money as follows:

> Money is the general medium of exchange, the thing that all other goods and services are traded for, the final payment for such goods on the market.[59]

With the help of this definition, Mises explained that the economists of the Currency School had overlooked a major component of "money in the broader sense". Irrespective of whether circulating currency consists of banknotes or gold coins, fractionally reserved banks will create additional fiduciary media *ex nihilo*, by extending credit. Without the backstop provided by a central bank, these additional claims can never be paid back, unless all debtors repay their debts. The term *fiduciary media* for such uncovered deposit money that is used in English for the German term "Umlaufsmittel" is based on the Latin word *fiducia*, which means trust. Fiduciary media entirely depend on the trust of depositors. Excepted from these considerations are so-called *mutuum* contracts, in which the bank acts merely as a credit intermediary, lending out money it holds either in the form of time deposits, or out of its own equity capital. These activities do not increase the money supply.

4. The Monetary System

Loans that are extended on the basis of fractionally reserved demand deposits, however, do create additional means of payment in the form of fiduciary media. As long as such uncovered claims on standard money exist, they can indeed be used as a "final payment for goods and services on the market". However, many official money supply aggregates contain significant components which do not represent money according to the above definition, but rather represent credit instruments. Retail money market fund units, which are a large component of M2 in the US, are a prime example. These are not money, but shares in an investment fund. They must first be sold in the market before they can be used for payment. The fact that credit cards are often tied to such investments in money market funds does not alter this fact, as money market funds lend the money they receive to third parties. They invest in short-term debentures (whether commercial paper or treasury bills), thus they are clearly extending loans. If one includes these funds in a money supply aggregate, one is double counting the money concerned.

"Savings deposits" are however included in the "broad Austrian money supply" TMS-2 (TMS= true money supply). These are indeed available on demand. There exists a legal objection with respect to this inclusion, as in the case of savings accounts, US banks are theoretically entitled to delay payment by up to 30 days. In practice, no bank will ever make use of this right, as regulators would be knocking at its doors the very next morning, not to mention that such an action would provoke a bank run within hours. The subjective assessment of depositors is definitely that money in savings accounts is "available on demand", and it is this assessment that is decisive in determining the "moneyness" of such deposits. However, it is nevertheless sensible to construct a narrow money supply aggregate TMS-1 for analytical reasons, simply because money held in savings accounts is less often used in exchanges than money held in current accounts.

There are also a number of items that are included in "Austrian" monetary aggregates, but are not part of the "official" aggregates. Among these are so-called sweeps, which are part of TMS-1 (these are demand deposits, which are "masquerading" as savings deposits overnight

– so-called MMDAs, or money market deposit accounts – for the purpose of evading minimum reserve requirements), or the Federal Reserve's so-called memorandum items, such as demand deposits of foreign official institutions or US treasury deposits with the Federal Reserve (the so-called general account).

Why is this relevant? Although modern-day money in a wider sense is a kind of credit money (because it is generated when credit is granted), one must still be able to differentiate between money and credit. If one lends $100 to one's neighbor, outstanding credit in the economy has increased by $100 – however, the money supply has obviously not changed. If a bank lends $100 to one's neighbor, then the money supply will in most cases have increased as well, as the bank does not extend the loan in "cash", but in the form of additional deposit money created in the course of fractional reserve banking.

Since various central banks have in the recent past begun to implement so-called "quantitative easing" (colloquially known as "money printing"), the development of excess bank reserves has become important. Apparently there exist a number of misconceptions in this respect. At the time the ECB performed its LTRO refinancing operations, the financial press widely reported something along the lines of: "It did not make a difference, as the banks immediately re-deposited the money with the ECB". This mainly shows that few people actually understand how the fractionally reserved banking system works. As soon as a central bank purchases securities with money it has created from thin air, both the assets and liabilities on its balance sheet increase. Securities purchased are a central bank's assets, bank reserves (as well as currency) are its liabilities. To put it differently: bank reserves represent the cash assets of banks.

Just as private clients deposit money at commercial banks, banks deposit money with the central bank. These excess reserves can be transformed into banknotes at any time, for instance if customers withdraw money from their deposit accounts and a bank's vault cash is insufficient. Other than that, reserves can be used for interbank lending of reserves (e.g. in the US federal funds market). The monetary base consists of currency in circulation, as well as bank reserves (which in turn consist of required and excess reserves). Bank reserves are essentially the demand deposits of private banks, which are deposited with the central bank. Minimum reserves are those reserves that are required for the "backing" of customer deposits. New loans and deposits can be pyramided atop base money. This is done on the basis of the required minimum reserve, which currently stands at just 1% in the euro area, for example. Theoretically, the European banking system can extend loans of 100 euro for every euro in reserves held at the ECB.

Since the 2008 crisis, private banks in many cases no longer increase the money supply on their own initiative, and if they are doing so, then only reluctantly, as credit demand has weakened and many willing borrowers are regarded as too risky. Thus monetary inflation is now actively pursued by central banks. They give the banks the means to at least theoretically increase the money supply immensely. It is therefore even more important at the current juncture that central banks also create large sums of deposit money directly with their monetization activities.

As figure 4.5 shows, the broad money supply TMS-2 has increased from $5.3 trillion at the beginning of 2008 to $10.871 trillion as of March 2015. In other words, the US money supply has more than doubled since the beginning of 2008. Since the excess reserves of banks have increased to approximately $2.6 trillion at the same time, the "backing" of the existing money supply in terms of standard money has increased significantly. This means that the banks could in theory create an additional $10 trillion, or even up to $20 trillion or more in new deposit money. For a variety of reasons, which we will discuss in more detail below, this is not very likely at the current juncture, however, it would at least be theoretically possible. Thus the basis for a still much larger degree of monetary inflation already exists.

The Money Supply

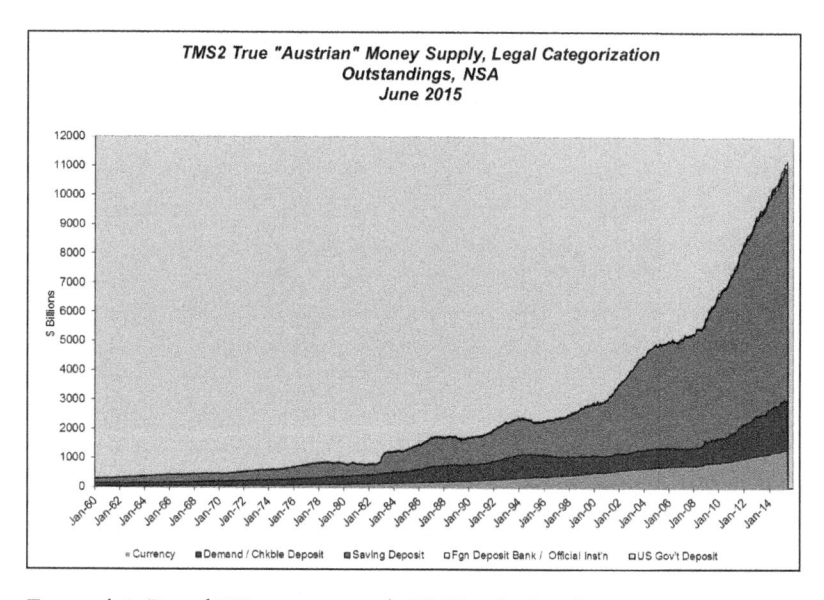

Figure 4.5: Broad US money supply TMS-2, by legal categories (Sources: Federal Reserve St. Louis, Incrementum AG)

5. Monetary Tectonics

Inflation

Today, the term inflation is commonly used to describe a rising price level and conversely deflation a falling price level. However, this is not the only definition. Originally, inflation (Latin: *inflatio* = expansion, enlargement), was used to denote the "expansion of the circulation of paper money"[60]. The definition popular today was only adopted later, and can be traced back to Irving Fisher. The US economist decided at the beginning of the 20th century that the purchasing power of money should be measured, and thereby contributed greatly to a confusion of terminology. According to Henry Hazlitt, four different definitions of the term inflation are in use:

- any increase in the supply of money and credit generally
- an increase in the supply of money that exceeds the increase in the supply of goods
- an increase in the price level
- any type of economic boom

Why is it even important to discuss the different definitions of the term at this juncture? Firstly, because the Austrian School's definition of inflation is the first, not the third one in the list above. Secondly, because the third definition harbors great danger. The rate of price increases is an inadequate measure for the debasement of money: it arrives with a great lag, it is compensated for by productivity increases and cannot be measured objectively. Official "inflation rates" are prettified numbers based on arbitrary methods and assumptions, which

5. Monetary Tectonics

veil the true extent of devaluation. A great many "adjustments" to the calculation method have been responsible for this as well. According to John Williams, the owner and operator of *shadowstats.com*, more than 20 fundamental changes have been implemented in the calculation of price inflation since 1980, including geometrical weighting, hedonic indexing and the substitution approach.

This semantic confusion leads to a misapprehension of the cause-effect relationship in the context of money creation and thus represents an obstacle to finding solutions to the associated problems. An increase in prices can happen for a variety of reasons. It is, however, only *one* of the great many problems caused by an expansion of the money supply. If one regards inflation merely as the increase of a certain price level, then everything that leads to a price increase must be called inflationary. Thus supply bottlenecks, bad harvests or entrepreneurs charging usurious prices come to be seen as inflation problems. It is not our monetary system that is to be blamed for inflation, no, instead there are many different and vague causes, which are held responsible for rising price levels. As a result the central bank is magically transformed from the engine of inflation into an inflation fighter – the arsonist becomes a firefighter.

The continual devaluation of money's purchasing power by approximately 2% per year is an explicit mandate of central banks. In this context, the Federal Reserve is focused on the so-called core inflation rate, which does not take the prices of food and energy into account. The reason for this is allegedly the "great volatility" of these expenditure items. In reality though, it is one of many means to veil the loss in purchasing power while at the same time carrying on with inflationary policy. Even though these inflation statistics are relatively worthless, it is important nowadays for investors to keep an eye on official inflation data, in order to better anticipate future central bank policy. As soon as the level of CPI's change rate is below or above the "comfort zone" of 1.5 percent, monetary policy interventions by the central planners become likely. These efforts can be clearly discerned in figure 5.1.

Inflation

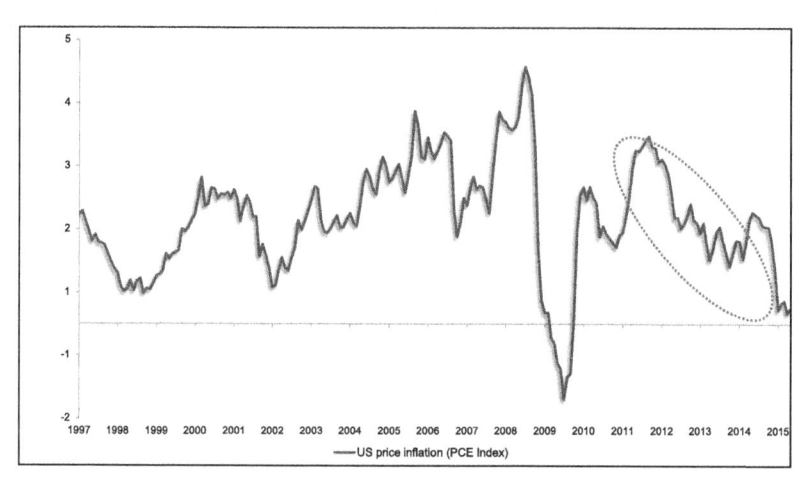

Figure 5.1: US inflation rate (PCE price index)
(Sources: Federal Reserve St. Louis, Datastream, Incrementum AG)

The Federal Reserve attempts to counteract a contraction of the broad monetary aggregates by aggressively inflating the base money supply (also called the monetary base, or high-powered money). The incredible extent of these measures can be seen in figure 5.2.

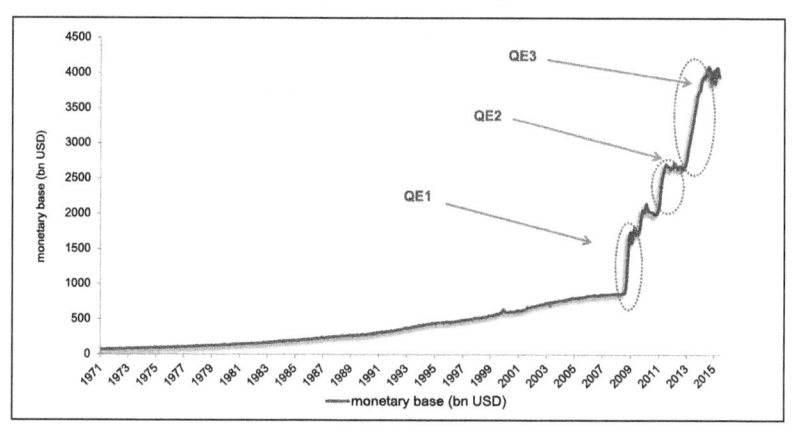

Figure 5.2: Trend in the US monetary base since 1918
(Sources: Federal Reserve St. Louis, Incrementum AG)

At the moment, asset price inflation is far outpacing consumer price inflation. This can be seen in figure 5.3: The broad stock market (represented by the S&P 500 index) has more than tripled from its lows in 2009. Especially strong however were the share prices of companies that are able to benefit disproportionately from inflationary policy, such as luxury goods producer Louis Vuitton Moet Hennessy (LVMH) or auction house Sotheby's.

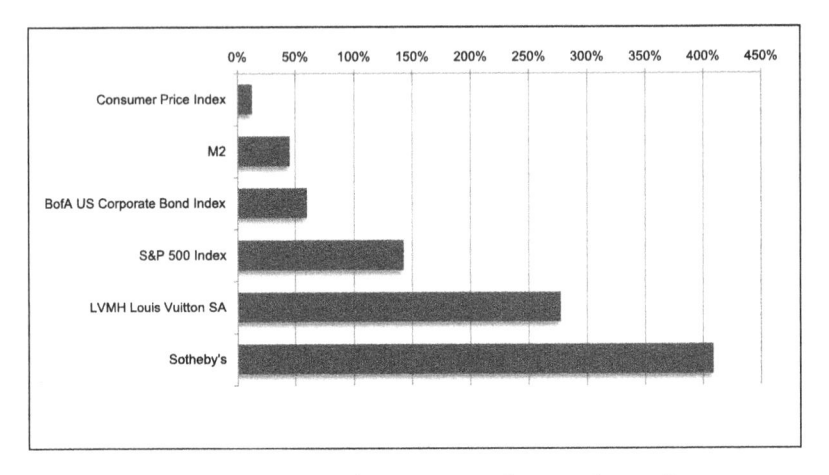

Figure 5.3: Consumer price and asset price inflation: change from 2009 to the beginning of 2015 in percent
(Sources: Bloomberg, Federal Reserve St. Louis, Incrementum)

Inflation is one of the oldest scourges of mankind. It not only leads to the stealth expropriation of savers, but to a continual wealth redistribution toward the centers of money creation: the State, banks and big business. Rarely in history have the ruling classes refrained from employing this hidden tax, which at the same time continually distorts the economy for the benefit of their cronies. Hence, the greatest threat to every private investor and saver is and will remain the State. As recent events dramatically illustrate, one of the most important considerations for an investment strategy today is to protect one's wealth in the long term from the acquisitive hands of governments.

Deflation

From the Austrian School's perspective, deflation as the opposite of inflation describes a decrease in the quantity of money and an increase in the quality of money. Analogous to the term inflation, the definition of deflation has also changed significantly. Originally, deflation denoted a decrease in the quantity of money in circulation. In the meantime, deflation is used to describe a declining price level of an arbitrarily defined basket of goods and services, often without taking their quality properly into account. As might be expected, economists of the Austrian School prefer the older definition of deflation, i.e., as a contraction of the money supply. Although most central banks are obligated to prevent price inflation, they never tire of warning of the danger emanating from the monster of deflation, which allegedly lies in wait around every corner, whereas "moderate" price inflation is fulsomely praised. As Jörg Guido Hülsmann writes on the "danger" emanating from deflation in his book *The Ethics of Money Production*:

> The harmful character of deflation is today one of the sacred dogmas of monetary policy. The champions of the fight against deflation usually present six arguments to make their case. One, in their eyes it is a matter of historical experience that deflation has negative repercussions on aggregate production and, therefore, on the standard of living. To explain this presumed historical record, they hold, two, that deflation incites the market participants to postpone buying because they speculate on ever lower prices.
>
> Furthermore, they consider, three, that a declining price level makes it more difficult to service debts contracted at a higher price level in the past. These difficulties threaten to entail, four, a crisis within the banking industry and thus a dramatic curtailment of credit. Five, they claim that deflation in conjunction with "sticky prices" results in unemployment. And finally, six, they consider that deflation might reduce nominal interest rates to such an extent that a monetary policy

5. Monetary Tectonics

of "cheap money," to stimulate employment and production, would no longer be possible, because the interest rate cannot be decreased below zero. However, theoretical and empirical evidence substantiating these claims is either weak or lacking altogether.[61]

Price deflation is only a threat in our current monetary system and even in this case it only threatens the continuation of an artificial boom. This is the economic situation we are in. Keeping an eye on the various credit and money supply aggregates is therefore extremely important for investors. It is fascinating to observe that credit inflation has become sluggish in recent years. In figure 5.4, it can be seen that total credit market debt relative to US economic output has been in decline since 2008. This temporary halt in credit expansion had a deflationary effect on the broad money supply, which the Fed's interventions however more than compensated for.

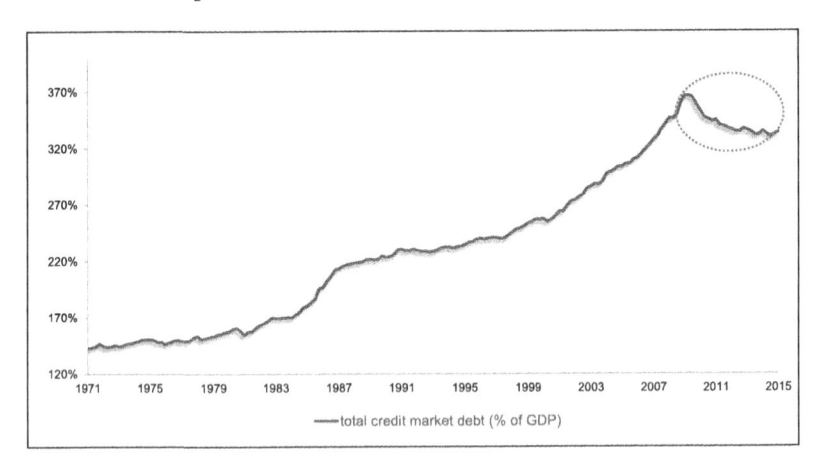

Figure 5.4: Total credit market debt as a percentage of US GDP (Sources: Federal Reserve St. Louis, Incrementum AG)

Tectonic Pressure Build-Up

Let us return to the topic of money creation: central banks are only *one* possible source of new money. An important aspect in understanding the dynamics of the money supply is today's fractional reserve banking system. Money substitutes are no longer backed by a real asset like gold in today's monetary system. Currency is partly created by central banks and partly by commercial banks. Ludwig von Mises already explained this fact and its wide-ranging consequences in 1912. He referred to the uncovered portion of the money supply as fiduciary media. In modern times, a major portion of the circulating money supply is indeed created by commercial banks. Usually a much smaller portion is created directly by central banks (the post 2008 crisis era is an exception to this rule).

As a result, the behavior of commercial banks is decisive in whether an inflationary expansion or a deflationary contraction of the money supply takes place. This means that there is no uniform force of inflation or deflation. If the central bank wants to achieve a rising price level, but commercial banks decrease the amount of outstanding credit, these forces are superficially offsetting each other. This interaction of deflationary and inflationary forces can be compared to the pressure building up between two tectonic plates: underneath a seemingly stable surface, pressure is gradually increasing, and is subsequently released in the form of volcanic eruptions or earthquakes. These eruptions are the inevitable consequence of processes taking place far below the earth's surface.

5. Monetary Tectonics

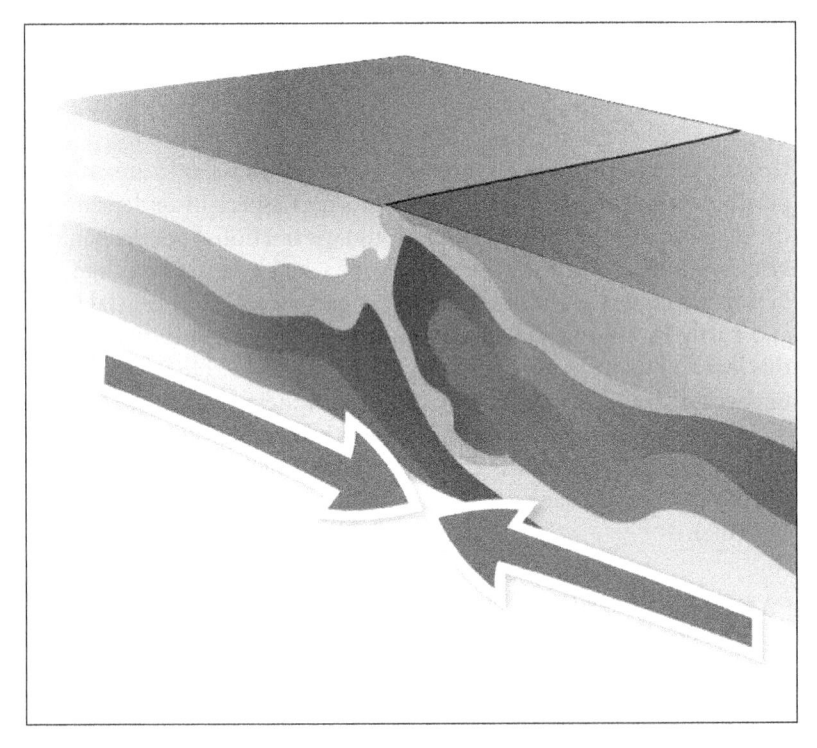

Figure 5.5: Monetary tectonics
(Source: Incrementum AG)

The "inflation or deflation?" question has been a major point of contention among economists in recent years. The Austrian School offers an alternative, and in our opinion, a much more profound perspective on this important topic for investors than mainstream economics can. In order to explain the "tectonic pressure" phenomenon, we have put together the following overview of current and potential influencing factors:

Inflationary Forces	Deflationary Forces
Zero interest rate policy	Balance Sheet Deleveraging: Under-capitalized banks – still recovering from the crisis – are reluctant to lend
Communications Policy (forward guidance)	Sluggish Credit Growth: Over-indebted consumers are reluctant to borrow
Quantitative Easing	Regulation: Basel III
Operation Twist	High Demand to hold Money (low inflation exp.)
Currency Wars	Productivity gains
Eligibility Criteria for Collateral (ECB)	Defaults and Bail-ins (Europe: Greece, Cyprus)
	Demographics

Figure 5.6: Inflationary vs. deflationary forces

It is hardly surprising that all the inflationary forces enumerated in figure 5.6 are directly related to the monetary policy of central banks. Zero interest rate policy makes it possible for commercial banks to borrow central bank money essentially for free. Forward guidance has become a very popular tool of central banks in order to exert influence on market participants in the financial markets. "We will keep interest rates low until 2017!" or: "As long as the economy has not sustainably recovered, we will not change our policy!" Such future-oriented statements attempt to build up confidence among market participants and thereby alter their behavior.

By means of quantitative easing and Operation Twist, the Federal Reserve has attempted to increase inflationary pressures, as the instrument of interest rate cuts was already fully exhausted. In the course of

5. Monetary Tectonics

the former, it has purchased securities directly in the markets, and thus increased the money supply directly; in the course of the latter, the central bank sells short-term securities from its holdings and replaces them with long-term securities. The aim is to put pressure on the yield curve on the long end as well and thus lower not only short-term, but also long-term interest rates. The term "currency war" refers to competitive devaluations of irredeemable currencies against each other. Devaluation of one's own currency promotes exports and is therefore an economic necessity, or so it is universally held. As central bank independence is not all it is cracked up to be, this provides yet another welcome reason to inflate. Inflation is also promoted by easing the eligibility criteria for securities collateral. As a result, central banks issue credit to commercial banks on the basis of ever more dodgy collateral.

The beginning of the financial crisis in 2007 marked the end of the massive expansion in commercial bank balance sheets. In the past few years, the aggregated bank balance sheet total in the euro area has even significantly declined. This has a strong deflationary effect. Many banks continue to suffer from structural problems. Loans that have been hived off into "bad banks" in the course of the financial crisis have still to be written down. In many cases, balance sheet totals are also decreasing because loans that are paid back are no longer replaced with new ones.

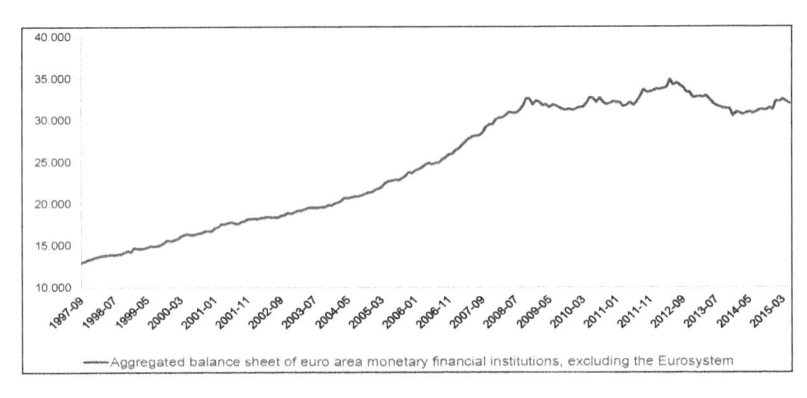

Figure 5.7: Aggregated balance sheet total of monetary financial institutions in the euro area (in EUR bn) (Source: bundesbank.de)

The sum of extended loans is rising a lot less quickly than prior to the beginning of the financial crisis. Potential borrowers often no longer conform to the perceptions of banks that have changed in the meantime. One has generally become more cautious. This can clearly be seen in figures 5.8. and 5.9, both in absolute terms as well as in terms of annual growth rates. However, in the US in particular, banks have become less reluctant to expand credit since 2014. Strong growth in commercial and industrial lending has resumed, much of which appears to be used for financial engineering purposes, such as stock buybacks and the financing of merger and acquisition activities. By contrast, capital expenditure growth has only been tepid.

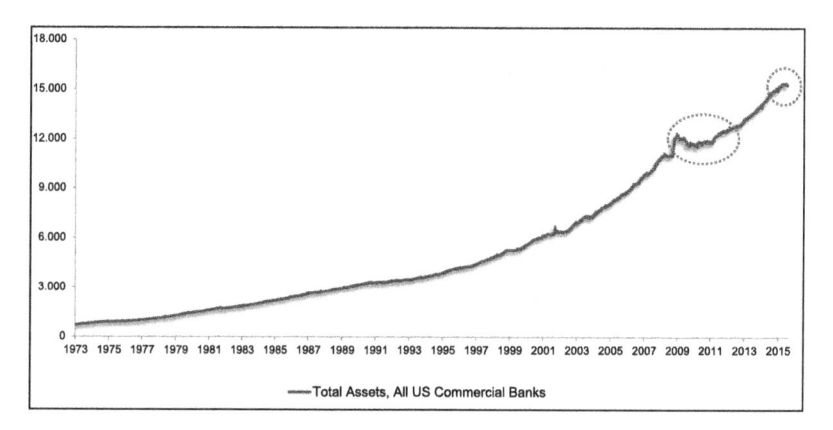

Figure 5.8: Total bank credit of US commercial banks in USD bn (Source: Federal Reserve St. Louis)

5. Monetary Tectonics

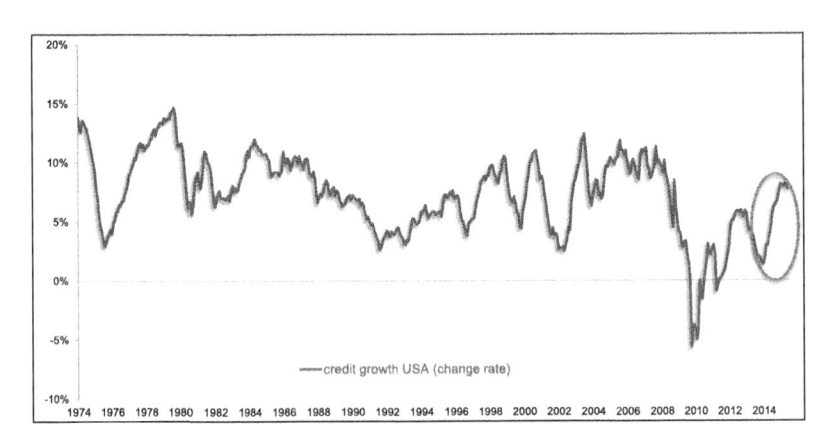

Figure 5.9: Annual rate of increase in bank loans extended by commercial banks in percent (Source: Federal Reserve St. Louis)

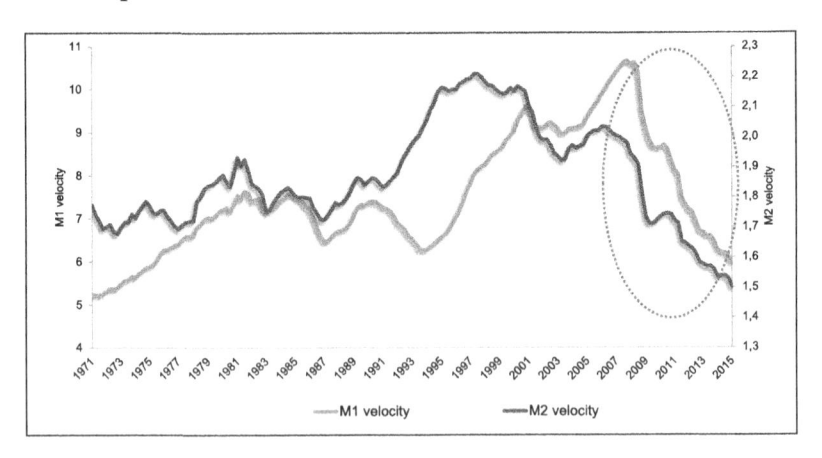

Figure 5.10: Velocity of the US dollar (Source: Federal Reserve St. Louis)

In addition to this, bank regulations have become subject to stricter guidelines that are set to be tightened even further until 2018. This has an immediate deflationary effect. One force that has an effect that is very similar to an actual change in the money supply is what monetarists refer to as the velocity of money. It represents a rough indicator of the demand for holding cash balances. Figure 5.10 illustrates the average annual rate of turnover of a monetary unit in the US.

As the highlighted area shows, money velocity has declined almost steadily since the 2007 financial crisis. This is currently raising the tectonic pressure on the deflationary side. Investors must pay close attention as to when this dynamic changes. Note though since "velocity", which is a fudge factor in Irving Fisher's tautological quantity equation, is calculated as a ratio of the money supply to economic output, its decline may simply represent the fact that central banks are creating a lot of new money, while economic activity concurrently remains subdued.

It therefore cannot be stated with certainty to what extent a decline in "velocity" is due to rising demand for holding cash balances and to what extent it simply mirrors the degree of monetary inflation. For instance, the sharp rise in the prices of certain assets like stocks, works of art, expensive trophy real estate and so forth, is an indication that among the richer strata of the population, the demand for holding cash balances is already decreasing sharply.

The last deflationary force listed above is an increase in productivity. This is not a factor relevant only today, as one must assume that human striving and economic activity continually increase productivity. Price deflation is therefore by no means a phenomenon purely induced by monetary factors similar to price inflation, but is rather the rule in an unhampered economy. One can buy more and more goods for the same amount of money as time passes, simply because enterprises become ever more efficient.

5. Monetary Tectonics

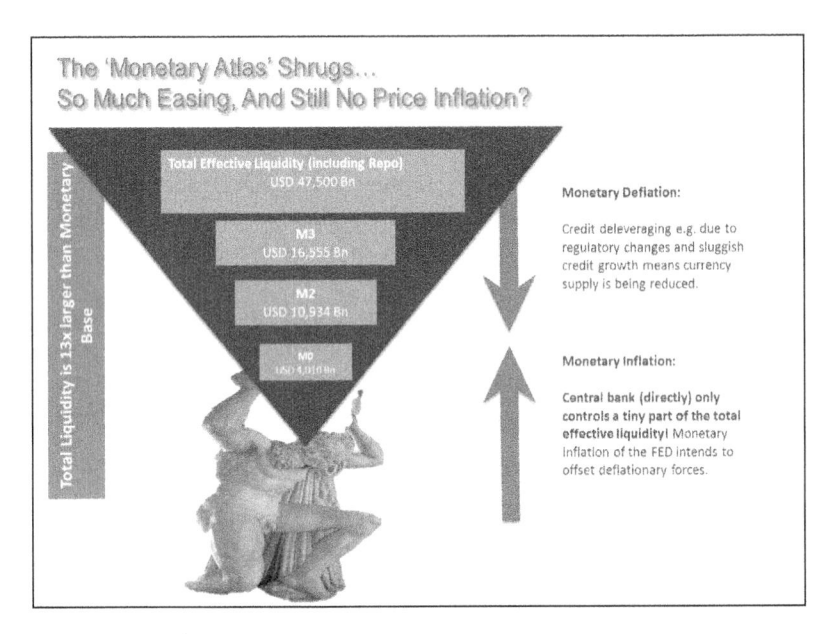

Figure 5.11: The pressure increases
(Sources: Nowandfutures.com, UBS Research, Federal Reserve St. Louis)

Without the massive interventions on the part of central banks, the financial crisis would have been a highly deflationary event, as the malinvested capital of the 2000's would have been painfully revealed and expurgated. Credit deflation and price deflation in its wake would have been far stronger in the absence of countervailing monetary policy measures. With the aid of extremely expansive central bank policy, deflationary tendencies were - and still are – successfully counteracted. This can be seen in the crossing curves in figure 5.12. It is a dangerous balancing act, which will sooner or later fail.

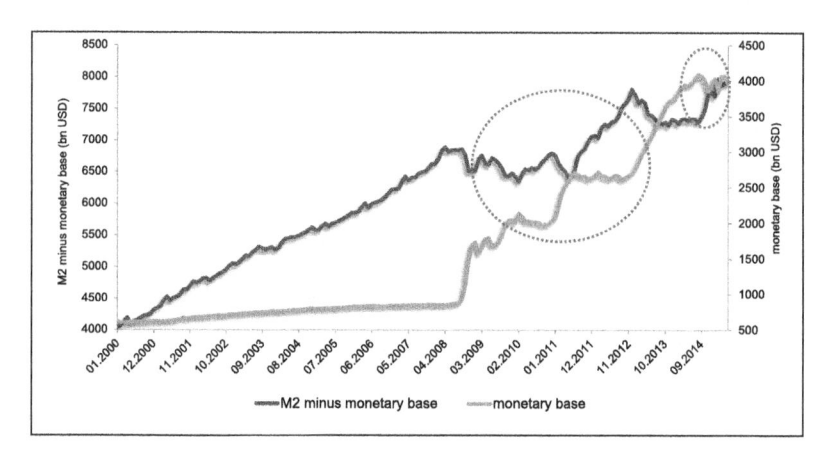

**Figure 5.12: Broad money supply stagnates, monetary base explodes
(Source: Federal Reserve St. Louis)**

Figure 5.13 demonstrates that deflationary pressures are increasing. It depicts the ratio of gold to 20-year US treasury bonds as a performance index. The line marks the current downtrend.

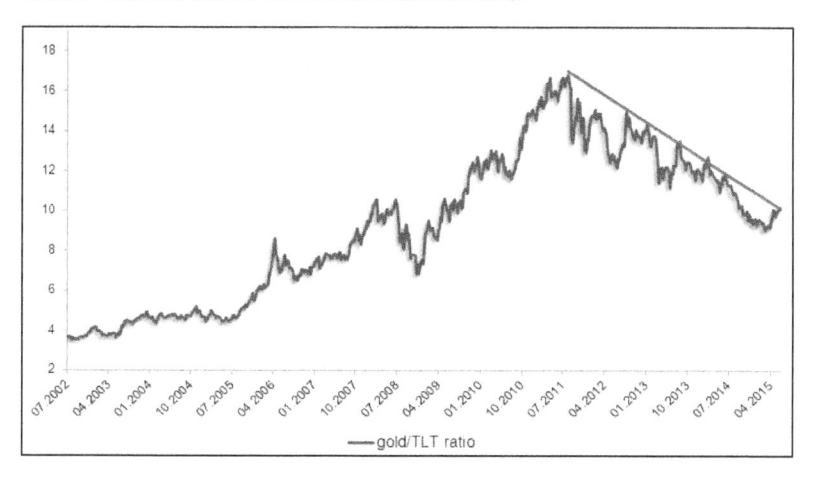

**Figure 5.13: Ratio of gold to 20-year treasury bonds
(Sources: Paul Mylchreest–Thunder Road Report, Federal Reserve St. Louis)**

5. Monetary Tectonics

Another sign that commercial banks are contributing to pressures on the deflationary tectonic plate can be seen in the extent of excess reserves. These are directly connected with required minimum reserves commercial banks must hold with the central bank. Required reserves are an important monetary policy tool of central banks. They make commercial banks dependent on the central bank in terms of their own loan issuance, as the central bank can lower or raise required reserve minimums. Commercial banks in turn require central bank credit.

If a commercial bank holds an amount with the central bank that exceeds the required minimum reserve, the excess is termed an excess reserve. Normally excess reserves are very small. They are equivalent to demand deposits of commercial banks with the central bank, minus required reserves minus vault cash of commercial banks that is made available for the cash withdrawals of bank customers. Not too long ago – prior to the collapse of Lehman Brothers – there were in effect no excess reserves at all. In the meantime, the amount has increased to an incredible 2,600 billion dollars (figure 5.14).

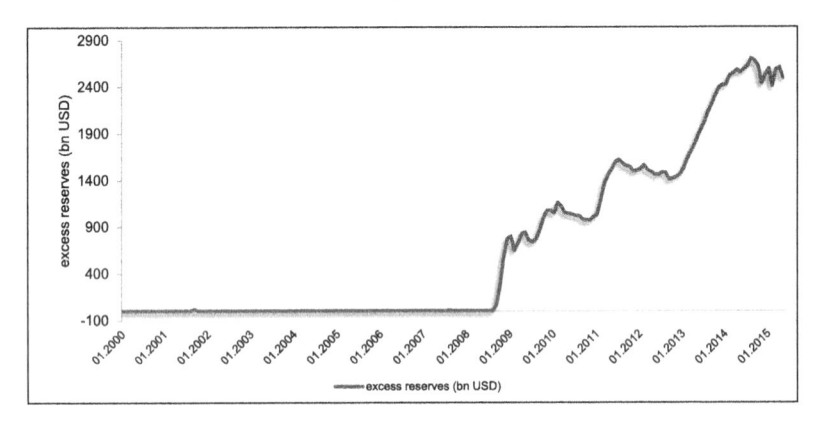

Figure 5.14: Excess reserves held at the Fed
(Sources: Federal Reserve St. Louis; Incrementum AG)

At the end of 2014, the Fed began to pay interest on both required and excess reserves. This promoted the enormous increase in excess reserves and has created a subsidy for commercial banks by giving them a share in seignorage profits. Initially, the deposit rate was calculated with the help of the base rate. Since December 18 2008, it is fixed directly by the Fed, as was already the case at the ECB. Since that day, it has amounted to 0.25%. This is significantly higher than other short-term money market rates.

The trend of the central bank deposit facility rate is shown in figure 5.15. As can be seen, the ECB's rate on the deposit facility has been at zero percent for some time (in the meantime, the ECB has set a negative deposit rate). The reason why the Fed decided to introduce interest payments on its reserves deposit facility has to do with the "zero bound" and quantitative easing. Normally, it would not be possible for the Fed to successfully raise the Federal Funds target rate without significantly reducing its balance sheet by selling the assets it has acquired in the course of the "quantitative easing" policy.

Such an asset sale would dramatically shrink the broad money supply, it would amount to a severe monetary deflation with all the associated effects, such as crashing asset prices and the cessation of all bubble activities in the economy (the major central banks all have a slightly different modus operandi, and in the Fed's case quantitative easing almost dollar for dollar creates new deposit money as well. Thus, a reversal of "QE" would also reduce the money supply). Hence it could not possibly raise its base rate without causing a major deflationary contraction first.

Paying interest on excess reserves allows the Fed to circumvent this problem: it can now hike the Federal Funds rate, as long as it increases the rate paid on excess reserves in tandem, without having to reduce its balance sheet. It can be assumed as a virtual certainty that the Fed will never actively shrink the money supply. Interest payments on reserves not only represent a small subsidy to commercial banks, but can also be used to keep them from flooding the interbank lending market with

5. Monetary Tectonics

supply once the Federal Funds rate is hiked. Without this tool at its disposal, the Fed could not maintain control over interbank lending rates without shrinking its balance sheet.

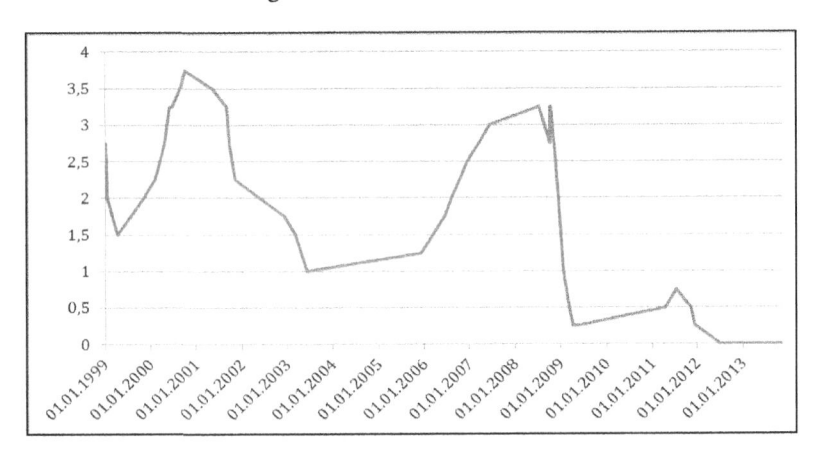

Figure 5.15: Deposit facility rate of the ECB
(Source: ecb.int)

Excess reserves in the euro zone declined significantly prior to the recent decision to once again expand the ECB's balance sheet by a large-scale new quantitative easing program. This was hitherto a major difference between the dollar and the euro areas. Excess reserves in the dollar area are many times larger than those denominated in euro at the ECB. While a significant reduction of excess reserves has taken place in recent years in the euro area, they remain near an all time high at the Fed.

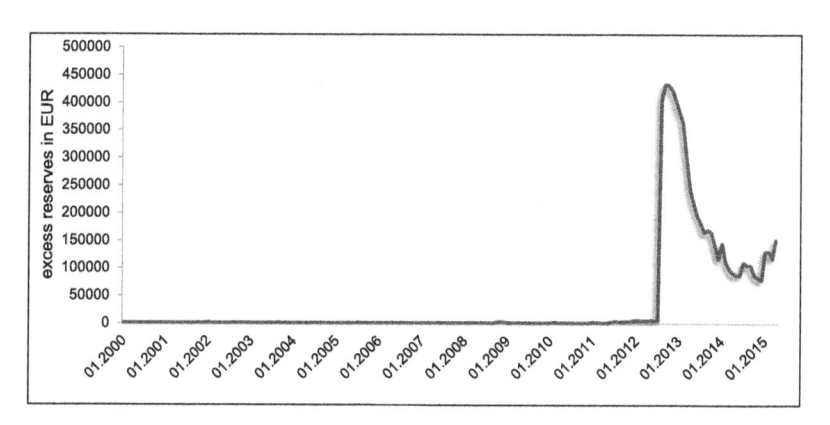

Figure 5.16: Excess reserves held at the ECB
(Source: ecb.int)

The ECB can move the deposit rate above or below zero, with correspondingly deflationary or inflationary effects. The effect of a negative interest rate policy by the Fed would however be commensurately larger, due to the far higher volumes involved. Sweden's central bank already lowered this interest rate to minus 0.25% before the ECB and the SNB followed suit. The Federal Reserve still has room to maneuver in this respect, as it can still lower the deposit rate to zero. Up until 2014, demands to lower the rate on excess reserves have steadily grown. Prominent market commentators like former Fed board member Alan Blinder have been increasing the pressure through the media in this respect.[62] Similar steps have already been implemented in Sweden in 2009 and in Denmark in July of 2012. The ECB followed suit, shortly after ECB president Mario Draghi in reply to a question on the topic, stated that the ECB was "operationally ready". The Swiss National Bank (SNB) has likewise imposed strongly negative interest rates on deposits at the central bank, and is actively targeting a negative interest rate on 3 month LIBOR.

Choosing this option has considerable economic consequences. Penalty rates can only be avoided if commercial banks extend more loans.

5. Monetary Tectonics

Potential effects are the intensification of speculative bubbles, such as in the stock market, the art market, commodities, etc. Moreover, the cost of charging banks for excess reserves is passed on to bank customers. The most important factor is probably going to be the ultimate opening of Pandora's box, with negative interest rates being extended to customer savings deposits. This would lead to an even more pronounced decline in thrift, and have fatal effects on long-term capital formation. The fact that from the perspective of both the Fed and the ECB, new monetary policy tools to promote inflation are required is shown in figure 5.17.

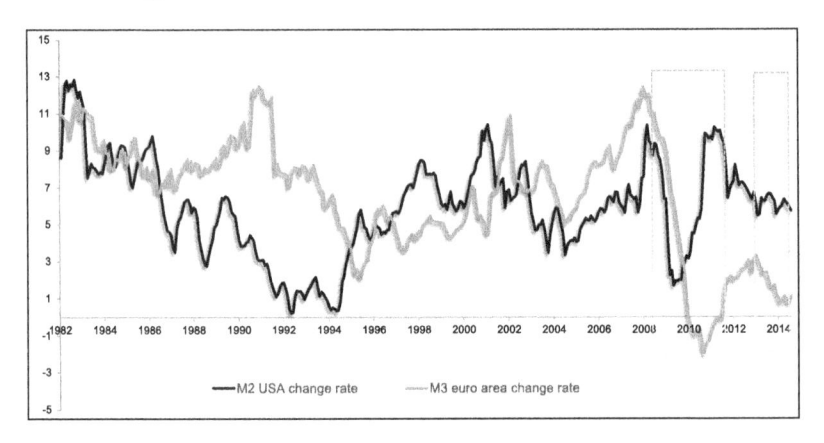

Figure 5.17: Annual rate of money supply growth in the US and the euro zone in percent
(Sources: ECB, Federal Reserve St. Louis)

It can be seen that money supply growth rates have slowed since 2012. It can be assumed that the central banks will attempt to aggressively counter this trend and indeed, the ECB has already acted in this respect and money supply growth in the euro area has markedly re-accelerated accordingly. In the next chapter, we will discuss the question of why central banks will always try to avert a slowdown in monetary inflation.

A few words on the differences in the *modus operandi* of major central banks: as mentioned above, quantitative easing by the Fed results not only in an expansion of excess reserves, but also in a direct increase of deposit money in the economy. The reason for this is that the counterparties of the Fed are the so-called *primary dealers*. Although most of them are subsidiaries of commercial banks, they are legally organized as non-banks. When the Fed buys securities from a non-bank, money will be deposited in an account the non-bank holds with a bank. The banks in turn will redeposit the check arriving in the accounts of primary dealers with the Fed, so that at the conclusion of the transaction, both bank reserves and deposit money have increased. In effect, the Fed "finances" its asset purchase by crediting the reserves account of the banking intermediary where the primary dealer's account is held. From the perspective of the bank, both its assets in the form of reserves as well as its liabilities in the form of customer deposits have increased; similarly, the securities the Fed has purchased are increasing the asset side of its balance sheet, while the new bank reserves represent the required balance on the liabilities side.

When the ECB buys securities, many of its purchases are also from non-banks (insurance companies, pension funds and the like). Banks are in fact reluctant to sell high quality assets to the ECB, as they need to hold them both for regulatory purposes and because they need high quality collateral for repo market transactions. The effect is a corresponding increase in the money supply as well. When the ECB introduced the first "securities market purchase program" (SMP) to manipulate the interest rates of Greek, Portuguese and Irish government bonds, it "sterilized" its purchases by auctioning short-term securities on a weekly basis so as to prevent an increase in the money supply. No such restrictions accompany its new QE program, which is purposely designed to boost the euro area's money supply. In addition, the ECB excludes non-resident owned euro accounts from its monetary aggregates. As a result, the actual amount of extant money in the euro area is larger than the official statistics would suggest.

5. Monetary Tectonics

The Bank of Japan has hitherto bought most of the securities it purchases from banks themselves, which are among the largest holders of JGBs. As a result, the BoJ's QE operations have increased bank reserves greatly (in this case, the BoJ's balance sheet grows, but for the banks there is merely a shift on the asset side: they hold more reserves and fewer securities), but have only had a modest effect on the money supply, mainly because commercial banks have concurrently continued to decrease outstanding credit to the private sector. In other words, the BoJ has relied on banks to employ their excess reserves in pyramiding more credit atop them, but the banks have failed to comply.

However, the BoJ has become such a big buyer of JGBs, that banks no longer want to sell to it, as similar to European banks, they need to hold a certain inventory of government bonds for regulatory reasons as well as for use as collateral in repo transactions. At the same time, Japan's largest pension funds have adopted a policy of purchasing riskier assets such as stocks and selling part of their large inventory of JGBs. It is therefore to be expected that the BoJ will also begin to acquire more securities from non-banks in the future. Moreover, the BoJ also buys ETF securities in the stock market, and many of the sellers must be assumed to be non-banks. Japan's money supply growth could therefore begin to accelerate, even if Japanese commercial banks remain reluctant to increase the amount of fiduciary media in the economy by extending new credit.

Another peculiarity concerns the monetary statistics compiled by the Bank of Japan, which have been revised several times in recent years. In contrast to other central banks, the BoJ has a very narrow definition of so-called "money holders", whose bank deposits are included in monetary aggregates. Specifically, the BoJ excludes e.g. the central government, all insurance companies and government-affiliated financial institutions, non-resident accounts, as well as securities and *tanshi* companies from the class of "money holders". In the past, most analysts assumed that Japan's money supply M1 was a fairly close representation of money TMS (i.e. currency plus demand deposits). In light of the above-mentioned Japan-specific statistical quirks, this view will likely have to be revised. It is therefore also possible that Japan's money supply growth has in effect been much larger than was hitherto assumed, although the fact that commercial banks have been reducing outstanding credit and the associated fiduciary media has without a doubt put a great deal of pressure on the BoJ's attempts to inflate.

6. Business Cycles

Business cycles are periodically repeating, successive periods of booms and recessions, which is the term employed nowadays to describe economic collapse, respectively a bust. Since this represents a significant risk for investors, a profound understanding of the causes and the process of business cycles is of the utmost importance. One of the unique features of the Austrian School is precisely that it offers an explanation of business cycles. "Austrian" business cycle theory (ABCT), which can be traced back to Ludwig von Mises, who first elaborated it in his habilitation treatise "The Theory of Money and Credit", can explain why economies experience business cycles and periodic economic crises. They are by no means a feature inherent in the market economy, but a direct consequence of the interventionist monetary system. One can explain the theory based on a number of different concepts. We will begin doing so by looking at the economy's production structure.

Undistorted Production Structure

An example often used to illustrate a production structure under the division of labor was provided by German economist Wilhelm Roscher. In order to understand the distortion of the production structure, we will first show an example of a healthy structure as it would exist in an economy with a non-state, free market monetary system. For this purpose, we follow Roscher's thoughts, far back to the point when human beings began to be differentiated from animals. He considers a group of fishermen near a body of water rich in fish, which at one point must have been utterly destitute. An individual fisherman can probably just

6. Business Cycles

about survive on the work he performs in an entire day, by spending the day in shallow waters and hunting for fish. How could these fishermen improve their situation?

Isolated fishermen who receive no outside help must create the means to increase their productivity themselves. However, this will necessarily weigh on near-term returns. If a fisherman is able to catch two fish per day with his bare hands, he must try to subsist on only one fish for two successive days so that he can take a day off from fishing, which he can use for the construction of a simple tool to help improve his catch. This tool, for example a simple net, is what Carl Menger called a higher order good: higher compared to the consumer good fish, which Menger calls a first order good. That he begins to count at this point, the goal of human action, illustrates the reverse order of causality governing production. Consumption was temporarily reduced by half in this example, while a higher order good was created, which increased the overall time period it takes to produce fish (one day for making the net, a second day for fishing). This ratio between achieving a consumable return and the duration of production can be imagined as a triangle, which becomes deeper and flatter. It is called a Hayekian triangle, after Austrian economist Friedrich A. Hayek.

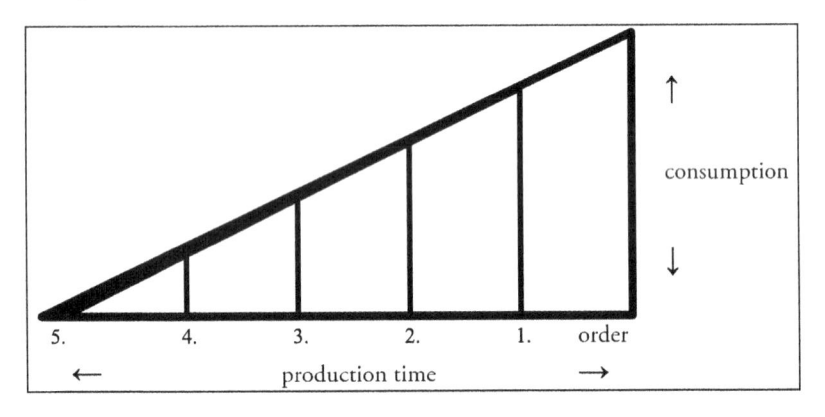

Figure 6.1: Hayekian triangle I

Undistorted Production Structure

On the right hand side of the triangle is the consumption good. At that point, at the end and the goal of the production process, Menger begins to enumerate goods and differentiates them according to their order. After the consumer good, which is a good of first order, follow goods of second order, third order, and so forth. Higher order goods are called capital goods. In an advanced economy, the number of capital goods increases strongly, and production processes become ever longer and encompass numerous stages. One speaks of a lengthening of the production structure, if new stages are added and as a result a longer time period is required to complete the production process *ab initio*.

A lengthening of the production structure by means of employment of additional capital goods will as a rule produce a higher output. This higher output can consist of a larger amount of consumer goods, such as the fish in the example discussed here. A higher return can however also consist of an increase in the quality of consumer goods. Improving the quality of consumer goods requires capital accumulation as well. This is referred to as the increased return of "roundabout" production. Every lengthening of the production structure entails taking detours – time and scarce resources are no longer employed directly in the production of consumer goods, but are employed in early and intermediate stages and thereby contribute indirectly to the production of consumer goods.

In the example of the group of fishermen, the next step toward lengthening the production structure could consist of the production of ropes, which can be woven into nets in the next stage, making a bigger catch possible. Every lengthening implies that one begins at an earlier stage, further removed in time from the final result (in this case the catching of fish). In a modern society, many years can lie between the first stage of a production chain and the consumer goods it helps to produce.

The higher return of roundabout production is by no means guaranteed. However, only those detours are chosen and continued which ultimately result in a higher output. Thus more capital-intensive production structures as a rule result in a larger output than less capital-intensive ones. Otherwise they would be abandoned, as no one would adopt a roundabout production process that does not result in an output of either more goods or better quality goods. A detour that fails to result in a higher return would be existence-threatening.

Due to capital accumulation, the sacrifice of abstaining from consumption today can lead to a multiplication of future output. Ludwig von Mises spoke of "apparent sacrifices"[63] in this context – although abstention from consumption initially feels like a sacrifice, it increases prosperity in the long term. Mises regards it as an exchange through time: today's renouncement of satisfaction is exchanged for greater satisfaction tomorrow. US economist Frank Fetter coined the term "time preference" for this, based on Eugen Boehm-Bawerk's thoughts. High time preference means that more value is placed on the factor time, this is to say, acting man regards it as important to reach his goal as early as possible, while a low time preference indicates the willingness to wait longer in order to reach loftier goals.

Reorganization of the Production Structure

In the simple example above, the dynamics of changing the structure of production were already hinted at. The decisive point is that prior to capital accumulation, there has to be a change in behavior: in the example of the fishermen, people were able to temporarily lower their consumption and create savings – by making an "apparent sacrifice". It is only an *apparent* sacrifice because it is outweighed by the higher return achieved in the end.

Let us now look at the associated dynamics in the context of a more complex society. The change in behavior which impels a change in the production structure consists of a change in the desire to save. It happens all the time that thriftiness increases or decreases on average on a society-wide basis. For instance, the desire to accumulate savings has increased dramatically in China in recent decades, as the protection of private property improved.

Economically, every action incurs a cost. When people save more, it means necessarily that they must consume less. This consequence is strongly feared today. However, this fear is unfounded and based on bad economics, which only considers static aggregates and circular flows, while neglecting dynamic processes. Let us take a closer look at these dynamic processes: the first consequence of lower consumption is of course a decline in demand. However, this decline is not distributed evenly across the entire economy. Less consumption only means less demand for consumer goods. Thus there is at first a slump at the outermost right-hand boundary of the Hayekian triangle. Retailers cannot sell all their goods anymore. The profitability of their business evidently declines. Which dynamic process is set into motion by this?

Let us observe the changes on the real level of individual people. Let us imagine that a group of entrepreneurs is meeting at its regular haunt to discuss business. The retailer is going to complain loudly about his losses. However, retailers only represent a small segment of all business people. The large majority is engaged in stages of production that are far removed from consumption. They are not experiencing any change. The retailer will reduce his next order from the wholesaler due to the slump in demand. The wholesaler in turn will reduce his orders from the producer. In this manner, the change moves down along the production structure. For the moment, however, only retailers are complaining; entrepreneurs in other lines continue to enjoy strong order books. A new investor or a new entrepreneur who joins the meeting in the pub gets a clear signal: avoid sectors close to consumption! New entrepreneurs will now be more inclined to become engaged in stages further removed from consumption, investments are thus shifted.

However, this is not the only dynamic process at work here. The assumed shift from consumption to saving alters the supply of goods across time. More present goods become available for capital formation, because actors renounce present consumption and exchange it for the promise of (more plentiful or qualitatively better) future goods. The larger supply of unconsumed present goods leads to a decline in the prices of these goods relative to those of future goods. This price ratio is expressed by the market interest rate. It thus becomes cheaper to employ present goods in longer-term projects.

The decline in consumer demand has the consequence that many retailers become unable to sell some of their goods. In reaction to this, they will lower sales prices in order to get rid of these goods. When consumption decreases, one therefore observes as a rule that on average, and *ceteris paribus*, the prices of consumer goods decline. Expressed differently, falling prices mean rising real incomes. Employees are now able to afford more and better goods as long as they receive the same amount of nominal wages. The increase in real incomes however also means that human labor becomes relatively more expensive compared to capital goods. This in turn leads to the replacement of labor-intensive production processes by more capital-intensive production processes. As a rule, labor-intensive processes tend to be closer to consumption than capital-intensive ones – the latter are tying up more capital and thereby exhibit greater temporal depth.

All the dynamics described above point in the same direction: a change in human behavior leads to a deepening of the production structure, to a widening of stages far removed from consumption and a flattening of stages close to consumption. This change can be seen in figure 6.2., which was created by the "Austrian" economist Roger Garrison.[64] In addition to the Hayekian triangle, the change in conditions is illustrated by the so-called production possibilities frontier. This curve illustrates the trade-off between consumption and investment.

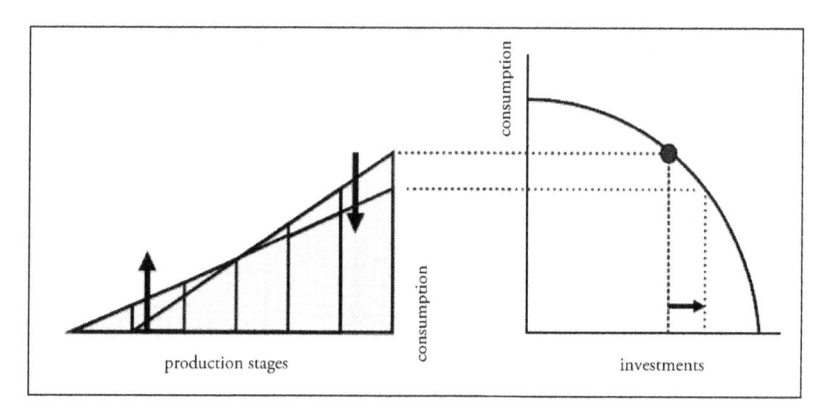

Figure 6.2: Hayekian triangle II and production possibilities frontier (source: Roger W. Garrison, Time and Money. The Macroeconomics of Capital Structure)

A widening of the production structure goes hand in hand with greater output. Capital accumulation only takes place in those projects that offer the prospect of higher returns. This means that ultimately, more and/or better consumer products are produced. This increase in returns implies that the temporary restriction of consumption is by no means permanent, but that ultimately, a sustainable increase in consumption is made possible. The decision to save is not a decision against consumption as such. It only represents a temporal shift in consumption: the restriction of consumption today enables greater consumption tomorrow.

Due to the dynamic processes this sets into motion, the production structure is adjusted to consumer preferences. The decision of consumers to save means that they prefer greater consumption in the future to present consumption. In order to satisfy this want, capital must be formed. This capital formation is only possible in a sustainable manner by the creation of savings. If the savings ratio remains at the same level, these higher returns ultimately enable a further deepening of the production structure. This process represents sustainable economic growth. On the production possibilities frontier, this growth is illustrated by a shift that forms a pattern not unlike tree rings.

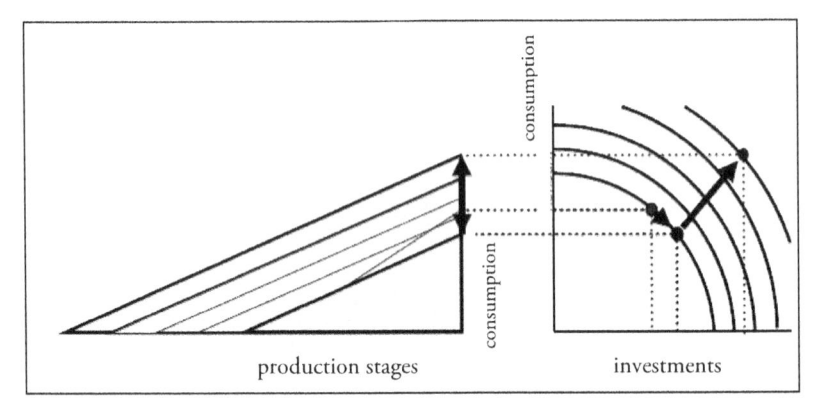

Figure 6.3: Hayekian triangle III and production possibilities frontier (source: Roger W. Garrison, Time and Money. The Macroeconomics of Capital Structure)

Capital Structure

The question of whether capital can in some way be regarded as a homogeneous magnitude was also a major topic of the so-called capital controversy. Adherents of the Austrian School always distinguished themselves by emphasizing the heterogeneity of capital, i.e., the impossibility of standardization or aggregation. We want to take a closer look at this approach through the lens of one of its most consistent proponents, Ludwig Lachmann. Lachmann summarizes the problem of capital by the following statements, which build on one another:[65]

- Heterogeneity of capital means heterogeneity in its use
- Heterogeneity in usage implies multiple specificity
- Multiple specificity implies complementarity

Capital Structure

- Complementarity implies capital combinations
- Capital combinations form the elements of the capital structure

We want to explain these points step by step:

Heterogeneity of capital means heterogeneity in its use: the decisive point is always that capital is a means for the attainment of the subjective goals of human actors. Its physical characteristics are therefore only of secondary importance. The same capital can be employed for the attainment of different goals and can hence be valued differently; a capital good is never defined in material terms, but by how it is employed. If the subjective goals of people change, a capital good, in spite of not having materially changed, can lose its capital function from one moment to the next and can even become completely worthless.

Heterogeneity in usage implies multiple specificity: the lower the order of a good, i.e., the closer to consumption it is, the more specific it will tend to be. Specificity means that a good only allows certain employments. The highest degree of specificity in case of a capital good means that it can only be transformed into a single good of lower order. The fact that capital goods have a different role in relation to our goals thus means that they can only be used for specific purposes; as a rule however, for several purposes. Hence multiple specificity.

Multiple specificity implies complementarity: two goods are complementary, if they can only be transformed into a good of lower order together. Since individual capital goods as a rule are only suitable for a small number of uses, they are always employed in combination with complementary capital goods. This is an important complication: even the largest accumulation of capital good A is worthless without the complementary capital good B. Therefore, speaking about a kind of "automatic" capital accumulation is only possible from an unrealistic perspective, which assumes capital to be homogeneous.

Complementarity implies capital combinations: since different specific capital goods require other, complementary goods in certain ratios, they only have an effect in combinations. The precondition for the creation of goods of lower order, this is to say the satisfaction of human wants and goals, is therefore the proper combination of capital, not its "mass".

Capital combinations form the elements of the capital structure: since capital must be combined most of the time at every stage of a very long production process, capital must be regarded as a highly complex structure, not a simple metric. Capital is a structure, the composition of which does not come into being on autopilot, but requires human choices and actions of anticipation and combination.

The actions that result in building up the capital structure are called investment. Investing is therefore a process of dehomogenization of capital. Homogeneous capital, "free capital", must be tied up. A consequence of the above insights on the structural nature of capital is the irreversibility of investments. An existing capital structure can rarely be transformed into a different one without cost and effort. Many components that were highly specific pieces fitting in the structure of a production process cannot be inserted anywhere else, respectively require completely different complementary capital goods in alternative employments.

The insight that capital has a structure makes clear that the popular conception of capital as an amount of money is fundamentally wrong. Investment, this is to say, capital formation, begins with the dehomogenization of money (the ultimate present good) into a concrete structure, which requires at least partially irreversible decisions. The term "investment" comes from the Latin term for "clothing" (*investire*). In other words, one invests capital with a different form, so to speak tailors and transforms it into new clothes.

Distorted Production Structure

Up until now we have assumed an interest rate that has formed freely in the marketplace. It depends directly on the desire of market participants to save, this is to say, their time preferences, and thus by definition cannot be manipulated by a central bank. It is called the "natural interest rate" after Knut Wicksell. Wicksell developed his influential contribution to interest theory in his work *Interest Rates and Prices* (1898). He differentiated between the natural interest rate and the monetary interest rate. The monetary interest rate is the rate that can be observed in financial markets. It represents the rate for credit, respectively loans and is entirely a financial construct. The natural interest rate is the rate that would form on the capital markets in equilibrium. In Wicksell's words:

> There is a certain interest rate on loans which is neutral in relation to commodity prices and neither raises nor lowers them. This is necessarily the same interest rate that would be determined by supply and demand if money were not employed and the entire extension of loans would take place in the form of real capital goods. In essence this can be described as the current level of the natural interest rate on capital.[66]

According to Wicksell, a divergence between the two types of rates leads to a situation where the demand for investment no longer conforms to the amount of savings. If the gross market interest rate is below the natural interest rate, economic expansion takes place and prices will – all else equal – rise. Conversely, if the market rate is above the natural rate, an economic downturn takes hold.

The idea that there exists a discrepancy between two interest rates is a similarity to the views of the Austrian School. Its adherents suggest that an artificial increase in the money supply, respectively artificially suppressed interest rates, lead to the business cycle. In contrast to Wicksell, Ludwig von Mises and Friedrich Hayek succeeded in developing the theory further into a consistent theory of the business cycle and pointed out Wicksell's errors. Wicksell believed that prices would be stable if the natural and the monetary interest were in equilibrium. This idea was *inter alia* refuted by Hayek in 1931.[67]

The natural interest rate can be seen as a price ratio (between future and present goods), and thus is determined by supply and demand like every other price. It occupies an economically relevant coordinating function between consumption and investment. Thus the following applies: interest rates fulfill an irreplaceable coordinating function in the economy. They are not arbitrarily determinable numbers; they express something. If they are centrally manipulated, they can no longer fulfill their coordinating function and take on a misdirecting role.

What does this coordinating function consist of? Interest rates coordinate production inter-temporally. They make it possible for entrepreneurs to gauge the future profitability of investment decisions taken today, by indicating how many resources remain unemployed today and can therefore be used for investment. If they are not manipulated, they therefore reflect the time preferences of market participants. High interest rates indicate a relatively higher time preference than low interest rates. By steering interest rates, one cannot alter the time preferences of market participants to the same degree. While manipulation of interest rates influences the order of preferences and thus time preference as well (since the costs of consuming today have changed relative to future consumption), this intervention nevertheless distorts the direct relationship between time preferences and the interest rate. As a consequence, the resources available for investment are no longer properly correlated with the interest rate.

If one saves, one effectively leaves resources in the economy instead of appropriating them for one's own purposes, leaving them for investors to use. These resources cannot be created by means of credit expansion. Let us say that Fed chair Janet Yellen were to meet the press and declare *sotto voce*: "I will do whatever is in my power to push interest rates to a low level". Through this or any other monetary policy, not one whit of additional resources is created. The economy's pool of real funding remains initially completely unaffected by monetary policy decisions; the effects that do occur over time are entirely negative. What happens when interest rates are manipulated, especially when they are lowered, is described by Mises as follows:

> But now the drop in interest rates falsifies the businessman's calculation. Although the amount of capital goods available did not increase, the calculation employs figures which would be utilizable only if such an increase had taken place. The result of such calculation is therefore misleading. They make some projects appear profitable and realizable which a correct calculation, based on an interest rate not manipulated by credit expansion, would have shown as unrealizable. Entrepreneurs embark upon the execution of such projects. Business activities are stimulated. A boom begins.[68]

Central banks that manipulate interest rates downward to an unnatural level, are not releasing additional resources into the economy. What changes, however, in an environment of artificially suppressed interest rates, is the number of investments that appear profitable. The same pool of real resources now has to suffice for the realization of a great many more investment projects. The normally coordinating function of interest rates is now misdirecting entrepreneurs, as no natural interest rate is allowed to form. Mises likened the situation of entrepreneurs to that of a master builder, who does not know that the building materials at his disposal are insufficient to construct a building of the intended size and shape:

> The whole entrepreneurial class is, as it were, in the position of a master-builder whose task it is to erect a building out of a limited supply of building materials. If this man overestimates the quantity of the available supply, he drafts a plan for the execution of which the means at his disposal are not sufficient. He over-sizes the groundwork and the foundations and only discovers later in the progress of the construction that he lacks the material needed for the completion of the structure.[69]

The height of the natural interest rate also expresses the scarcity of real savings, which so to speak are standing behind the veil of money. The natural interest rate harbors the price of market participants renouncing a certain portion of possible present consumption. Economic growth results from capital accumulation which is based on a change in behavior that is expressed by a lower natural interest rate. An artificially suppressed interest rate not accompanied by the necessary change in the behavior of market participants by contrast cannot possibly enable sustainable economic growth.

Monetary policy interventions mean *de facto* that price controls are applied to interest rates. Commercial banks are induced by the central bank's measures to extend ever more consumer and business loans. An artificial expansion of credit ensues, which is enabled by the institution of the fractional reserve banking system. Moreover, the central bank's role as a lender of last resort, that is an institution that stands ready to supply commercial banks with near unlimited amounts of fresh capital at all times, has led to the shrinking of required reserve ratios to an absolute minimum.

As financial institutions only have to hold a tiny fraction of their deposits in the form of cash reserves, they have the legal privilege of creating deposit money from nothing. From nothing, because banks can create new "virtual money" through the act of extending a loan by simply enlarging their balance sheet. From a balance sheet perspective, both a claim on and a liability of the same borrower is created. What makes the entire process absurd is the fact that the balance sheet claim or asset, is based on the bank's own liability, and moreover the bank demands interest payments from the borrower. Mises referred to these uncovered loans as "circulation credit". This artificial expansion of credit hands new purchasing power to the recipients of loans. In the economy as a whole, this monetary inflation is however not offset by a commensurate retention of real resources.

The combination of expansive monetary policy of central banks and the expansion of circulation credit by commercial banks induces many companies to invest in projects that turn out to be unprofitable down the line. This is essentially because future returns are discounted by an interest rate that is too low as a result of the monetary expansion. This inevitably results in a distorted, too high present value of long-lived capital goods. Capital intensive long-term projects suddenly appear profitable. This is reflected in an increasingly distorted production structure – distorted because it does 'not incorporate the actual time preferences of market participants. Production and consumption are increasingly imbalanced.

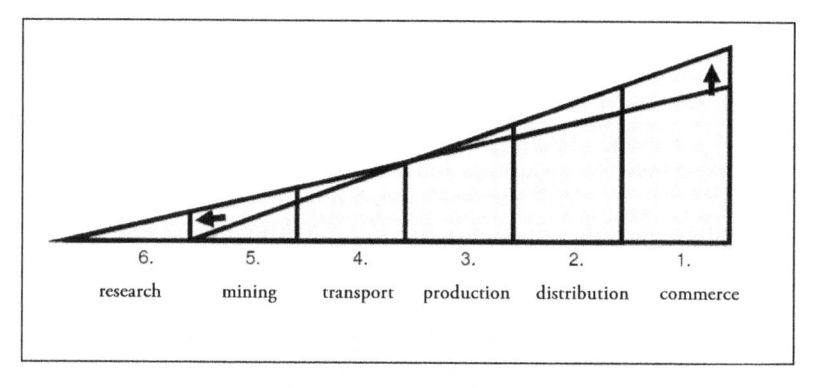

Figure 6.4: Hayekian triangle IV

Figure 6.4 shows this causal connection. The artificially induced money supply expansion, respectively the artificially suppressed interest rate, leads to a lengthening of the production structure. However, in contrast to the previous case, this is not the result of an increase in savings. The production structure does not flatten now, but is buckling. The reason is that the desire to save has not only not increased, but tends to even be reduced, as saving is no longer as remunerative due to lower rates. Thus a rising inflow of funds into stages of production close to consumption will occur, usually with a slight lag, as the illusory accounting profits made in the higher stages are distributed. These accounting profits are illusory because they are based on erroneous economic calculation due to the shift in relative prices. Much of what is regarded as "profits" will later turn out to have been capital consumption. The triangle of the production structure is distorted and the business cycle is set into motion. We are now entering the boom phase. The resources required for the new, higher stages of production far from consumption are no longer retained, but are concurrently consumed. One attempts to have one's cake and eat it at the same time. Roland Baader gets to the heart of the matter in his characteristically trenchant manner:

> What we have eaten in advance in recent decades in the paper credit binge, we will have to starve for in coming decades.[70]

The new money brought into circulation drives a wedge between savings and investment. Previously they were two sides of the same coin, now they are no longer complementing each other. The wedge becomes a tug-of-war between producers and consumers over the proverbial cake.

Naturally, companies that are active in capital-intensive sectors, where capital is tied up in the long term and projects are of far longer duration than those of companies in the consumer goods industries, are much more sharply affected by these distortions. Artificially suppressed interest rates induce companies that would not have invested in a project at the previous interest rate to undertake capital malinvestment. Due to the low cost of credit during the boom years, many of the above mentioned firms appear rock-solid and promising, and are enticing more and more investors in the capital markets through a self-reinforcing spiral of optimism to engage in malinvestment as well. The Spanish "Austrian" economist Jesus Huerta de Soto[71] in this context criticizes the international accounting standards (IAS) introduced in recent years, which convey a false "wealth effect" during boom times. De Soto finds fault with the fact that these guidelines have led to abandoning traditional principles of caution, as rising securities prices are immediately booked as gains in balance sheets, which are subsequently distributed and/or used as the justification for additional artificial increases of securities prices. However, the crisis of 2008 brought an equally unwise movement in the opposite direction. After asset prices and the value of many loans on the balance sheets of banks fell, "mark-to-market" accounting that previously produced large artificial profits for banks was abandoned again. De Soto is of the opinion that assets should be valued either at cost, or at their market value, *whichever is lower*. This kind of prudent accounting would help to avoid many problems, but the opportunity to introduce it was missed.

The distortions described above increase all the more, the longer the expansive monetary policy of central banks lasts. The resultant investments in projects that would under normal circumstances be regarded as unprofitable are only unmasked as unsustainable and corrected once the inevitable recession strikes. Even a number of classical value investors who ignore monetary policy trends and traditional economic relationships become victims of the erroneous economic calculation that results from artificial credit expansion.

Let us take a look at empirical confirmation of the Austrian business cycle theory described above. Figure 6.5 shows the segmentation of the productive factors in the US economy, whereby the ratio between spending on capital goods versus consumer goods production is depicted. A rise in the ratio shows that the capital structure increasingly shifts from lower order to higher order stages. This phenomenon is primarily explainable by an unsustainable, credit-induced boom. While the ratio cannot show how large the extent of misallocations is, it is clear that the economy is increasingly distorted if the relationship between capital and consumer goods production diverges enormously within a few years. After a strong increase in the ratio, the short-term trend tends to be reversed as soon as a recession strikes. During these periods, the production structure is partially readjusted to the actual consumption and saving intentions of market participants. However, as the reaction of monetary policy to recessions is usually not long in coming, the process of reallocation of previously malinvested capital is never fully completed. Contrary to widespread opinion, the boom is actually kept on artificial life support.

6. Business Cycles

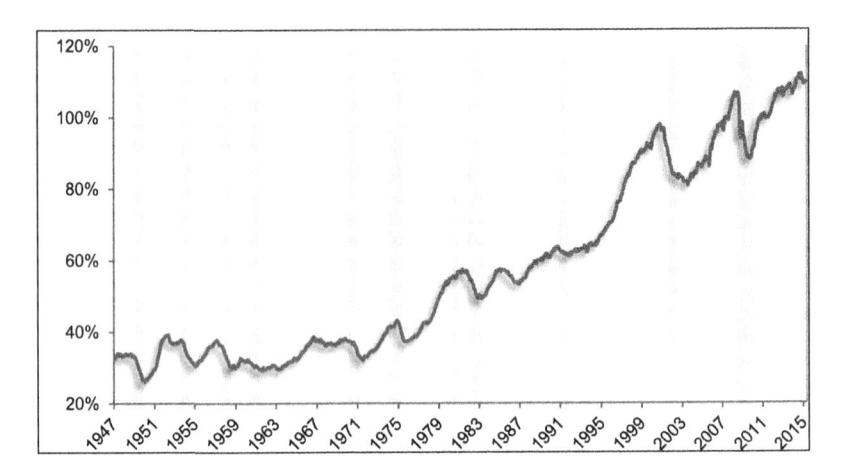

Figure 6.5.: The ratio of capital to consumer goods production (Source: Federal Reserve St. Louis)

Investors can use this ratio in practice as an indicator that signals whether a boom induced by monetary policy is taking place. Currently we still remain in the boom phase of the overarching economic cycle.

The economic cycle begins with an expansion of the money supply (in the middle of Figure 6.6). The foundation of the boom is created and the business cycle is set into motion. It is propelled by new loans and often by rising government debt. The increase in the money supply begins to affect price levels step by step. This does not necessarily have to result in a strong increase in consumer prices, which are the main object of official statistical observation. More often one can observe price increases in financial market assets. A diagram of the possible outcome of the cycle is shown in the next figure. As soon as malinvestments become obvious, there can be, depending on the duration and extent of the preceding money supply expansion, a high danger of a chain reaction of cascading payment defaults and ultimately insolvencies. This tends to have a deflationary effect and harbors two dangers: on the one hand, a decline or even a mere reduction in the pace of growth in money supply expansion can already lead to the impression that not enough resources for the completion of all the investments undertaken are available.

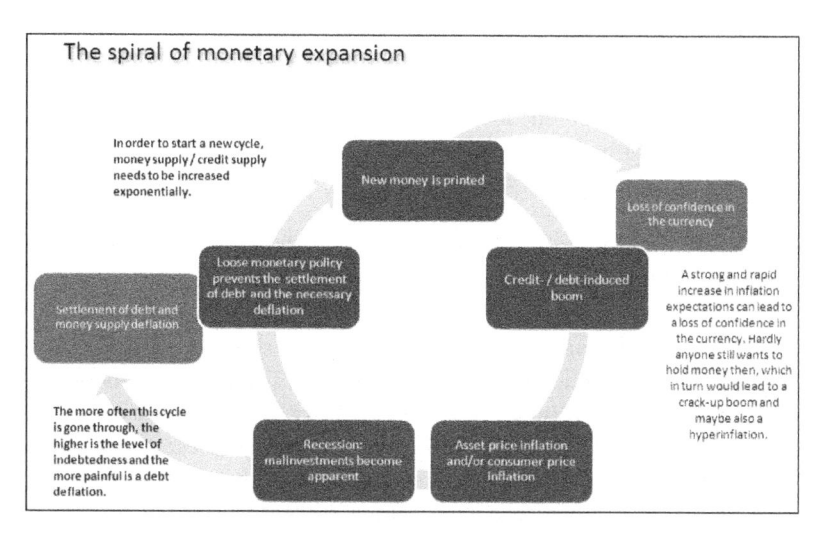

Figure 6.6: The spiral of money supply expansion
(Source: Incrementum AG)

On the other hand, many companies and banks can be economically intertwined with insolvent companies and banks, which can lead to additional write-offs. This process is usually presented as the actual problem in public debate, which often conveys the impression that "Austrian" economists practically pine for a crisis. In reality, they simply regard the inevitable and necessary deflationary correction as an opportunity to lay the foundation for growing prosperity that is sustainable in the long term. Contrary to mainstream economists, they therefore do not regard the bust phase as a problem that needs to be prevented at any price, but simply as a necessary evil. The erroneous perspective of the boom as an upswing induces monetary policy makers to try to avert the outcome shown in figure 6.6. at the lower left as long as possible, and gives them an incentive to continue to inflate. Poison is used as a medicine; the drug dosage is increased further, withdrawal is postponed. Friedrich A. Hayek warned:

> To fight a depression by increasing credit expansion is akin to the attempt to fight an evil by its own causes; because we suffer from a misdirection of production, we want even more misdirection – an approach that necessarily leads to an even more serious crisis once the credit expansion ends.[72]

The more often the boom-bust cycle occurs, the more sensitive market participants become to the demeanor of central bankers. Every frown is subject to interpretation and can affect the stability of financial markets. We have become so accustomed to this situation that it barely registers as peculiar anymore. However, this is simply government-created uncertainty that is by no means necessary. Resources are employed in order to anticipate monetary policy decisions. These expectations in turn influence the decision makers. Historical market patterns have radically changed in recent years. Since 2009, the Fed has reacted to every slowdown in economic activity by taking further inflationary measures, so that a paradoxical situation can be observed in the meantime: disappointing economic data lead to price increases in stocks, as a continuation, respectively expansion, of inflationary policy is priced in.

On the other hand, better than expected economic data often lead to price declines, as they suggest the possible abandonment of inflationary policies. Prior to the beginning of the first "quantitative easing" exercise, the rate of change of the Fed's balance sheet displayed a 20% correlation with the S&P 500 Index. Since 2009, this correlation has increased to more than 86%. Money supply expansion has thus a bigger effect on stock prices than trends in corporate earnings. This is now even acknowledged by the Federal Reserve. The strong dependency of the stock market on inflationary policy can be discerned in figure 6.7. As soon as inflationary policy is slowed down or discontinued (or if plans to do so are announced), stocks suffer strong price slumps, before cries for more "quantitative easing", and the renewed adoption of the policy ultimately leads to the rally's continuation.

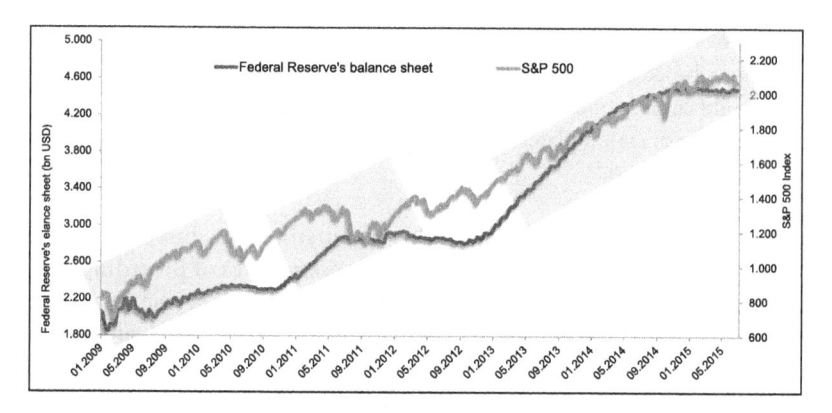

Figure 6.7: S&P 500 Index and US money supply; the shaded areas designate periods of quantitative easing
(Source: Federal Reserve St. Louis)

This stock market rally is one of the many effects of the artificial expansion of the money supply, which always sets a business cycle into motion:

> Thus, bank credit expansion sets into motion the business cycle in all its phases: the inflationary boom, marked by expansion of the money supply and by malinvestment; the crisis, which arrives when credit expansion ceases and malinvestments become evident; and the depression recovery, the necessary adjustment process, by which the economy returns to the most efficient ways of satisfying consumer desires.[73]

Alan Greenspan in 2001 and Ben Bernanke in 2008 prevented precisely this recovery in order to avert a short term, painful correction, at the price of a significantly worse recession in the future. The economic structure was unable to heal, but instead was inundated with painkillers. A significant amount of capital continues to be tied up in unprofitable projects. Too many investors continue to lay claim to an insufficient pool of resources. Ludwig von Mises explains where this must lead:

6. Business Cycles

There is no means of avoiding the final collapse of a boom brought about by credit expansion. The alternative is only whether the crisis should come sooner as the result of a voluntary abandonment of further credit expansion, or later as a final and total catastrophe of the currency system involved.[74]

According to the Austrian School, the bursting of a bubble and the subsequent hangover are the inevitable consequences of preceding misallocations of capital, which are ruthlessly exposed in the recession. The reasons for the slump are an artificially lowered level of interest rates, as well as excessive monetary expansion by the central bank and commercial banks, which were employed to stimulate a weak economy previously (weak employment data, low economic growth, rescue packages, etc.). From the Austrian perspective, the slump is contrary to popular opinion not a negative consequence of the market economy, but rather the necessary healing process of the effects of previously practiced interventionism.

The boom is purely a monetary phenomenon, while the recession represents a structural adjustment. Such structural problems cannot be solved with monetary policy means. The causal confusion of economic growth with monetary expansion is even partially recognized by mainstream economists. Robert Lucas (a representative of the "Rational Expectations" School) remarked in his Nobel Prize address that monetary expansion is nothing but a deception of market participants.[75] The interest rate – the central price ratio in the market economy – is falsified and the function of money as a store of value gradually destroyed. This then leads to the misallocation of capital. According to Lucas, monetary policy – regardless of whether it is expansive or restrictive – is not able to alter the level of economic output. This also explains why the currently extant problems cannot be solved with monetary stimulus. One might be tempted to think that such a business cycle is not all that bad. At times, the economy is doing well, at other times a little worse. This opinion is however simply incorrect. Malinvestment actually destroys real wealth, which subsequently must be rebuilt anew. It is not simply a redistribution between generations – wealth is destroyed outright.

The Cantillon Effect

Irish economist Richard Cantillon (1680-1734), an important forerunner of the Austrian School, was the first person to recognize that money is not neutral, but that every change in the money supply also alters the structure of the economy. Newly created money is neither uniformly nor simultaneously distributed among the population. This means that some users of money will benefit from rising prices, while others will be harmed. Money supply expansion is a transfer of wealth: market participants who receive the newly created purchasing power earlier benefit relative to those who receive newly created money only later or not at all. The former are still able to buy consumer or capital goods at relatively low prices, the latter only after prices have already increased. The Cantillon effect – the fact that newly created money enters the economy at specific points and propagates from there – is the very reason an expansion in the supply of money can never be "neutral".

If the money supply expands in a period of subdued economic activity, the money supply expansion can also fail to raise prices. However, even in this case there is redistribution, even though it is not immediately obvious: the larger money supply prevents a decline in prices to the level they would have attained had it not grown. Thus producers benefit, because the prices of their goods remain artificially high. Consumers, on the other hand, lose out, as the money supply expansion prevents a decline in goods prices and an increase in money's purchasing power. Inflation has the effect of a regressive tax, which due to the so-called Cantillon effect tends to hit the least affluent strata of the population the hardest.

Friedrich August von Hayek compared the Cantillon effect to pouring honey onto a saucer. The honey only distributes itself slowly from the center outward. Transposed to the effects of inflation, this means that governments and companies that are close to the source of money creation benefit from it. They receive the new money before prices in the economy have risen due to the additional demand they are able to exercise because of it. One can also transpose the Cantillon effect to the international currency system. The issuer of the reserve currency – currently the US – is the primary beneficiary of inflation and the Cantillon effect. This is reflected in a structurally negative trade balance. The US exports dollars and imports real goods and services from all over the world in exchange.

According to Austrian business cycle theory, capital goods tend to rise first in the course of an inflation process (asset price inflation), while consumer price inflation only occurs later. Currently asset price inflation is rampant, as many examples show. Prices of antiques, fine wines, old timers, but also real estate and stocks have increased sharply in recent years. The phenomenon is especially conspicuous in the art market: in 1980, the most expensive painting in the world only cost $ 6.4 million. Thereafter, prices began to rise exponentially, the barrier of $100 million was first breached with the sale of Picasso's "Boy with a Pipe". Up until recently, Cezanne's "The Card Player" was the most expensive painting at $260 million. This record was broken in February 2015, when Paul Gauguin's "Nafea Faa Ipoipo (When Will You Marry?)" sold for $300 million. The number of billionaires is likewise a conspicuous indicator of inflation: while there was not a single billionaire in the 1970s, there were already eight in the 1980s, while the number of billionaires currently stands at more than 1,400 according to Forbes. The reason for this is the gradual bloating of asset values and the associated Cantillon effect. This is also shown in figure 6.8.:

Chart showing ownership of stocks by income segment:
- top 10%: direct ownership of stocks 48%, pension plans 90%
- middle 10%: direct ownership of stocks 12%, pension plans 33%
- bottom 10%: direct ownership of stocks 4%, pension plans 11%

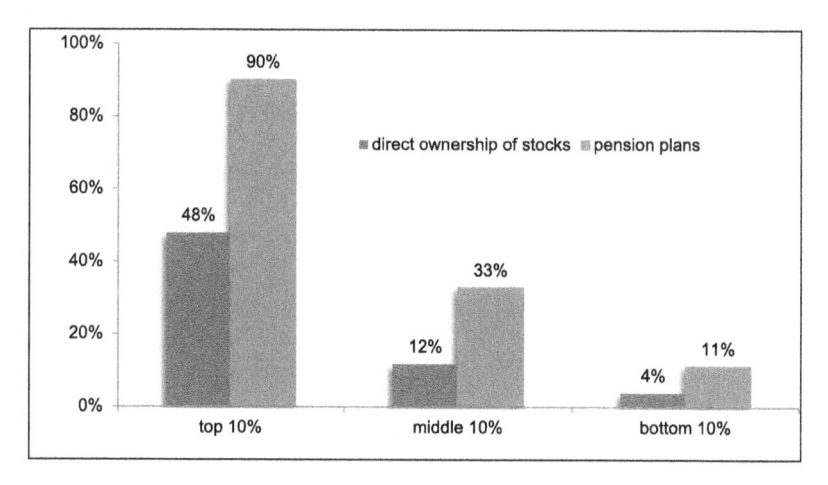

Figure 6.8: The Cantillon effect. Ownership of stocks by income segment (Source: Incrementum AG)

The Federal Reserve always justifies its money printing programs with the so-called wealth effect. The argument is that a large portion of monthly incomes can be spent on private consumption, as private wealth continually increases due to rising prices of stocks and real estate. Inflating asset values are thus used as a justification for conspicuous hedonistic consumption. However, even Keynes was aware of the consequences of long-term monetary debasement:

> By a continuing process of inflation, governments can confiscate, secretly and unobserved, an important part of the wealth of their citizens. By this method they not only confiscate, but they confiscate arbitrarily; and, while the process impoverishes many, it actually enriches some. [...] Those to whom the system brings windfalls become "profiteers," who are the object of the hatred [...] the process of wealth-getting degenerates into a gamble and a lottery. [...] Lenin was certainly right. There is no subtler, no surer means of overturning the existing basis of society than to debauch the currency. The process engages all the hidden forces of economic law on the side of destruction, and does it in a manner which not one man in a million is able to diagnose.[76]

6. Business Cycles

The hotly debated disparity in income distribution is currently escalating and leads to growing social tensions. Between 1979 and 2011, the average household income rose by 64%, while the income of the upper 1% of households rose by nearly 300% and the income of the lowest quintile rose by a mere 18%. This strong rise in the concentration of wealth can be seen in the Gini coefficient, which has reached record levels in many countries. This means that the extremes at the lowest and highest boundaries of the income scale become ever more pronounced, while the importance of the traditional middle class declines.

In the US, the Gini coefficient is thus at the same level today as on the eve of the Great Depression in the late 1920s. This is no coincidence, as there was also rapid monetary inflation at the time that led to an artificial boom and the associated inflation of asset values. Due to the strengthening of moral hazard (the temptation to engage in highly risky ventures in the knowledge that one will be bailed out in case things go wrong) in the framework of today's "too big to fail" paradigm, the momentum of wealth redistribution has increased further. The strong increase in inequality is also visible in the ratio of executive salaries vs. those of average employees. While a chief executive officer earned about 24 times as much as an average employee in 1980, manager salaries are currently 425 times the average employee wage. This is definitely a consequence of fractional reserve banking, respectively the Cantillon effect, which in the case of managers is augmented by the "halo effect".

The Skyscraper Index

Can the hubris of city planners be seen as a reliable warning of misallocations? The skyscraper index, which was developed by Andrew Lawrence in 1999, attempts to answer this question.[77] In his study "The Skyscraper Index: Faulty Towers" he was the first to systematically examine the connection between the erection of skyscrapers and the business cycle. Mark Thornton made an important contribution to the further development of this idea in 2005.[78] He incorporated Lawrence's idea in an economic framework based on Austrian business cycle theory. His analysis led him to conclude that the skyscraper index indeed represents a reliable warning signal that the end of a boom is near:

> The building of world's tallest building is a good proxy for dating the onset of major economic downturns.[79]

However, many critics regard the skyscraper index as a spurious correlation. How is the construction of the world's tallest building supposed to trigger an economic downturn? It is, of course, not the skyscraper as such that represents the decisive criterion. As we will show below, the erection of the tallest skyscraper primarily stands for the economic interdependence between a strong expansion of the money supply, the business cycle, the hubris of city planners, and the ensuing financial crises. The skyscraper itself is not the object of study, but merely represents a symptom that can often be observed at the end of artificially created boom periods. The megalomania of many skyscraper projects is visible proof of the correctness of Austrian business cycle theory. As noted above, interventions into the level of interest rates and the growth of the money supply lead to momentous distortions of incentives. In reference to the Cantillon effect and its derivations, Thornton's monograph succeeds in proving the theoretical validity of the skyscraper index with respect to these incentives. He derives three further effects from the Cantillon effect, which correlate with the Cantillon effect insofar as they lead to the same consequence, namely a redistribution of real wealth. All three effects need to be examined in conjunction, as they are not independent of each other, but rather reinforce each other.

The first one concerns the effect interest rates exert on land and capital values. Declining interest rates make real estate more attractive, as the opportunity costs of purchasing property decrease. *Ceteris paribus*, a decline in interest rates will lead to rising demand for real estate and land. Consequently, real estate prices will rise.

6. Business Cycles

The second effect concerns the fact that low interest rates also affect the size of companies. Low interest rates not only increase the size of companies, they also lower the cost of financing capital goods. Long-term investments in capital goods appear viable. The confidence of entrepreneurs and speculators increases. As the cycle continues, excessive speculation and economic ignorance increase in tandem. A "this time everything is different" mentality begins to take over, which ultimately serves to justify the construction of megalomaniac projects.

The third effect concerns the connection between innovative technologies and the construction of ever larger structures. Not only skyscrapers, which reach ever greater heights, but also capital-intensive production processes always require the adoption of new methods to successfully implement them in the marketplace. Moreover, additional problems require solving, such as engineering and construction problems, as well as environmental, transportation and communication problems, such as the need to construct faster elevators, or taking into account various environmental influences when building at hitherto unattained heights, and so forth.

These are the reasons why the three effects connected with the Cantillon effect provide a convincing explanation of the skyscraper index. The construction of the tallest building illustrates the inefficient allocation of resources and a euphoric assessment of the future. Due to the long preparation and construction time it is not surprising that an investment and construction decision is often taken close to or at the peak of a boom. The confidence, euphoria and hubris of entrepreneurs and speculators reaches its peak at the same time. As a result the completion of the building often occurs during the subsequent bust.

The index exhibits a very good hit rate, although it was not able to forecast every recession with precision, such as e.g. Japan's crisis in the 1990s. In spite of such exceptions, impressive historical correlations can be found with the help of the index. Thus the construction of the Singer Building (1906-1908) and the Metropolitan Life Building (1907-1909) heralded the panic of 1907. The Great Depression was accompanied by the completion of the Chrysler Building (New York) in 1930 as well as the Empire State Building (NY) in 1931 (due to offices standing empty until the 1950s, the Empire State Building was for a long time referred to as the "*Empty* State Building"). The completion of World Trade Center One and Two (NY) and the Sears Tower (today: Willis Tower, Chicago) in 1972, 1973 and 1974 coincided with the oil crisis of the 1970s. The Petronas Tower in Kuala Lumpur was completed in 1997, just as the Asian crisis began. Figure 6.9 summarizes these and other examples.

Completed	Building	City	Height	Stories	Economic crisis
1908	Singer	New York	186 m	47	1907 Bankers' Panic
1909	Metropolitan Life	New York	213 m	50	1907 Bankers' Panic
1913	Woolworth	New York	241 m	57	---
1929	40 Wall Street	New York	282 m	71	Great Depression
1930	Chrysler	New York	318 m	77	Great Depression
1931	Empire State	New York	381 m	102	Great Depression
1972/1973	World Trade Center	New York	416 m	110	Stagflation in the 1970s
1974	Sears Tower	Chicago	441 m	110	Stagflation in the 1970s
1997	Petronas Tower	Kuala Lumpur	452 m	88	1997 Asian financial crisis
2014	Shanghai Tower	Shanghai	632 m	94	China

Figure 6.9: The world's tallest buildings and economic crises (Source: Mark Thornton, "Skyscrapers and Business Cycles")

6. Business Cycles

There are also astonishing examples in connection with the 2008 financial and economic crisis. At the beginning of the implosion of Spain's real estate bubble, three of Europe's tallest skyscrapers were built in Madrid (Torre Caja Madrid, Torre de Cristol and Torre Sacyr Vallehermoso).[780]The construction of the Burj Khalifa in Dubai – which is currently the world's tallest building – began in 2004 and was completed in 2010. Although Dubai's royal family initially wanted to finance the construction on its own, the Emirate Abu Dhabi had to assist with a financial injection, as the state-owned company Dubai Worlds had begun to experience financial difficulties as a result of the financial crisis.[81]

India and China are especially conspicuous in this context at present. Both countries plan the construction of giant skyscrapers in the near future in order to create living space for workers moving into cities. Over the coming six years, China alone intends to complete half of the 124 skyscrapers currently under construction worldwide. Figure 6.10 shows that not only are ever more skyscrapers being built, but that their average height also continues to increase. According to the Barclay's Skyscraper Index, this will not only alter the dimension and number of Chinese skyscrapers, but also their geographical profile. While skyscrapers were mainly built in first and second tier cities in the past, they will in future be predominantly built in third tier cities.

The Shanghai Tower, currently China's tallest building, was completed in 2014. At a height of 624 meters and an incredible construction cost of $2.4 billion, it is the pride of the People's Republic and at the moment the second tallest building in the world. In the near future, China will be home to five of the ten tallest and 14 of the 20 tallest skyscrapers (see figure 6.10).

#	Building	City	Height	(Scheduled) completion	Utilization
1.	Kingdom Tower	Jeddah (SA)	1000 m	2019	office / hotel / living space
2.	Burj Khalifa	Dubai (AE)	828 m	2010	office / hotel / living space
3.	Pingan Finance Center	Shenzhen (CN)	660 m	2017	office
4.	Wuhan Greenland Center	Wuhan (CN)	636 m	2017	office / hotel / living space
5.	Shanghai Tower	Shanghai (CN)	632 m	2015	office / hotel
6.	Makkah Royal Clock Tower	Mecca (SA)	601 m	2012	hotel / various things
7.	Goldin Finance 117	Tianjin (CN)	597 m	2016	office / hotel
8.	Lotte World Tower	Seoul (KR)	555 m	2016	office / hotel
9.	One World Trade Center	New York City (US)	541 m	2014	office
10.	The CTF Guangzhou	Guangzhou (CN)	530 m	2017	office / hotel / living space
11.	Tanjin Chow Tai Fook Bintai Center	Tianjin (CN)	530 m	2017	office / hotel / living space
12.	Zhongguo Zun	Beijing (CN)	528 m	2018	office
13.	Taipei 101	Taipei (TW)	508 m	2004	office
14.	Shanghai World Finance Center	Shanghai (CN)	492 m	2008	office / hotel
15.	International Commerce Center	Hong Kong (CN)	484 m	2010	office / hotel
16.	International Commerce Center 2	Chongqing (CN)	469 m	2018	office / hotel
17.	Guangdong Building	Tianjin (CN)	468 m	2017	office / hotel / living space
18.	Lakhta Center	St. Petersburg (RU)	463 m	2018	office

Figure 6.10: The tallest buildings in the world (Source: The Skyscraper Center).

6. Business Cycles

Andrew Lawrence, the developer of the skyscraper index comments on China's situation as follows:

> The Skyscraper Index has a good 150-year correlation between the world's tallest buildings and economic slowdowns and recessions [...]. For China, there is no reason that correlation will change.[82]

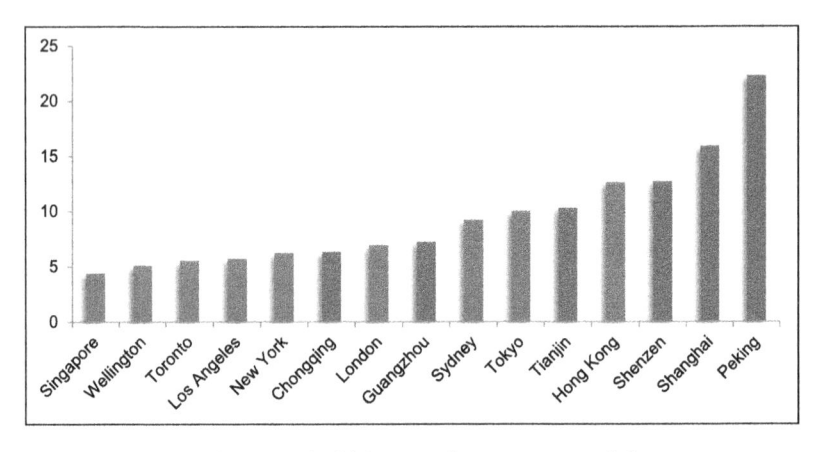

Figure 6.11: Real estate bubble in China? Ratio of home prices to annual incomes (Sources: Global Financial Stability Report: The Quest for Lasting Stability, IMF, April 2012; Incrementum AG)

In India, giant construction projects are also being pursued. In the next five years, fourteen skyscrapers will be built. The India Tower in Mumbai at 718 meters is set to become the world's second tallest building. However, after beginning in 2010, construction was interrupted in 2011.

Apart from the projects in China and India, the Kingdom Tower and the Azerbaijan Tower are of interest as well. The goal of these projects is the erection of the tallest building in the world. Construction of Saudi Arabia's Kingdom Tower began already in 2013. It is supposed to reach the incredible height of 1,000 meters (~3,280 ft.) at the end of 2018. The Azerbaijan Tower is still in the planning stage. According to press releases, it is supposed to reach an even loftier 1,050 meters (~3,445 ft.). The construction project includes the creation of 41 artificial islands in the Caspian Sea, on top of which the skyscraper is to be built. Azerbaijan is supposed to become the "Dubai of the Caspian Sea". Construction is planned to begin in 2015 and with completion targeted for 2019.

When tall buildings are erected based on strong demand for space and high land prices, they can be very profitable over a building's entire life-cycle. If the construction is however only a symbol of the "greatness and pride of a nation", it rings alarm bells. The Barclay's Skyscraper Index not only shows a correlation between skyscrapers under construction and economic slumps, but also a correlation with the height of skyscrapers. The current developments in China and India should therefore serve as a warning to investors that an overheated situation is possibly at hand. In China, not only are the number of skyscrapers in the planning stage and under construction increasing, but also their average height. A looming end of China's boom can no longer be ruled out.

The oil price is especially noteworthy in this context. The assumption that oil and gas prices will remain high recently ended with a rude awakening. Considering that Azerbaijan's oil and gas sector accounts for 50% of GDP, the skyscraper index could in this case have been interpreted as a long-term warning signal for the oil price.

7. Scenarios

Hyperinflation versus Hyperdeflation

The expansion of fiduciary media – inflation – cannot be continued at will. At some point, a majority realizes that the currency is no longer useful as a store of value. In such a case, incomes and savings will increasingly be used for consumption and investments – a currency that is no longer useful for hoarding is "dehoarded". As a result, the currency's purchasing power declines even more. A self-reinforcing spiral can be set into motion, at the end of which stands hyperinflation. Then the velocity of the currency's circulation explodes – everyone attempts to pass currency on as quickly as possible. Even the most naïve and clueless people eventually realize that the currency is crashing when the caloric value of paper money begins to exceed its purchasing power. At this point, people burn currency in their ovens or begin using it as wallpaper. Ludwig von Mises noted:

> An inflationary policy can only be continued as long as the opinion that it will cease in the foreseeable future still prevails. Once the conviction that inflation will no longer come to an end has become entrenched, panic breaks out.[83]

In the 20th century alone, there have been 25 episodes of hyperinflation. The most famous of all is that of the Weimar Republic in 1923, when the government's bankruptcy due to World War I was delayed with the aid of the printing press. Prophetic observer Felix Somary would have preferred a government insolvency, as would have all adherents of the Austrian School, as it would have been akin to a one-off surgical

7. Scenarios

procedure, while the inflation was akin to a permanent blood poisoning. Our recent history is testament to the consequences of this blood poisoning:

> Thus defrauding the saver became a patriotic maxim and remained so with a brief interruption for an entire generation; from inflation, this is to say, expropriation without law and limit, Bolshevism and Hitlerism arose. Back when we uttered our warnings in the beginning, we were mocked as monomaniac money-men, as mean-spirited financiers, denounced as pessimists. But even the deepest pessimism was vastly exceeded by the frightfulness of the actual consequences.[84]

We find this pattern throughout history: warfare and welfare lead to government overindebtedness, and the State sidesteps bankruptcy by remaining nominally solvent and expropriating its creditors in real terms. Without inflationary policy, the big world wars would have ended after a short period of time for lack of funding.

A glance at the history books reveals interesting analogies to the status quo. An analysis of monetary policy cannot be undertaken without analyzing government policy more generally. After all, at its core, inflation is not an economic, but a political problem. Nicolaus Copernicus already warned:

> Although there are countless scourges which in general debilitate kingdoms, principalities, and republics, the four most important (in my judgment) are dissension, [abnormal] mortality, barren soil, and debasement of the currency. The first three are so obvious that nobody is unaware of their existence. But the fourth, which concerns money, is taken into account by few persons and only the most perspicacious. For it undermines states, not by a single attack all at once, but gradually and in a certain covert manner.[85]

In antiquity, the perfidious goal of inflation was still achieved by lowering the precious metal content or the weight of coins. Thus the weight of the Aureus, the largest Roman coin, declined from 10.5

grams (approx. 20 BC) to 0.77 grams (260 AD). The silver content of the Denarius was gradually lowered as well, in order to finance "bread and circuses" as well as Rome's overly large bureaucratic apparatus and rising military expenditures. In the first century BC, the silver content was still at nearly 95%, by 286 AD the Denarius consisted only to 0.02% of silver.

Ancient Rome flourished in times of low taxation. However, over time, its rulers began to buy the support of the citizenry with gifts. Slowly but surely, excessive administration, increasing over-regulation and rising taxes undermined the government's budget. The peak of Roman inflation was reached in the third century, as Rome was increasingly transformed into a welfare state. When the population of Rome reached approximately one million inhabitants, wheat and later bread were distributed to 300,000 citizens for free. Emperor Diocletian (284–305 AD) in particular used inflation for his purposes. He increased the money supply enormously, lowered the precious metals content of coins and issued brass and copper coins. Taxes were hiked in order to finance the military, which was supposed to safeguard the borders against "barbarians". In 301 AD, Diocletian released his famous edict on prices and thus fixed the prices of goods and services (similar to what recently took place in Venezuela and Argentina). Anyone who was found in breach and either offered goods above the fixed price or did not offer any goods for sale at all anymore faced the death penalty. Diocletian's belief that speculators and the hoarding of goods were responsible for price inflation naturally proved misguided. The draconian punishments had little success, as the actual cause of rising prices was not targeted.

This resulted in the first documented episode of hyperinflation. While a pound of gold cost 50,000 denarii in 301 AD, its price had risen to 2.12 billion denarii 50 years later – an increase of 42,000 times. Price inflation – measured in terms of the price for Egyptian wheat – rose to 15,000 percent within a century. By the time Diocletian's reign ended in 305 AD, his edict on prices began to be widely ignored. The edict sought to double the value of bronze and copper coins and set maximum

7. Scenarios

prices for more than a thousand different goods as well as wages. The economic disruption this caused was vast, and although economics was not well understood at the time, the edict was criticized by Lactantius of Nicomedia, who blamed the emperors for the inflation and pointed out that tampering with prices had led to violence and bloodshed. The example of the Roman Empire's downfall is a striking demonstration of how a growing bureaucracy and increasing misallocation of resources eventually leads to inflation and ultimately to complete collapse.

Swiss economist Peter Bernholz has compared the properties of historical hyperinflation episodes from Roman times to modern times in an extensive study.[86] He specifically analyzes 29 hyperinflation episodes, and illustrates their causes: money supply inflation, devaluation of exchange rates, budget deficits and lastly various phases of currency substitution. What seems especially relevant in Bernholz's work is the role of politics in hyperinflation periods, as well as his phase model of currency substitution in an environment of strongly rising price inflation. According to Bernholz, all hyperinflation episodes have taken place in the framework of paper money standards, globally there were only very few instances in which an increase in central bank money did not lead to rising prices (e.g. in Japan). Gold and bimetallic standards exhibited no, respectively much lower inflationary tendencies than paper money standards. According to Bernholz, there are in fact no examples in history in which hyperinflation was not set into motion as a result of money creation due to an exorbitant public debt. Budget deficits amounting to 40% of government expenditure are a near certain path to hyperinflation, as the political class finds itself facing a dilemma: one tries on the one hand to "boost the economy" with additional monetary stimulus, and on the other hand to finance budget deficits.

However, in this phase, budget deficits tend to increase very quickly due to "Tanzi's Law". The law states that budget deficits are bound to increase even faster in times of rising inflation rates if tax revenues fail to rise at a commensurate pace. Since there is often a long time lag between a transaction that is taxed and the point in time when the tax payment occurs, the real value of these tax revenues declines considerably in times of high inflation rates. For instance, sales tax and income tax payments are as a rule only made with a delay of several months and will in the meantime decline significantly in value if inflation rates are high.

Similar to many other economic phenomena, one characteristic feature of high inflation episodes is that they build up slowly. However, once a certain threshold is reached, the trend accelerates very quickly. Gresham's law only applies in the early stages of inflation, when it is e.g. attempted to defend a fixed parity under a bimetallic standard. In this phase, the population often flees into real assets such as real estate ("gold made from concrete") or gold. Due to "Thier's Law", the velocity of circulation increases, a number of market participants return to engaging in barter transactions, and the real value of the inflated money supply rapidly declines. Thier's law – also known as the "reverse Gresham's law" - states that due to the ever more rapid devaluation, acceptance of the currency abruptly declines. The lack of a stable means of payment increasingly leads to chaos in trade and production and results in foreign currencies being used for payments. People thus chose to employ the money that they deem to possess the greatest long-term stability.

A concrete example for this is "dollarization", this is to say the increased use of the US dollar (or the Deutschmark) following the collapse of the Eastern Bloc. Zimbabwe provides another example, where use of the Zimbabwe dollar was discontinued in 2009 as it was no longer practicable to employ in everyday transactions. It was replaced by the US dollar and the South African rand. In the final stage of Zimbabwe's inflation episode, people began using the banknotes of their worthless currency, which were adorned with amounts in the trillions, as wrapping paper for gold dust to effect payments.

Our current system clearly has an "inflationary bias". This means that the scattershot approach to stimulus and election promises is the basic precondition for money supply expansion. According to Bernholz, many central bankers underestimate the psychological pressure they are under when they discontinue stimulus measures and attempt to decrease the outstanding amount of central bank money. While reducing the money supply seems technically easily possible, it is difficult to push through politically. As soon as stimulus is reduced, the economy's enormous dependency on cheap liquidity means that recession risks rise significantly. This in turn puts political pressure on central bankers.

If the economic environment improves slightly and the population's confidence increases, interest rates should be hiked quickly and the money supply reduced. However, pressure from the media and the population makes this unlikely from a realpolitik perspective. This could be seen among other things in the recent debate that accompanied "tapering", the gradual reduction of the third phase of quantitative easing in the US. Considering all of this, it cannot be ruled out that the present currency system will end in hyperinflation. The uncomfortable side effects of deflation significantly increase the probability that a large number of inflationary measures will be taken over the medium term in an uncovered paper money system so as to "vanquish" deflationary pressures. The creativity of central bankers with respect to furthering credit expansion by the commercial banking sector seems likely to increase markedly in the future.

As time goes on, it will be more and more difficult for central bankers to control the balancing act between inflation and deflation. Due to this monetary tectonic effect, investors should be prepared for stronger eruptions of both inflationary and deflationary phases. Every investment strategy should therefore be designed to be able to react flexibly to changes in the inflation regime.

The matrix below should serve to classify the current economic situation and illustrate as many possible developments as possible. Figure 7.1 shows different scenarios segmented by their growth and inflation rates. At present, we are stuck in between three potential forms of a renewed iteration of an artificial boom, stagflation as well as recession. The natural state of affairs cannot be reached directly. This would necessitate a recession first, during which unsustainable capital structures are liquidated in order to free up resources for better employments.

It is hardly surprising that the political class has so far opted for reflation, this is to say for feeding the artificial boom with ever more newly created money. What is more surprising is the absence of significant price increases and the intermittent decline in precious metals prices. Inflation and deflation are, however, not opposites, but rather accompanying and mutually interdependent sides of political intervention. In the final analysis, the price decline in gold and silver was only a symptom of a deflationary undertow that has set been into motion by central bank policy.

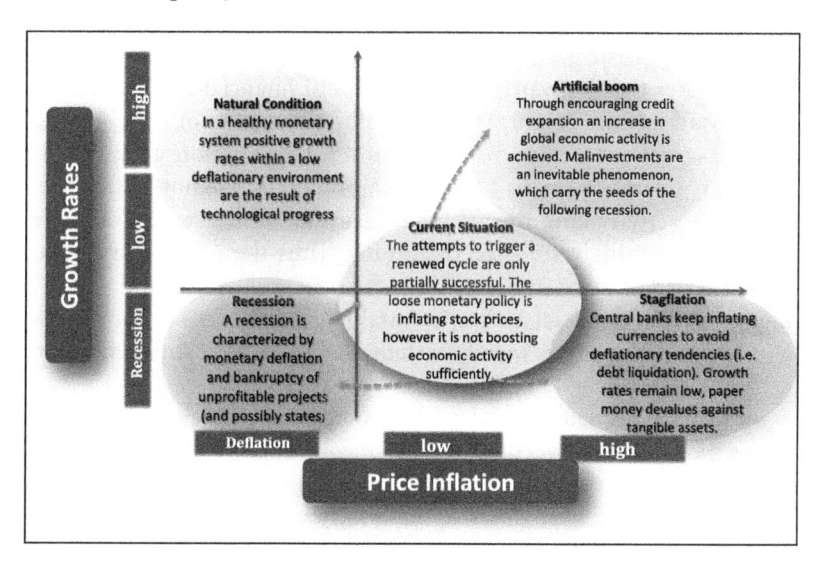

Growth Rates (vertical axis: high / low under "high"; low / Recession under "Recession")
Price Inflation (horizontal axis: Deflation / low / high)

- **Natural Condition**: In a healthy monetary system positive growth rates within a low deflationary environment are the result of technological progress
- **Artificial boom**: Through encouraging credit expansion an increase in global economic activity is achieved. Malinvestments are an inevitable phenomenon, which carry the seeds of the following recession.
- **Current Situation**: The attempts to trigger a renewed cycle are only partially successful. The loose monetary policy is inflating stock prices, however it is not boosting economic activity sufficiently
- **Recession**: A recession is characterized by monetary deflation and bankruptcy of unprofitable projects (and possibly states)
- **Stagflation**: Central banks keep inflating currencies to avoid deflationary tendencies (i.e. debt liquidation). Growth rates remain low, paper money devalues against tangible assets.

Figure 7.1.: Scenarios and their effect on inflation and growth rates

This may appear paradoxical and requires an explanation. Reflationary policy can only attain its goals if the money pumped into the economy actually reaches the real economy. Its goal is however never attainable, namely the temporary provision of liquidity to markets that is then taken back in a timely fashion. As the Austrian School explains with great precision, this is only the hubristic view of central bankers, as the distortions that are created cannot be fixed by means of a centrally planned monetary policy. Just as an organism can die from regular overeating alternating with hunger, the real economy is damaged by this unsustainable monetary bulimia.

However, why is not even the short-term goal of monetary force-feeding of the economy attained? Only if newly created money is used for investment in concrete capital goods with low liquidity can it reach the real economy. If it is, however, invested in highly liquid assets, the new funds are merely "parked" and do not enter the economy proper. And now for the explanation of the paradox: the more inflationary the policy, the greater the premium for holding purely financial assets. If real interest rates trend toward zero, the prices of financial assets seemingly rise toward infinite height. "Parking" of money now not only does not involve a cost, one even earns a premium. More and more areas become monetary "parking spaces". Circulating media are removed from real economic activity (and this includes hoarding of real savings) in order to obtain seemingly risk-free premiums. Thus the inflationary policy creates a deflationary undertow, which sucks real capital and real savings away into financial assets. As Antal Fekete explains, hyperinflation and hyper-deflation are merely extreme swings of the same pendulum:

> At first, the pendulum was swinging towards infinite interest, threatening the dollar with hyperinflation. Right now the pendulum is swinging to the other extreme, to zero interest, spelling hyperdeflation. This is just as damaging to producers as the swing towards infinite interest was in the early 1980's. It is impossible to predict whether one or the other extreme in the swinging of the wrecker's ball will make the world economy collapse. Hyperinflation and hyper-deflation are just two different forms of the same phenomenon: credit collapse. Arguing which of the two forms will dominate is futile: it blurs the focus of inquiry and frustrates efforts to avoid disaster. In the meantime, the wrecker's ball keeps swinging, with ever wider amplitude, and ever greater force.[87]

A deflationary scenario can be accompanied by price increases in certain goods. Especially those goods - *honi soit qui mal y pense (shame on him who thinks ill of it)* – that are increasingly removed from "inflation indexes": necessities of life, such as food and energy. Ultimately, there is a tug of war between deflationary and inflationary forces, as we have already mentioned above. Hyperinflation in most cases goes hand in hand with a breakdown in government financing, this is to say, tax revenues, hyper-deflation with the write-off of book values and the destruction of balance sheets – price declines and mass insolvencies. Can the central bank blow up new bubbles faster than they burst? This is a question no economist can answer in general. In concrete circumstances, one can at best follow economic indicators. These exhibit the evil of artificially created volatility.

Stagflation

The term "stagflation" is a compound of the terms stagnation and inflation. This designates an economic situation in which economic stagnation (declining economic growth as well as high unemployment) and high inflation (price increases) occur concurrently. The term was coined during the persistent economic crisis of the 1970s, when the US experienced rising price inflation and a contracting economy simultaneously. This combination was previously held to be impossible by most mainstream economists.

However, stagflation was already first observed in the 1960s in Great Britain and the US. In the 1960s, the Federal Reserve believed that there was a stable inverse relationship between unemployment and inflation. The Fed's monetary policy had the goal to stimulate overall demand for goods and services and keep unemployment rates low. The only trade-off in the eyes of economists at the time was rising inflation – albeit to a controllable degree.

The wage-price spiral that was caused by high inflation (which represents an adjustment process of wage and price increases between households and companies) was however not the trigger of the grave stagflation of the 1970s. Inflation rates increased dramatically over the decade. The transition also had severe effects on capital markets and the real returns of investors. Due to the monetary inflation of the 1970s (and the subsequent price inflation), the decade turned out to deliver below average returns for bonds and stocks, while commodities and precious metals rallied. Between 1979 and 1980, the then still young paper currency US dollar suffered an acute confidence crisis. Due to ongoing inflation, a flight from the dollar ensued. Only a dramatic change in monetary policy under the new Fed chairman Paul Volcker succeeded in defusing the currency crisis. As a result of drastic interest rate hikes implemented by Volcker, the economy suffered the most severe recession since the Great Depression.

According to mainstream economics, stagflation is most often a result of supply shocks (price shocks), which influence the general level of prices due to rising cost pressures. Sharply rising input costs (such as energy prices) drive entrepreneurs to raise their sales prices. With overall demand remaining unchanged, a decline in sales sets in, which ultimately leads to a decline in production and consequently to the dismissal of employees. In Keynesian economic theory, the so-called Phillips curve postulates that there is a proportional relationship between economic growth (resp. unemployment) and inflation. According to the Phillips curve, inflation rises when unemployment is low, while it decreases when it is high. Strong employment goes hand in hand with strong economic growth. A high inflation rate thus leads to strong economic growth. By definition, stagflation should therefore be impossible.

An alternative concept to Keynesianism is Monetarism. While the economic policy of Keynes's disciples is also referred to as demand-oriented, the representatives of Monetarism (monetarists for short) are characterized by a supply-oriented economic policy. Monetarists explain inflation by an excess supply of money rather than by demand influences. With the aid of Irving Fisher's quantity equation, they show that an increase in the money supply can indeed lead to price inflation concurrently with high unemployment rates. Monetarists stress that

Stagflation

an increase in the money supply has both a price as well as a quantity effect. If there are unused capacities in an economy, an increase in the money supply can lead to these capacities being employed (quantity effect) and new workers are hired for this purpose. Unemployment declines. If there are no unused capacities, only the price level rises.

Looking at the current situation, partial similarities with an incipient stagflation can be observed. Japan's economic history may be a herald of future developments with respect to stagnating economic growth. Japan demonstrates that Keynesian fiscal policies implemented in the past were unable to alleviate ongoing stagnation. Instead, subsequent Japanese governments have simply amassed an enormous debt load. In the wake of this lack of success, it is now attempted with Keynesian logic (which holds that it is not the Keynesian approach as such that is misguided, instead it was merely not properly applied) to cast out demons with Beelzebub, by adopting ever larger stimulus packages supported by loose monetary policy (this is called "Abenomics", after Japan's prime minister Shinzo Abe). High unemployment rates in Europe's peripheral countries on the other hand can be an indication of the potential for high unemployment in other countries as well. These unemployment rates were the consequence of an artificial boom, created by credit expansion.

Although we are observing that a historically unprecedented flood of additional money is pumped into the markets (quantitative easing by the Fed, securities purchases by ECB and BoJ), price indexes are not yet indicating rising price inflation for the time being. However, official price indexes exclude important parts of the economy (real estate and capital markets). Nearly all-encompassing high indebtedness (of governments, banks, households and companies) and the fear of deflation suggest that even more money supply expansion is in the offing. Therefore, the threat of stagflation cannot be ruled out. Rising interest rates on government bonds combined with the prevailing weakness in growth and high rates of unemployment could upset the apple cart.

How should investors position themselves in times of stagflation? A historical study of the stagflation era between 1966 and 1981 can definitely provide us with important information on this point. In figure 7.2., the nominal and real returns of different asset classes are listed.

	nominal	real
S&P 500	5,90%	-1,10%
Long-Term Corporate Bonds	2,90%	-4,10%
Long-Term Government Bonds	2,50%	-4,50%
International Government Bonds	5,80%	-1,20%
90-day Treasury Bills	6,80%	-0.2%
Price inflation	7,00%	

Figure 7.2: Nominal and real returns of different asset classes during the stagflation era from 1966 to 1982 (Source: Datastream)

During periods of stagflation, demand for goods and services can decline due to rising unemployment. As already noted, the high rate of inflation often exceeds the return on most investments. The most important task of investors is a thorough analysis of which securities are able to keep pace with inflation or may even exceed it in such an environment. Hence companies that are able to handle times of crisis well or can even benefit from crises can be attractive. Investors should primarily focus on necessities of life including oil, electricity, food and health care. It is to be expected that companies in these sectors will get through a crisis largely undamaged. It is also to be expected that the providers of these goods will be able to adjust their prices to inflation in times of crisis without having to fear a decrease in demand. In a second step, fundamental analysis can be an important tool to pick those companies from the potential candidates that exhibit sound balance sheets and good growth potential at a reasonable price. Real assets (commodities, real estate, etc.), which are essentially regarded as a natural hedge against inflation, should be examined with a critical eye. While a stagflation period is inflationary, it is also marked by high unemployment and stagnating growth. Commodities that are mainly used in industrial production – especially lumber, copper, tin and aluminum – will therefore be subject to price pressures.

Gold can be seen as a natural hedge against inflation as well. Since it is only used sparingly in industrial production, it is in our opinion going to produce a better return than the commodities mentioned above. It is, however, hard to assess what will happen to the gold price in an acute crisis situation. On the one hand, it is thinkable that gold could regain its monetary function, however, demand for commodities that are necessary for survival, such as oil, fertilizer and seeds could outpace that for precious metals such as gold and silver.

An additional possibility is offered by exchange traded funds (ETFs) and inverse ETFs. The former are useful for benefiting from possible price increases in vital commodities during stagflation. The latter are useful to bet on declining prices, which are to be expected in the stocks of vulnerable companies. Inflation protected securities (TIPs) can only be recommended with reservations, although they superficially appear to be investments that provide inflation protection. Their advantage is that their yields increase in line with inflation rates. However, their disadvantages predominate. Thus their yield is strictly tied to the trend in core inflation rates, which exclude food and energy. However, these are the components that tend to rise especially strongly in a stagflationary environment. Moreover, the capital protection feature is only applicable at the end of the bond's term. In the intermittent time period, there can often be significant price fluctuations, as a result of which these bonds can at times trade well below their face value. Lastly, inflation protected securities are often expensive for private investors (high bid/ask spread).

Financial Repression and Compulsory Levies

In light of over-indebtedness, policy makers are faced with the choice between drastic spending cuts ("austerity policy"), significant tax increases or financial repression. The term financial repression essentially describes an economic policy in which governments and central banks use capital controls and regulations to distort asset prices in a targeted manner. In this way, unpopular measures such as tax increases and spending cuts can be avoided. The resulting transfer of wealth from savers to debtors is tantamount to a quiet expropriation of savers. The goal of the policy is to create incentives and proscriptions for institutions such as banks and insurance companies as a result of which they will increasingly invest in government bonds, which in turn makes it easier to finance fiscal debt. Investment opportunities for investors are significantly restricted and funds that would normally flow into different asset classes are redirected into politically desired channels.

In order to increase the incentive for buying government bonds, governments and central banks have various means at their disposal, such as e.g. the introduction of strict investment regulations: Basel III and Solvency II. European government bonds can be bought without having to keep any capital in reserve, as these bonds have attractive liquidity metrics, while the regulatory risk weighting for European government bonds is set at zero. In the event that this approach fails, compulsory bonds could be introduced.

Another important pillar of financial repression is the level of interest rates. Measures such as the Fed's Operation Twist are interventions in the yield curve. A major goal of financial repression is to hold nominal interest rates below the rate of price inflation. The vast bulk of government debt is nominally fixed. When the currency is devalued, the government's nominal tax revenues increase proportionally, thus the real value of the debt burden declines. This circumstance explains why over-indebted countries are interested in a nominal interest rate below the rate of inflation. According to World Bank studies, real interest rates are currently negative in 23 countries, resulting in losses for savers of approximately €100 billion per year. In addition, interest rate caps can be introduced. These artificially fixed upper limits for interest rates result in long-term interest rates being far lower than would otherwise be the case. Additional tools are government interventions in the economy, such as nationalizations or direct controls over the extension of credit and capital controls, such as is e.g. the case in China. The latter are currently also implemented in Brazil, where a levy on foreign capital inflows is charged.

Furthermore, direct interventions often occur during times of financial repression. Measures such as interventions in pension funds, as took place inter alia in Portugal, Poland and France, have the aim of shifting investment in favor of government bonds. The same applies to haircuts on bank deposits, as was the case in Cyprus. Two additional pillars are prohibitions and taxes. By prohibiting unwanted trading practices such as naked short selling or prohibitions on the possession of certain types of assets such as precious metals, governments can restrict investment opportunities further. A similar effect can be achieved by passing special taxes or hiking already existing taxes. Examples are financial transaction taxes, various forms of wealth taxes or increased sales taxes on gold and silver. In the course of history, governments have already employed financial repression measures on many occasions in order to ease their fiscal burden. Financial repression for instance played a decisive role in the effort to reduce public debt in the post war era in the US. The government was able to reduce its total debt from 116% of GDP to 66% of GDP between 1945 and 1955, while real interest rates stood at -0.8% and the inflation rate at 4.2%. One must, however, not lose sight of the fact that the economic upswing owed much to reconstruction and that private debt was comparatively low due to favorable demographics.

An additional example that shows how inventive governments can be in terms of financial repression is the obfuscation of real inflation rates in Argentina. Officially the rate of inflation is stated to be around 10%, realistically this figure should be closer to 25%. The Big Mac Index, which allows a global comparison of purchasing power parities, indicates a level of 20%, which caused president Kirchner to put pressure on the McDonalds chain to lower the price of its hamburgers.

The lessons provided by these historical examples of financial repression are worrisome. Such a policy merely postpones the problems by pushing their resolution into the future, at a very high price. Necessary structural reforms have only rarely been adopted, and instead of generating long-term growth, ultimately only fleeting efforts at stabilization were undertaken. All in all, a policy of financial repression leads to future collateral damage and a worsening of the crisis that should be fought. Financial repression is a policy that has been adopted in a number of countries and it must be expected that the types of measures described above will in future become more widespread. The most often discussed new revenue source for governments currently is a wealth tax, this is to say a compulsory levy on savings, securities and possibly real estate. The public debate was intensified after a publication on the topic by the International Monetary Fund (IMF). The basic idea of the wealth tax was presented as follows:

> The sharp deterioration of the public finances in many countries has revived interest in a "capital levy" — a one-off tax on private wealth — as an exceptional measure to restore debt sustainability. The appeal is that such a tax, if it is implemented before avoidance is possible and there is a belief that it will never be repeated, does not distort behavior (and may be seen by some as fair).[88]

The cat was out of the bag with this. The media quickly seized on the proposal, which caused great uncertainty and an uproar. As a result, the IMF felt compelled to mitigate its statement, by issuing assurances that it was merely a purely theoretical deliberation. However, that the proposal is not a mere thought experiment is shown by the fact that various influential think tanks and research institutions have taken up the idea of a capital levy and are discussing it as a possible option to fix government finances. For instance, the German Bundesbank has stated:

> With this special context in mind, the following outlines the various aspects of a one-off levy on domestic private net wealth, in other words, a levy on assets after liabilities have been deducted. From a macroeconomic perspective, a capital levy – and even more so a permanent tax on wealth – is in principle beset with considerable problems, and the necessary administrative outlay involved as well as the associated risks for an economy's growth path are high. In the exceptional situation of a pending sovereign default, however, a one-off capital levy could prove more favorable than the other available alternatives. […] If the levy is referenced to wealth accumulated in the past and it is believed that it will never be repeated again, it is extremely difficult for taxpayers to evade it in the short term, and its detrimental impact on employment and saving incentives will be limited – unlike that of a permanent tax on wealth.[89]

After the Bundesbank, the German Institute for Economic Research (DIW) took up the topic as well. The DIW released a statement that it believes that compulsory bonds would be an effective means against over-indebtedness. This instrument has been employed quite often in the course of history, usually however, for the financing of wars. Such a compulsory levy amounting to 10% of all fortunes exceeding 250,000 euro would bring in revenues of 230 billion euro for Germany's public finances. Daniel Stelter, a senior partner at Boston Consulting Group, believes a mere tax on bank deposits such as in Cyprus is not enough. He proposes a mixture of capital levies, wealth taxes and an inheritance tax. According to him it is:

> obvious […], that those, who own assets and are ultimately laboring under the illusion that these are still fully covered and will be paid back, should be subjected to a tax, by means of which one would so to speak clean up after the party, this is to say, tidy up the legacy of the past 30 years.[90]

It can be observed that some policy makers are already trying to pave the way for a potential wealth levy. In order to take the wind out of the sails of critics, a putative wealth levy is referred to as a "millionaire's tax".

7. Scenarios

One should however be very cautious about that. The well-known statement of the former chairman of the euro group (now EU president), Jean-Claude Juncker, should always be kept in mind:

> We decide something, put it out there and then wait a little while to see what happens. If there is no big uproar and no upheaval, because most people do not even understand what has been decided, we continue – step by step, until we are past the point of no return.[91]

The collection of a wealth tax alters saving behaviors and therefore has a long-term negative effect on capital formation. In order to avoid a future wealth tax, people save less or do so in different forms. The capital structure is distorted and capital accumulation becomes more difficult. While savings were in the past built up in capital markets, other paths are sought in order to avoid the levy. Since new paths are only sought because of the wealth levy, they represent as a rule less efficient forms of capital formation, as they would otherwise already have been used previously. The actual causes of government indebtedness are not resolved by a wealth tax, instead the levy primarily punishes market participants who are not responsible for the mistakes that have been made.

Special Drawing Rights as a Global Currency

Another possibility to postpone national currency problems is to move them to an international level. The next step in the monetary system going to seed could be special drawing rights, which former French president Valery Giscard d'Estaing called "monetary LSD". Economist James Rickards expects that the next big financial market crisis will see the IMF becoming engaged. Since the balance sheets of Western central banks have already been blown up strongly in the course of the 2008/09 crisis, Rickards sees only limited scope for additional monetary rescue operations without risking a fatal loss of confidence in paper currencies. According to Rickards, the next higher authority, i.e., the IMF, will have to step in to reflate the system:

> But the problem is, the Fed printed trillions of dollars without a liquidity crisis. What is going to happen when we do have a liquidity crisis, which I expect in the next couple years, where there is a 2008 panic starting again? What are they going to do? Print $6 trillion? $9 trillion? There is a limit on what they can do. And so at some point, it is going to get handed over to the IMF, and they are going to have to print SDRs (special drawing rights). That is the IMF world money. Because none of the central banks have clean balance sheets at this point; they look like hedge funds.[92]

The special drawing right (SDR) is an artificial accounting unit introduced by the IMF in 1969, which is not traded on foreign exchange markets. Special drawing rights consist of the four most important global currencies: US dollar, euro, yen and British pound; the exchange rate is fixed every day anew. Once the governing council of the IMF decides that additional capital market liquidity is required, special drawing rights are distributed among member countries. These represent a deposit with the IMF, which can be used to pay debts to creditor countries. According to the statutes, all member nations are obliged to accept payments in the form of special drawing rights. What is not widely known is the fact that special drawing rights are already used in many places. Thus they are employed as accounting units in international claims, in air transport, shipping and in the event of oil-related accidents at sea. They are also used in payments for international postal services as well as for the calculation of tolls in the Suez Canal.

The most important metrics for a currency's weighting in the SDR are the issuing country's share in global trade, as well as the reserves held by IMF members. The weighting of the currency basket is determined anew every five years. Since January of 2011, one special drawing right contains the value of the sum of 0.66 US dollars, 0.423 euro, 0.111 pound sterling and 12.1 yen. Figure 7.3 shows the weightings of the SDR currency basket over time.

7. Scenarios

	USD	DEM	FRF	JPY	GBP
1981–1985	42%	19%	13%	13%	13%
1986–1990	42%	19%	12%	15%	12%
1991–1995	40%	21%	11%	17%	11%
1996–2000	39%	21%	11%	18%	11%

	USD	EUR	JPY	GBP
2001-2005	45%	29%	15%	11%
2006-2010	44%	34%	11%	11%
2011-2015	41.9%	37.4%	9.4%	11.3%

Figure 7.3: Weightings of the SDR currency basket (Source: imf.org)

In their current composition, special drawing rights are a pure fiat money, this is to say neither covered nor redeemable. The SDR was created during the end phase of the Bretton Woods system in 1969 and once was referred to as "paper gold". Jim Rickards calls this term "the greatest oxymoron of all time". It is ever more often said that a "grounding" with metals or agricultural commodities should be instituted, in order to create confidence in special drawing rights. From our perspective this does not make much sense. Nevertheless, such proposals continue to find ever more prominent supporters. Robert Mundell (who is often called the "father of the euro") for instance proposes that central banks should fix the exchange rate between the US dollar and the euro in order to create a currency anchor called the "Eurodollar", which is responsible for nearly 50% of global economic output, would be a decisive step toward the creation of a uniform global currency. The Eurodollar could, with a revival of special drawing rights and by including the renminbi, form the basis of the global currency INTOR. "Int" stands for international, and "or" for the French term for gold.

More and more often representatives of emerging markets are also demanding to expand the role of this artificial currency, possibly coupling it with gold and establishing it as a "supranational" reserve currency: The governor of China's central bank called special drawing rights the "light at the end of the tunnel for the reform of the international currency system". In his essay "Reform the international monetary system", Zhou Xiaochuan among other things demanded a supranational global reserve currency based on special drawing rights, as well as a strong weighting of the Chinese yuan.[93] Russia wants gold to receive greater importance in the global currency system as well. Thus the Kremlin's chief advisor opined that Russia would support the inclusion of gold in the weighted basket of a new global currency. The IMF's special drawing rights should be the basis of the new currency. It would however be logical that the ruble, the yuan and especially gold should take on a greater role as well.[94]

The next big crisis will likely lead to a reorganization of the international currency system. Most of the proposals for an intensified use of special drawing rights do not appear to make much sense from an "Austrian" perspective, since acceptance and confidence in them among the population at large would likely be small. Special drawing rights are derivatives of derivatives, it is therefore doubtful that such an instrument would meet with much confidence. One should nevertheless not underestimate the political will behind this idea. An expansion of special drawing rights and the development of the IMF into a global central bank would not only be in line with the mentality of the central planners in East and West, but would from their perspective also have the advantage that governments could continue to finance their various projects with a hidden inflation tax. The sesquipedalian term "special drawing right" moreover sounds a lot more comfortable than "currency reform" and could enable such a reform by the back door. This solution would also be politically desirable because no-one could really be held responsible in the event of run-away inflation, as the IMF is just as intangible for most people as are terms such as QE, LTRO or OMT.

8. Austrian Investment Philosophy

Since we cannot foresee the future, it seems sensible to take investment decisions that are as independent as possible from future developments, but cover the entire range of possible scenarios. It follows from this that it is rarely a good strategy to bet everything on a single horse, it rather seems reasonable to create a diversified portfolio. A thorough examination of one's goals is necessary from the subjectivist perspective of the Austrian School before one thinks about putting together a portfolio. The economic portfolio is preceded by a philosophical portfolio so to speak. This entails clarifying the dimensions of accumulation of wealth, investment of wealth and use of wealth.

Since human beings have different goals and under uncertainty always choose different ways and means, there exist no answers that are correct for everybody, but a number of questions that are applicable and important to everybody. Good investments are the ideal of an investment strategy, but realistically they are only a part thereof. The typical investor is not a gifted venture capitalist who puts liquid funds in arbitrary amounts at arbitrary points in time into safe undertakings with high returns.

If one asks the question: "In which companies should I invest my savings in order to increase their value?" one is seeking the wrong answers. Investing is the central core of a successful investment strategy, but it is not everything. In the spirit of the Austrian School, value investing – value oriented investment – must be complemented by value preservation, value oriented consumption and value-oriented endowment. Investment, as opposed to speculation in the narrow sense, is not only the risking of liquid funds on the side, after work in front of the screen in a search for ever newer and better tips, but a question of one's economic way of life. There are five different aspects to this, which have to be taken into account and differentiated. However, why should one save at all?

The Morals of Saving

"Investment" as a rule describes the attempt to sensibly employ what is hopefully a positive difference between income and expenditures in order to create long-term value. Many focus too much on this remainder and not enough on the factors determining it: namely, income and expenditures. Building up a positive difference between them is generally referred to as "saving". The etymological root of the term means "to save" in the sense of "keeping safe and sound". The first discipline of economics in the original sense is to keep an eye on income and expenditures.

Investment decisions differ from normal purchasing decisions in terms of the time dimension: they are aimed at the future. This is the essence of thrift. The Austrian School lauds thrift as a virtue, as Carl Menger taught his famous pupil, the crown prince Rudolf:

> I am referring to the industry and economy of citizens: thrift, work and earning a living in an honorable way are genuine civic virtues, that provide a reliable basis for a major upswing of material and immaterial culture.[95]

The low interest rate policy and the devaluation of money associated with it appear to make saving increasingly nonsensical. Inflation is a steady, hidden expropriation of savers. One could say that anyone saving today is actually an idiot, or an incorrigible idealist. In any case, he has not recognized the signs of the times. His renunciation of consumption – this is what saving ultimately means: one keeps money aside for tomorrow, instead of using it for consumption today – is not rewarded. On the contrary, there is a great danger that his saved money will be devalued – steadily and imperceptibly, by means of inflation. Therefore, a contemporary man willing to save in principle may perhaps decide, so to speak as a result of a higher understanding, to rather consume, if involuntarily. He buys things he actually does not need. And at some point, he buys things he actually cannot afford. Welcome to today's debt-financed consumerism.

"Consumerism" has a negative connotation. Is consumption immoral? Neither consumption nor credit are per se tainted with a moral blemish. How come then, that times during which consumption and debt begin to dominate saving, go hand in hand with moral decline? History provides plenty of evidence for this correlation, from the downfall of the Roman Empire to modern-day inflation episodes. The reason for this is simple: excessive consumption is tantamount to a total fixation on the present – after me, the deluge! All is laid bare, and all restraint is dropped. An especially impressive description of rising consumption on the one hand and moral disinhibition on the other hand is provided by Giovanni Boccaccio in his collection of short stories *Decamerone* – faced with the threat of impending death through the plague, people cling to whatever the day has to offer. Back then, one concluded that the best medicine against the epidemic was:

> ...to drink a lot, enjoy life, wander around singing, have enjoyable conversations, satisfy every urge as good as one can, to laugh about everything that happens and ridicule it, [...] Day and night they moved from one tavern to the next, and drank without metes and bounds. Their behavior was at its most uninhibited though in other people's homes [...].[96]

In Matteo Villani's chronicles it is recorded that:

> People [...] behaved with less restraint and more disgracefully than ever before. They abandoned themselves to idleness, and their shattered state led them to indulge in the sin of gluttony, to revelry, into taverns, to

8. Austrian Investment Philosophy

delicious foodstuffs and to gambling. Without a second thought they threw themselves into the arms of lust.[97]

What does "moral decline" mean though? Is not merely bourgeois bigotry to condemn an increase in the desire to consume? At a time when neither tradition, nor religion are of lasting conviction, and thus sufficient to provide orientation, a moral perspective is always under suspicion of being ideologically motivated. However, ethics are a part of practical philosophy and as such a part of the attempt to understand the world and human action.

Classical ethics condemns self-indulgence and thereby hints at an imbalance in action. The desire to consume and to save refer to each other: one consumes today, but one consumes in a controlled manner, because one wants to have the option to consume tomorrow as well, or to invest. If one only thinks of today, one takes on debt to consume. Credit becomes "imbalanced" if it leads to a debt spiral. Over-indebtedness means that a repayment of debt to its full extent is no longer possible, as for instance all income is already consumed by the burden of interest.

The imbalance is initially a temporal one: action in the present is strongly overrated in comparison to future consequences. Economists describe this behavior as the expression of a high time preference. A too low time preference on the other hand can lead to no longer treasuring the moment, and letting life pass one by because one is always focused on planning for an uncertain tomorrow. This would be a "life not lived", as Erich Fried expressed it poetically and Carl Gustav Jung psychologically. However, even while lauding the vitality of the moment, we must not lose sight of the fact that a large part of human culture, especially that of the Occident, is based on a spiritual, abstract overcoming of the moment, which is the basis of low time preference. The human individual exists between the poles of vitality and orientation, the sensory grounding and spiritual-transcendental orientation, immanence and transcendence, and must find his or her proper personal place between them.

The Morals of Saving

Overindulging in the life instinct focused on the moment has cultural and physiological consequences for the individual. On the one hand, many human goals, especially more complex ones, can only be reached in a roundabout manner. As Austrian economist Eugen von Boehm-Bawerk stated, roundaboutness results in greater productivity. In a specific moment in time, we must make do with what is available right then. With appropriate frugality and the grace of an abundant environment this was possibly sufficient to satisfy basic needs, but higher goals that are the essence of human culture would be out of reach. Culture comes from *colere* (growing something) and thus refers to the first big cultural achievement that required economizing through time: agriculture.

"Culture" is of course a label over which we can no longer come to an agreement nowadays; it is almost as impossible as agreement on morals. The most value-neutral approach probably consists of the recognition that humans would not discover their potential if they were not setting aside many lower ranking goals in favor of higher ranking ones. This is the cultural counter-argument against a too pronounced focus on the present.

The physiological argument acknowledges that people age: and their ability to earn an income declines. Thrift is therefore necessary because we are beings limited by time. If we were not providing for old age, our lives would either be miserably shortened or the earnings power of the young would be so overburdened that their life would be unbearably restricted.

All "signs of moral decay" are simply over-extensions of a *per se* positive life instinct, gluttony and alcoholism exaggerations of enjoyment. Saving, consumption and credit are actually not opposites, but are mutually dependent. Correctly understood, saving, as well as correctly understood consumption, are oriented toward life. The political disintegration of the connection between saving and consumption is thus ultimately inimical to life. It shortens the perspective of our actions,

8. Austrian Investment Philosophy

and robs the economy of sense. Roland Baader, who tirelessly admonished against the devaluation of money, bemoaned that:

> Everyone involved is endlessly chasing around for income, trying to counteract the diminishing purchasing power of their money. In the process, people are losing their moral inhibitions about public debt, about financing their whole lives with debt, and about irresponsible financial acrobatics.[98]

Finding the correct measure between discipline and life instinct is already not easy for individuals. For entire societies it is especially difficult, as there are massive reinforcement effects due to our tendency to imitate others. Once certain behaviors begin to predominate and the basis that feeds them disappears, human beings often react with exaggerations in the opposite direction. A harmless expression of this phenomenon can be observed in fashions. The devaluation of saving leads to an exaggerated emphasis on forces of immanence. Such forces are e.g. youth, lust, passions and the Left. With that however, dangerously excessive mirror images are fed as counter-exaggerations. A paradoxical and devastating consequence of the artificial bloating of illusory values that thwarts the meaningfulness of saving, is the devaluation of pleasure, which provokes a prudish backlash.

However, it is only the second feature of moral decay that makes the first so devastating: the disintegration of society. The term "morals" (from the Latin *moralis*) refers to traditions, the customs of a society. This means: a focus not only on today, but also on tomorrow and the day after tomorrow, not only on oneself, but also on one's neighbors and others, it means reliability, honesty, self-restraint, courage and sound judgment. Without a basic stability in one's expectations with respect to one's neighbor, no society can survive. If society threatens to disintegrate, a panicky reaction to the previous over-extension ensues. History provides sobering evidence for this. The last great period of devaluation was described by Stefan Zweig as follows:

The Morals of Saving

> How wild, anarchic and unreal were those years, years in which, with the dwindling value of money all other values in Austria and Germany began to slip! It was an epoch of high ecstasy and ugly scheming, a singular mixture of unrest and fanaticism. Every extravagant idea that was not subject to regulation reaped a golden harvest: theosophy, occultism, spiritualism, somnambulism, anthroposophy, palm-reading, graphology, yoga and Paracelsism. Anything that gave a hope of newer and greater thrills, anything in the way of narcotics, morphine, cocaine, heroin found a tremendous market; on the stage, incest and parricide, in politics, communism and fascism, constituted the most favored themes; unconditionally proscribed, however was any representation of normality and moderation.[99]

No one would have thought that the "youth movement" that was established at the time would ultimately lead to national socialism. Shortly before, one was still convinced that one was living in a "golden age of security". As soon as savings became insecure, all other certitudes fell by the wayside too.

Investment is thus always a long-term endeavor with far-reaching moral consequences and foundations. Thrift is not an end in itself, but a means to imbue our life in a roundabout manner with more quality and meaning. In times when thrift no longer seems to pay, it is especially important. The most beautiful and valuable things are often not immediately available, but require patience. It seems bitter that time is running out for us human beings. However, this is the precondition for the unfolding of our potential: practice, experience, acquisition of knowledge, memories and items of material wealth which can store human energy, only increase our prosperity because of the influence of time. Saving is the attempt to rescue a piece of each moment for the future. Thus properly understood, thrift is actually not the opposite of a conscious living of life in the present, but an expression thereof.

Consumerism by contrast, the desire to have as much as possible immediately, wastes one's life for short-term fun without joy, for a kick without adventure, it means having without being. The subjectivism of the Austrian School calls on individuals to shape their lives in a more conscious fashion: to deal with life carefully and appreciatively. Investment of money in the narrower sense, the accumulation of material wealth, is only one aspect of thrift – the decisive question is always: how does one enhance one's daily efforts and one's life time, by imbuing every moment with a perspective that goes beyond the moment?

Profit and Interest

In the course of the debt spiral following the monetary revolution, the old critique of interest has returned. Profits also appear increasingly suspect – after all, losses are ever more often socialized. Bank rescues, insolvencies that leave creditors nearly empty-handed, the negligent delay in declaring the insolvency of public finances and many a bank balance sheet and the discredited profits of many a corporate management, while interest rate arbitrage, leveraged speculation and negative interest rates discredit interest in the eyes of the common man. Is it even morally legitimate to strive for interest and profits? This question is going to be asked ever more frequently, criticism of interest and profit is likely to continue to grow, we must therefore deal with this question. After all, investment would be pretty much superfluous without interest or profit returns. Readers may well be a bit impatient by now in view of all these excursions into the history of ideas. They should however heed the warning that even the best investors in the bubble economy of the last century have been caught napping by the history of ideas.

Profit, or entrepreneurial profit, only exists because people make mistakes and the real economy is not an automatism in equilibrium, but a process of discovery. The world around us is changing all the time, just as we human beings are changing. This is a good thing, standstill equates to death. The future is not predetermined, because people learn, but also because they can always make new mistakes. Almost every progress in knowledge, culture and technology is tied to new errors, some of which are so large that they are giving the lie to talk about progress. This is the price of human liberty. There exist two ideologically motivated exaggerations with regard to how these changes should be handled, which always reinforce each other. On the one hand, there is the reactionary fear of change with its panicked clinging to the existing order and yearning for a romanticized past. On the other hand, there is euphoric techno-optimism, which expects progress to bring salvation from all human defects and evils. Both tendencies are important for investors: the latter strengthens the stock prices of companies which are part of a progressive story, the former reacts with a longing for simpler, more grounded things.

A company produces profits if it closes a gap in the structure of the economy, which exists due to the mistakes made by other actors. The value added is not at the expense of other factors such as labor, but a signal that certain factors have not received their full valuation by the marketplace. Profits tend to lead to their own demise over time, as they represent signals for other companies and investors that incentivize them to correct these mistakes and to pass on all possible value added to the factors involved. The biggest incentive to discover such gaps is personal responsibility. In a politicized world, companies can however even make profits without possessing this intuition: when market access is restricted due to privileges, when they have easier access to credit and therefore can grow more quickly, when they are fed with government contracts, or their risk of loss is partially insured, which favors more risky, and thus potentially more profitable undertakings.

However, in the long term, all these distortions lead to diminishing the entrepreneurial talent to retain an intuition for changes and take responsibility for the uncertainty of the future. Accordingly, there is a cyclical pattern in evidence with respect to such companies: they rise to the very top, and then fall especially hard. In the long term, companies with such bloated earnings tend to be losing propositions. However, as the government has deep pockets, because it can dig ever deeper into the pockets of its citizens, the long-term nature of this process

8. Austrian Investment Philosophy

may well exceed the patience of most investors. They are happy with obtaining short-term returns and dismiss the necessary corrections as "black swans".

Inflationary policy itself leads to excessive profits being reported. Ever since the monetary revolution, one can never be sure whether a highly profitable company is not merely consuming its capital especially quickly. Since bonuses for managers, who are increasingly detached from the ownership structure, are growing along with reported earnings, there are devastating incentives to consume capital, especially at large companies that are widely held.

Skepticism with respect to high profits should however not lead one to despise entrepreneurial profit as such. Companies are a means for value creation. Their profit orientation should not be underestimated as a disciplining instrument. It leads to them handling the funds that have been entrusted to them with care, and entices them to create as much value as possible for fellow human beings. Many non-profit institutions, ostensibly working for the common good, are by contrast vanity projects that waste funds or misdirect them into self-serving channels.

Interest rates are subject to even more criticism than profits. Under this term, numerous, quite complex issues are mixed up. Before one ponders the legitimacy of interest rates, one should attempt to examine what real phenomenon they represent, and why they exist. Past criticisms of interest failed mainly because they were based on moral arguments, while ignoring the economic basics.

The phenomenon most often discussed is not a payment or a fee for using or renting something. Rather, it is interest in the sense of a claim, or the payment of an additional amount for the lending of fungible goods. The difference is the following: in the former case, rent is paid for using a good, which apart from wear and tear is returned in identical form. The borrower becomes its temporary user for a specific time period, while the lender retains full ownership. By contrast, interest rates are charged for the lending of goods, as a rule money, against the promise that other goods of the same type will be returned in the future. Not only the right of usage is transferred, but ownership as well.

This is similar to the difference between borrowing a cooking pot or "borrowing" a handkerchief. The quote marks point to linguistic negligence, as it is of course not expected that the used handkerchief will be returned. The moral question based on this example would look as follows: should one in return for lending someone a handkerchief demand the used one, none at all, a new one or two new ones in return? Handkerchiefs have such low value that this question does not seem to carry much weight in the real world. It is evidently quite different when talking about significant amounts of money. One cannot use money either without using it up.

It was an important insight of economic science, especially of the Austrian School, that the phenomenon of interest or at least a phenomenon that looks deceptively similar, also occurs when there is a conscious decision not to pay any interest. This concerns simply different valuations through time. The phenomenon became evident in the discounting of bills of exchange and the valuation of leaseholds. A bill of exchange is a promise to pay. Roughly speaking, the transfer of a bill of exchange amounts to the exchange of goods against promises. This process can also be expressed as an exchange of present goods against future goods. A bill of exchange is similar to a voucher that can only be redeemed from a specific date onward. It can be observed that on markets in which per definition people who do not know each other meet in order to engage in mutual exchanges, the prices for such vouchers are not precisely equivalent to the prices of the promised goods.

Let us take a simple hypothetical example (which does not, however, conform to the historical customs with respect to bills of exchange) in order to illustrate the phenomenon. A farmer issues a voucher on which he states: "Whoever presents this voucher to me, receives one bushel of wheat from my next harvest, which I will reap a year hence". He uses this voucher to pay an assistant. This assistant however needs to eat bread today already, not a year from now. "No problem", the farmer tells him, "you can sell this voucher in the market, because I am known, and so is the reliability of my promises". The seller of the voucher indeed finds willing buyers in the market, but no-one offers him exactly a bushel of wheat or its equivalent value. All offers are slightly lower. What is the reason for this? On the one hand, there is of course a confidence problem, that is to say, the redemption could be regarded as uncertain. However, even if there is complete certainty about the timely and full redemption of the voucher, there would still be a difference between the amounts offered in the present and the value of the future goods. A bushel of wheat available today is evidently valued higher in the market than a bushel of future wheat, even if that future is absolutely certain. What is the reason for this difference?

As mentioned above, a similar phenomenon occurs in the valuation of leaseholds. Let us look at a simple example in this context as well: a small field can produce an annual return of one bushel of wheat. We will use real goods for the lease, so as to leave aside the complications stemming from monetary debasement. This also creates a fairly safe basis for the lease, since in conjunction with the appropriate work effort and knowledge, the field can produce this amount of wheat by itself, the uncertainty of the market plays no role. How much wheat should one expend for buying such a field?

Such a purchase represents a transfer of wealth in exchange for income, which people have engaged in at almost all times and almost everywhere to provide for their old age. As long as one is able to work, one attempts to use part of one's income to purchase assets. Once one is no longer able to work, these assets should suffice to produce an income that compensates for the cessation of one's income from work. One possibility is to use savings to purchase property, which can produce a lease income during one's retirement. This income consists not of interest, but of *rent*. When evaluating the leasehold property, we can see the following problem: if every future bushel of wheat were valued at the same level as every present bushel, and the fertility of the soil and the possibility of such a sharecropping lease were assured for all times, the purchase price of the field would be infinitely high. Of course uncertainty cannot be sharply divorced from the other aspects, but here too it must be assumed that the price would not be infinitely high even if complete certainty were to be obtained. Both the offered and asked purchase prices are finite, even if safe income streams are expected. How many times the expected income should the saver offer for the field, how many times the expected income should the seller accept as reasonable?

These questions can be explained by the phenomenon of time preference. This term expresses the willingness to renounce present wants in order to be able to better satisfy future wants. This preference differs from individual to individual, and is by no means constant. High time preference designates the fact that the timing of an action is accorded especially high value.

We should, however, take a step back at this juncture and take a closer look at these strange markets that are referred to as "capital markets" today. Apparently, sums of money are sold there, and that seems odd: why sell money in exchange for money? Economically, this only begins to make sense once we look at the other side of these exchanges: in reality, promises are traded in these markets, namely promises to pay. These become tradable by creating debentures, i.e., legally enforceable claims on future payments. The increase in trading of such promises is a modern-day phenomenon. The fact that people increasingly trade not in present goods but promises of future goods, is a hint that time preferences are changing. In a positive sense one could speak of an increasing future orientation, in a negative sense however of life at the cost of the future. In the history of ideas, this expansion in trading with promises is closely tied to progressive ideologies, which put a lot of faith in technological progress and strive to overcome the present in favor of an idealized future. Walter Bagehot confirms this in his famous description of the historical banking system of London. He describes its closeness to the so-called Whigs, British liberals who were always seen as the embodiment of progressive thought:

8. Austrian Investment Philosophy

In the beginning, the Bank of England was not only a financing company, but an undertaking of the Whigs. It was founded by a Whig government, which was in desperate need of money, and supported by urban circles, as these circles consisted mainly of Whigs.[100]

Why do people purchase "promises"? It is an additional opportunity to gain an income from saved wealth. There is, however, a significant difference to agricultural or other capital returns which are based on real capital, which per definition is something completely different from money: the fact that in this instance, money is supposed to produce money. There is only one obvious way in which saved amounts of money can serve to create a monetary income: by "dishoarding", that is to say by using up savings. A money market is no help in this regard, as 100 monetary units can never be more than one hundred times one monetary unit. The miraculous increase happens due to the fact that both a current income (from interest payments) as well as the entire original amount are demanded back. One could thus live from savings without ever using them up. How is this even possible?

The only method consists of the transformation of the amount of money by the borrower into capital, which achieves productivity that is sufficiently high that it not only produces a recurring income over and above the interest demanded, but allows the original amount to be earned back as well.

If the money supply were constant, shares in companies would be preferred over debentures, as they make it possible to achieve an income, while the original amount can become a fixed asset. This does not have to consist of money and therefore does not have to be hastily removed again from the company. There is however an important argument in favor of borrowings on the part of the entrepreneur: they allow financing with external capital, which means that the degree of interference is far smaller. However, the freedom thus achieved is often only an illusory freedom: instead of investors interfering, there is now the cold-hearted capital provider who equally cold-heartedly looks only at his yield. The necessary average returns required to pay the growing interest burden can only be achieved by an expansion of fiduciary media.

What about interest charges on consumer loans? Since many consumer loans have to be regarded as problematic due to the consumerism mentioned above, interest charges seem especially unethical in this case. However, these charges are in principle equivalent to the terms and conditions of a merchant, who charges a fee for late payment. This is perfectly legitimate from a traditional perspective as well. The next step would be to transfer the collection of payments to a collection agency. The agency would then suddenly take on a lending function. It makes little sense to tie criticism of interest to this process, rather, consumer credit should be generally advised against.

There is, however, also another motive for consumer credit apart from a special short-term focus or impatient greed, namely an emergency. Historically, this was the most important motivation. This also explains why historically criticism was focused on interest rates: the interest charge makes the emergency situation even worse. In order to mitigate such emergency situations, clerical circles attempted to create alternatives to pawn shops. These special pawn shops still exist today, in French their name has been preserved as well: Mont de Piété – Mountain of Mercy, whereby "mountain" must not be understood literally. "Monte" was once the name for charitable funds.

If we look at the history of these pawn shops, we make an uncomfortable discovery that supports the sober perspective of economists: initially interest-free pawn shops all went bankrupt fairly quickly. The problem consisted precisely of the fact that their overhead costs could not be financed. This is an observation that can be made today in the case of micro-loans: the expenses associated with extending small loans are very high, so high that traditional banks are backing away from this business. The micro-credit movement attempts to compensate for this by voluntary engagement and more affordable funding sources, mainly however by innovative forms of payment collection. Nevertheless, interest rates on micro-loans are surprisingly high.

8. Austrian Investment Philosophy

Interest charges are therefore also allowed in Christian pawn shops in order to cover operating costs. This concession to reality was probably the final step leading to the abandonment of the canonical prohibition of interest. The Church thereby however also largely abandoned its role as a voice of admonishment with respect to credit restraint. The argument in favor of the pawn shops was that in this manner, it was at least possible to offer lower interest rates to people in need.

However, even this argument turned out to be misguided. To this day, the annualized interest rates charged by pawn shops are higher than bank interest rates. Profit-oriented pawn shops were ultimately able to undercut charitable pawn shops, even before modern-day credit expansion, which creates cheap fiduciary media from thin air. The allegedly "immoral" goal to live off interest income from consumer credit led to lower interest rates due to the increased competition of entrepreneurs in the business. This may be another reason why interest causes so much irritation: it cannot be suppressed. If one tries to fight interest rates, they simply reappear elsewhere at even higher levels.

Let us take a look at Islamic economies for comparison. These have experienced an enormous boom in recent decades. The market for Islamic financial services has been growing by high double-digit rates for years already, and the potential does not yet appear exhausted. Only six percent of all Muslims actually avail themselves of sharia-compliant investments and banking services. 3.5 million Muslims with an estimated wealth of around 20 billion euro live in Germany alone. Has the economic competence of Muslims therefore grown?

Islamic financing forms appear literally as "constructs", their complexity is partially very high. As a rule, it is all about creating roundabout solutions in order to avoid interest rates. Since the phenomenon of interest is however unavoidable, this essentially amounts to merely avoiding the *appearance* that interest is charged. Similar to Christianity, Islam has great problems with interest rates. Although the Qur'an contains no negative statements about them, the Hadiths (traditions of the prophet) contain very pointed rejections of *riba*, which can be translated as "excess". Whether customary interest already represents such an excess, or only usury, has been discussed over and over again. The majority of both the classical jurisprudents as well as of today's scholars are of the opinion that *riba* refers to any form of interest, and that therefore both the payment as well as receipt of interest is prescribed.

A possible alternative for credit transactions is a discounted purchase called *murabahah:* the bank becomes the owner of an investment for a "legal second" and requests the borrower to become active as its agent and to purchase the investment to be financed on its behalf. The price plus an agreed upon profit margin then has to be paid back to the bank in installments.

Especially clever and equally absurd appears the *murabahah commodity deposit*. In this case, it is not a specific investment that is purchased, which would make use of the loan inflexible, but a commodity. Since it would be too obvious in the case of gold that a surrogate for money was being used, platinum or palladium is most often employed. While the metals are traded, they are in fact only used to replicate a loan.

However, in the eyes of many sharia jurisprudents – if they understand what is actually going on – such tricks are taking things one bridge too far. The pragmatic Islam in South East Asia often turns a blind eye to these practices, while scholars in the Middle East tend to be far stricter. The justification of Malaysian scholars for their leniency is interesting, namely that any speculation about the intentions behind business transactions should be eschewed and that therefore such constructs need only be evaluated in terms of their formal aspects.

One often gets the impression that the art of Islamic finance consists of inventing a well-sounding Arabic name for conventional financial products and employing a "sharia board" - a representative "supervisory board" of Islamic scholars. Serious deliberations over Islamic financial investments are a modern-day phenomenon – the first attempts were made in the 1960s. Of course, there is a long tradition of economic activity and economic science in the Islamic sphere, but in the course

8. Austrian Investment Philosophy

of the downfall of Islamic culture, intellectual discourse over economic topics atrophied. In today's Islamic world, the economic sciences are dominated by often calamitous ideas imported from the modern West. The number of potential members for sharia supervisory boards is currently estimated to be barely above 50 – globally! This appears plausible, as knowledge about Islamic economic law and financial services rarely go hand in hand.

How did the sudden boom in Islamic finance get going? Everything points to a marketing trick invented by Western banks, akin to "ethical investment funds". Most "Islamic economists" are employees of Western banks. Did the hunt for customers and yield suddenly lead to ethical and religious reflection? One has the impression that just as the biggest prude puts a naked female on the title page to increase circulation, bankers are discovering ethics and religion. Thus one arrives at the paradoxical conclusion that Western, hardly religiously inspired bankers, are eagerly working on an "Islamization" of a different kind. The invisible hand of competition then gives the banks an incentive to outdo each other in terms of which one of them is following the most strict sharia interpretation, which will lead to a continual tightening of standards and with that ever more complex avoidance constructs ("innovations"). The big problem with this: the hypocritical emphasis on a strictly Islamic approach to individual financial services insinuates that competitors are indulging in "un-Islamic" behavior and thus leads to polarization and an absurd race.

The same can be observed in the area of so-called "ethical investments": ethical investment funds are putting competing products and lastly economic activity as such under a moralizing general suspicion, which one can only escape by paying indulgences. As grateful recipients of such indulgence payments, "ethics experts" on the one hand, and "sharia experts" on the other, are offering their services, whereby economic competence represents an obstacle rather than a precondition in order to make money from this business.

The pointedness of this critique has to be seen in the context of the sad state of economic science and the rampant economic ignorance of most academics, including theologians. Religion properly understood ought to and can offer guidance, also, and especially in the context of economic activity. However, as a superficial criterion the goals of which are confined purely to marketing purposes, it is nothing but a business engaged in the certification of nonsense – the business with a bad conscience, which has to be boosted so as to increase returns. One only needs to look at the absurd criteria employed by ethical investment funds. Apparently, they simply plagiarized the poorly conceived *Islamic finance* methods, as the criteria appear arbitrary and often bizarre. Thus "Christian" ethical funds have a proscription against investment in wine, as though even altar wine were already immoral as such, as opposed to possible individual alcohol abuse.

In principle, Islam exhibits a friendly attitude toward trade. Contrary to income obtained without labor from risk-free interest, the mutual bearing of risk is always held up as an economic ideal. Banks are regarded as fiduciaries (Wadiah principle) that may not pay interest on sight deposits.

In line with the traditionally high esteem in which precious metals are held, Islamic economists would almost appear predestined to see through the interest rate manipulation of today's financial regime. To this end, they should not however leave *Islamic finance* to Western commercial banks. A positive example is offered by the popular DMCC Gold Sukuk (gold fund): in return for providing capital, investors receive a return that it is paid out in the form of gold. It is remarkable what Alastair Crooke reports about Islamist circles:

> "Islamists have argued for some time that this huge injection of M3 liquidity has fuelled the consumer boom, and has also created dangerous imbalances in the financial system that threaten its stability. Equally, Islamists have argued that a culture of liberal credit [...] has led to massive indebtedness, which in turn leads to exploitation and to a form of modern bondage within the economic system. [...] Islamists

would argue the merits of a return to a financial system based on some standard – such as the gold standard of the past – that limits the creation of money by central banks, and which prohibits fractional reserve banking."[101]

Let us return to economics and the ethics of interest rates: interest rates as differences in valuation are a consequence of human preferences. However, these do not have to lead to the charging of interest on money loans. With respect to consumer credit, it must be taken into account that it leads the borrower into a relationship of dependency, and can increase his already high time preference further. It is therefore morally questionable to offer one's savings to one's fellow men for the purpose of consumption and acquire a debenture for future repayment in exchange, regardless of whether one aggravates the situation with a demand for interest or not. "Consume now, pay later" is a dangerous temptation.

A charitable gift without a demand for repayment is better suited for aid in an emergency. An alternative that would be still superior to this would be aiding with capital accumulation – the financial means necessary for this are however the least contribution. Founding a joint company would create far better incentives for both sides than a mere loan. An interest rate charge in addition to repayment of principal in the form of money (instead of shares in equity capital) is a push toward producing short-term returns and can ultimately result in the break-up of a company and over-indebtedness of the borrower.

The compounding effect of interest is an especially great burden – but it is not an automatic consequence of taking on debt. Compound interest is only possible if interest payments are serviced with the help of new debt. This is something only governments are doing on a long-term basis. Compound interest is therefore not an argument against interest, but a warning against over-indebtedness. It is not compound interest that leads to a growth compulsion, it is the growth compulsion which modern-day states believe themselves to be subject to, which leads to over-indebtedness and therefore to the accumulation of compound interest. All legal orders of the past forbade automatically levied compound interest, today it is a legal privilege reserved to banks. It would be reasonable for a debtor to file for bankruptcy before a postponement of debt repayments is put in place, and with that additional interest charges on the interest he owes. However, as such, the phenomenon of compound interest is merely an expression of reinvestment: reinvested returns can develop similar momentum, which makes it possible for successful companies to achieve internally financed growth.

To regard interest as the cause of today's problems falls far short of reality. An attitude to life that involves living at the expense of the future cannot be altered by prohibitions, only by good examples and bad experiences. The dominance of credit and thus also interest is a modern-day phenomenon, the root of which is the credit expansion pursued by banks and governments. Since this expansion is unsustainable, the dark side of the large extent of indebtedness will eventually become painfully evident. The freedom and independence bought on credit will turn out to be illusory: it ends as debt bondage.

The Problem with Debt

Indebtedness is a fundamental question concerning investment philosophy. In recent decades, many of the most successful investors and entrepreneurs have had positive experiences with credit financing. Many a fortune has been made with the help of leverage. Adherents of the Austrian School have never denied the importance of credit for a highly developed economy. However, today a warning seems appropriate: debt exposes borrowers to a greater extent to the artificial fluctuations of the economy that Austrian economists refer to as the business cycle. A critical examination of credit is therefore definitely necessary.

Today, the most prevalent form of credit is consumer credit. Even though durable consumer goods are often called investments, they

8. Austrian Investment Philosophy

represent primarily the consumption of funds that have not yet been saved. The most important reason for taking out consumer credit is the desire to balance consumption over the course of one's life. Why should one wait for home ownership until one is old? Should one only frantically enjoy the fruits of one's labor once one has grown old? Dogged financing of one's life from one's own savings, without employment of future income in advance, looks like an exaggeratedly low time preference. Our savings are at their largest when we no longer need them. This makes it seem quite reasonable to fund a suburban home and the car it invariably makes necessary on credit. The main task of investment would then be to find the most favorable credit conditions, take precautions against unforeseeable events and use one's savings in the long term for the repayment of one's debts.

This perspective is not entirely wrong, but it harbors a number of pitfalls. Especially in a historical comparison, it is conspicuous how this seemingly reasonable strategy for individuals cumulatively becomes a symptom of economic and political change. The necessity of consumer credit appears almost inescapable mainly because it seems indeed no longer possible for young people today to purchase a home and a car – the classical symbols of bourgeois life in the post war period, and with that evidence of success presentable to the parental generation – by financing them with their own funds prior to reaching old age. This is evidence for rapid impoverishment, which we do not discern due to the prosperity illusion and politically expedient statistics. With a tax burden that can reach a real level of up to 70 percent and rising real estate prices, this is not surprising.

In the historical capital of banking "capitalism", which is in reality creditism, the City of London, the average price of an apartment with two bedrooms suitable for a family, currently sells for a million pounds, while the average savings rate in the UK currently stands at a mere 42 pounds per month. This is certainly an extreme example, but in the meantime it is true almost everywhere in the world – especially in light of growing youth unemployment – that financing a home from one's savings upon founding a family has become impossible without significant parental support.

The problem with credit financing is however "debt bondage", a strong, but valid term, if it refers to dependency on the economic situation. Due to the increase in credit financing, the interests of the population are shifting – debtors will always have an interest in devaluation. In addition, they become dependent on "growth policy": nominal returns must grow faster than real values. Unwittingly, they therefore lean toward supporting the very policy that was responsible for their dependency in the first place. This is why the monetary revolution is feeding on itself – that is its genius. However, an important consequence of this revolution is rising volatility of the economy. Periods of credit expansion reinforce a false sense of security, which then suddenly collapses. The high monthly installments needed for the financing of home and car are tying debtors to their places of employment and are forcing them to run ever faster in the rat race on the artificially accelerated economic treadmill.

The generation that is just about to retire was lucky to experience the longest boom in history to date; since the end of World War II it has hitherto always been possible to transform sharp corrections into new bubbles by means of reflation. The growth in prosperity this generation has experienced was unfortunately based on a flimsy real foundation. It is mainly the result of an unwitting, but very convenient, looting of the next generation. This young generation is often accused of careerism today. However, this criticism misses the mark completely, as it misconceives the true state of society. The way young people of today approach things is misguided: if they protest against the "system", they sound like their parents. A recent TV commercial ends with an apposite punchline: "When I'm grown up, I want to be a square too!" The days of stuffy-uptight non-squaredom are over. This is more than just adolescent defiance: the self-image of the parental generation as non-conformists has an important flaw. Instinctively, today's youth sense that its anti-bourgeois ideals were only an act.

8. Austrian Investment Philosophy

The generation of grandparents failed miserably with its looting in the end, the parental generation ultimately succeeded. The bill will one day be presented to today's youth. Young people suspect that they cannot trust that enough will be left for them in old age. Their restless careerist striving, as empty and unimaginative as it may appear, has the following motive: exploit the fat years, because they may soon be over. In Robert Musil's work, we find the reply of a father to his rebellious daughter: "And what would you live from, if I were not a capitalist?" The anti-ideological pragmatism of today's youth contains a reply of the daughters to their fathers: "And what would you live from, if I were not a careerist?" It is legitimate not to be a square. However, in that case, it is not legitimate to want to live like a square. Today's youth are rebelling against the double standard of their parents, just as their parents did before them. However, they once again tend to exaggerate in the opposite direction.

The pressure that stands behind consumer credit is ultimately often a confusion between means and ends. Whether a bourgeois existence in youth is worth the price of possible debt bondage remains an individual decision. Undoubtedly, it is the correct decision for some. However, it is just as undoubtedly true that in the long term, it is the wrong decision for many. In their desire to bring life forward, typical debtors only manage to postpone it into old age anyway: when finally everything is paid off. Thus the typical excuse of debt serfs: once I am retired, I will have enough time to do what brings me joy!

Prior to the monetary revolution, there were better alternatives available to reach the goals that are driving young people into debt today. Ultimately, it is all about a fact that corresponds to human nature, namely that the young have rather more income than wealth, and old people have rather more wealth than income. The problem therefore consists of how to transform income into wealth and vice versa. Since the two aims are compatible, there should not be a shortage of solutions to mutual satisfaction in the economy. Traditionally, this process of transformation took place within families, later also in capital markets. Ever since saving and credit are no longer tied to each other, this social nexus has been destroyed. A good investment strategy nevertheless attempts to manage this process of transformation with as little indebtedness as possible. The aim is therefore to transform income into wealth, and to choose, build up and maintain those assets that will be able to generate income later.

The second reason for taking on debt is the attempt to generate income – with the aid of productive credit. External capital to finance a company has many advantages, some of which have been artificially created by politics, while others are based on economic principles. The disadvantages are, however, similar to those of consumer credit: an increase in the vulnerability of companies in the course of the business cycle. In addition, due to the interest burden there is a greater focus on maximizing short-term returns, which can harm long-term returns. This is an aspect of capital consumption. During a boom, it appears stupid to eschew leverage. The price of forgoing it is indeed high, too high for some companies. However, the artificial boom cannot last forever, certainly not again for an entire generation – which is the natural minimum duration of a sensible investment strategy.

The first step of investment in an era of business cycles and the obvious use for liquid funds is therefore – as the "Austrians" would advise – the repayment of debt. This lowers one's dependency on the distorted economic cycle and wrests a little increase in one's quality of life from the sick economic structure.

The recommendation of some critics of inflation to bet on inflationism with the help of leverage is reckless. There is of course hardly any evidence that the debasement policy will be abandoned, and in light of the degree of indebtedness it is clear that every political regime is dependent on supporting debtors relative to creditors. However, the modern economy is far less controllable than many "experts" seem to believe. The dynamics are far more complex, and often quite paradoxical. No-one should use his basic means of existence to place bets on a specific economic outcome.

8. Austrian Investment Philosophy

Anyone who has debts does not need any further investment recommendation aside from: pay it back as quickly as possible! After the 2008 crisis, one probably no longer needs to issue warnings about foreign currency denominated loans. One consequence of the monetary revolution are enormous exchange rate fluctuations. Riskier loans, which are subject to foreign exchange and interest fluctuations, should be restructured as quickly as possible. Due to the artificial volatility of the business cycle, dramatic interest rate moves cannot be ruled out either. Only one important caveat has to be added in the context of debt reduction: nowadays it can often be in conflict with considerations regarding tax minimization. This needs to be weighed on an individual case by case basis. With respect to debts that are fully covered by one's own wealth and which only exist as a result of tax incentives, the above objections are of course not applicable.

If after all necessary expenditures and after repayment of one's debt a positive residual remains, one can be congratulated. Only this privileged situation, in which a steadily decreasing minority of the population still finds itself in, allows further deliberations regarding investment. The "Austrian" investment philosophy leads to the differentiation and examination of five aspects, which at the same time form the "philosophical portfolio" of the "Austrian" investor: hoarding, investment, consumption, endowment and speculation.

Hoarding

Hoarding of money is the first aspect of a long-term investment strategy. While hoarding is denounced as damaging for the economy by many leading economists, and salvation can supposedly only be attained by reckless consumption, the Austrian School defends its economic necessity. The point is the retention of liquid funds, which ensure the capacity to act. Due to always-present uncertainty, it is necessary to

Hoarding

hold liquid funds. Sensible investments cannot be undertaken at any arbitrary point in time and in any arbitrary denomination.

Hoarding is often reproached for allegedly not adding any real value. It is asserted that hoarded money "does do any work". However, today it is already quite a feat to achieve mere value conservation, which is in any event the precondition for investment. Holding a precautionary stock is a traditional basic principle of any sustainable economy. In a dynamic world, in which uncertainty, mistakes, fluctuations and change are inescapable, inventories play an important balancing, coordinating and development role. In every economy that goes beyond the level of mere subsistence, such inventories at least partially take the form of money. The balancing function over time is thereby one of the most important functions of money, which in the best case can so to speak represent a store of human energy. Demand for holding money is therefore perfectly legitimate and under no circumstances morally more dubious than immediate consumption, on the contrary.

Moreover, hoarding is not in conflict with production. Money is a medium of exchange, and money prices enable rational economic calculation, without which no modern complex economy could exist. However, money does not fund production – it is ultimately funded by real goods. Workers who are engaged in stages of production far removed from the consumer stage need to eat, buy clothes, pay rent, and so forth, long before the efforts of their labor ripen into consumer goods. All the goods required for this must either be saved or be taken from ongoing synchronous production. If there are trillions of dollars but not enough bread, they will starve. Even a miser who hoards nearly every cent he gets and hides it under the mattress cannot possibly harm the economy. After all, to receive the money he hoards, he has to contribute something – his personal production – to the economy's pool of real funding. By not exercising his claims on the pool of real funding and hoarding money instead of consuming, this contribution remains in the economy as savings that can be employed in production activities. It is not mysteriously "lost" to the economy.

8. Austrian Investment Philosophy

The only effect the hoarding of money *ceteris paribus* exerts, is to increase the purchasing power of the extant money stock (in today's world it is merely a countervailing force to the devaluing effect caused by the steady expansion of the money supply). Production cannot be influenced by this, it will simply adjust to the change in money's purchasing power. It is far more difficult to adjust a lengthy production structure to a shortage in the goods needed to complete its processes.

Building up real value-creating structures requires an inventory of liquidity. A different term for liquidity is marketability. Carl Menger introduced this concept to economic science. He wrote:

> But the fact that different goods cannot be exchanged for each other with equal facility was given only scant attention until now. Yet the obvious differences in the marketability of commodities is a phenomenon of such far-reaching practical importance, the success of the economic activity of producers and merchants depending to a very great extent on a correct understanding of the influences here operative, that science cannot, in the long run, avoid an exact investigation of its nature and causes.[102]

Menger cites bread as an example of a highly marketable good and Sanskrit works as an example of a good with very low marketability. The greater the potential market for a good, the more homogeneous the good, the lower the transaction costs in selling it, the higher its marketability. As already mentioned above, high marketability expresses itself in a tight spread between bid and offer prices. Perishable goods like bread exhibit a drastically declining marketability over time, in spite of their initially high marketability. Due to technological progress, the same is true of appliances: currently, iPhones still exhibit a higher marketability after a year has passed than mobile phones made by competitors – purchase price and selling price are closer together. However, the time period of their marketability is too short for providing enduring liquidity. Almost every consumer good loses a large portion of its resale value shortly after purchase, and is therefore not suitable for a marketable stock. Inventories of consumer goods one uses up oneself, such as food inventories, can definitely cover a part of one's hoarding activity.

In economies operating above the level of subsistence, marketable inventories – i.e., inventories of media of exchange – will always play a greater role. If the importance of perishable inventories increases, it can represent evidence of impoverishment. As the liquidity bottlenecks that typically occur in the course of the business cycle also mean supply bottlenecks, the accumulation of inventories of consumer goods can definitely be a plausible part of a realistic long-term investment strategy. Moreover, managing such inventories is quite instructive; it shows how difficult it is to preserve valuable things in a changing and transitory world. Effective management of inventories was at the core of the oldest form of economics, household economics. It teaches modesty and skepticism with respect to promises of risk-free interest income and other "safe" investment recommendations.

At the moment, it is still possible for most people in the West to obtain incomes that are so far above the cost of basic necessities that food inventories only represent a small part of private hoards. That could well change again; if such inventories gain in importance again, the marketability of food items fit for storage will increase enormously. For the time being though, liquid assets certainly play a bigger role. The good with the highest marketability is per definition money; the simplest form of hoarding was always holding cash reserves. The importance of liquidity has been forgotten today, because the electronic world and the arrogance of believing oneself to be at the end and pinnacle of history in the modern-day Western world, are feigning a market certainty that does not correspond to reality. In the real estate crisis, many Americans found out to their chagrin that assets lacking marketability represent only virtual book values.

Figure 8.1. shows an example of the various degrees of liquidity associated with different asset classes, from the most liquid forms at the bottom to the least liquid ones at the top.

8. Austrian Investment Philosophy

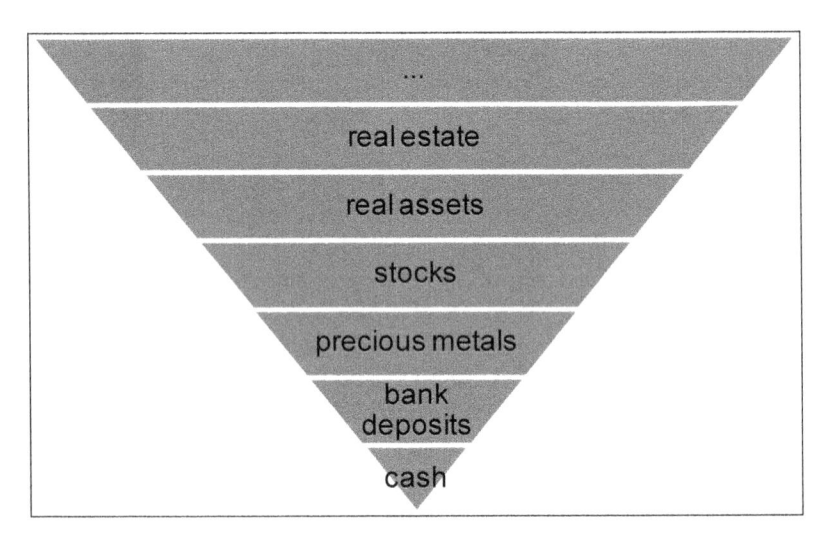

Figure 8.1.: Investment assets segmented by their liquidity

Based on Carl Menger's theory, Antal Fekete differentiates between two aspects of marketability, "large scale marketability" and "small scale marketability".[103] These aspects he calls marketability and hoardability. A good has large scale marketability if the bid/ask spread grows more slowly than that of other goods in the event of large volumes of it being offered in the market. Historically, cattle has proven to be especially marketable, i.e., even large numbers of cattle could be sold at a relatively small loss. The reason for this is the mobility of cattle, which means that the saturation of regional markets is less likely. On the other hand, if many property owners sell at the same time at the same location, the saturation effect leads to massive price declines – unless prices are lowered, the properties cannot be sold.

The small-scale marketability of a good is greater, respectively the good is more useful for hoarding, if the spread between bid and offer prices grows less than that of other goods when units of the good offered in the market become steadily smaller. Smoked, cured or dried beef is easier to hoard than cattle, as smaller units of cattle lead to a massive price loss: cattle that has been cut up into pieces is dead and immobile. While historically, cattle was the most marketable good prior to the use of money by the broad masses, salt was recognized as the most hoardable good. Especially in Austria, much prosperity can be attributed to the monetization of salt (i.e., the partial assumption of monetary functions by salt), as many place names still show, while the prosperity of Indo-Germanic tribes can be attributed to the monetization of cattle, as the oldest common etymological roots of the Indo-Germanic language show.

Other hoardable commodities in the course of history were wheat, tobacco, sugar, and alcohol. Fekete points out that it is probably no coincidence that all these goods were as a rule subject to massive government interventions, such as protectionism, prohibition and monopolies. The same applies to the two commodities that after the emergence of markets that went beyond tribal borders prevailed as the most hoardable and marketable goods: silver and gold. Due to its lower purchasing power, silver was traditionally the more hoardable good, the money of the "little guy" and of everyday use. Gold, by contrast, was the money of merchants and the State. Technically, it is nowadays far easier to divide gold into smaller units, and it has therefore pushed silver increasingly into the background; however, until today a typical gold coin still has a much too high purchasing power to be useful for everyday shopping transactions. Nowadays, hoarding is most likely to take place in the form of bank deposits and cash currency, which can be used to gradually build up other hoards.

Cash currency in the original sense no longer exists today. Due to the poor quality of today's currencies, which consist of debt claims that can be multiplied almost at will, hoarding has become quite a challenge. Even cash is nowadays a highly speculative asset class, as it is fully exposed to arbitrary political action – up to the prohibition of cash payments. Therefore, in hoarding one must not only consider the liquidity aspect, but also the sovereignty of different asset classes. This refers to the relative independence of an asset class from artificial debasement and burdens. Historically, while precious metals exhibited

8. Austrian Investment Philosophy

relatively strong sovereignty, even more sovereign are intellectual assets, such as talents, skills, contacts, ideas and knowledge. Figure 8.2. illustrates by way of example a breakdown of asset classes by the degree of sovereignty they convey.

```
            ...
           real
          estate
        bank deposits
        gold property
        cash currencies
        gold possession
        intellectual assets
```

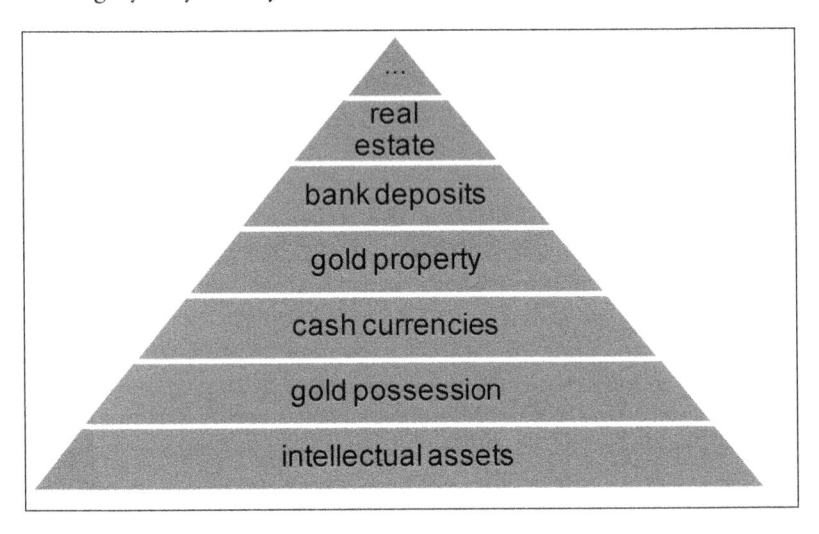

Figure 8.2: Asset classes by sovereignty

Typically reserves are nowadays saved at a bank. Widespread electronic payment methods and a high density of ATMs as a rule make bank deposits a sufficiently liquid asset. However, this liquidity can become subject to sudden restrictions. In banking crises such as the recent ones in Greece and Cyprus, and before that in Argentina, a panicky race for liquidity can be observed: people spend whole days driving from bank branch to bank branch in order to obtain control over part of their hoards. Typically only those with good connections to the political class or the banking cartel are truly successful in this; these people then tend to cross the borders with suitcases full of money. Due to the fractional reserve banking system, the withdrawal of low single digit percentages of bank deposits suffices to unmask the illiquidity of banks. Bank deposits enjoy only a small degree of sovereignty, because they are not the property of depositors, as is generally assumed, but are transferred into the bank's ownership. A bank deposit is legally nothing but a loan to the bank – which is why one receives interest payments on it.

Weighing liquidity versus sovereignty is a personal decision, for which no safe recommendation can be made – this is unfortunately true of most concrete investment decisions. This book can do no more than offer guidance for the necessary reflection. The initial intention of hoarding must be to bring one's financial circumstances to the point where one is in the black. Hoards are preconditioned on the plugging of gaps and the reduction of burdens. Once one has rid oneself of debt, the first priority must be to build up reserves for expenditures that are to be expected. Liquid reserves should at a minimum be equivalent to the expenditures of a whole year. Before one has built up such reserves, it is pointless to think about further investment. Roland Baader recommended the following segmentation:

> One third of one's investments should be placed as if everything was right with the world, one third should be invested cautiously and very conservatively, one third as if "red alarm" had been sounded.[104]

In "red alarm" situations historically, either cash (in one's home currency during times of deflation, in foreign currency during inflation) or precious metals have proved their worth. In the case of precious metals, relative liquidity can be easily discerned by comparing bid and ask prices: the more standardized their form, the more liquid they are. As long as "everything is right with the world", deposits in current accounts are the most liquid form for everyday payments. However, the banking sector's structural illiquidity suggests that it would be wise not to hold deposits that are too large relative to the savings held by the population on average, under no circumstances above the threshold of the supposed "deposit insurance". In emergencies, deposits above certain maximum thresholds that are configured along the lines of ensuring majority support, are always frozen, confiscated or devalued by politicians.

After cash currency, precious metals and bank deposits, investments in money markets are an obvious means of hoarding. If there were no market distortions, these investments would actually be topping the list of recommendations. This part also has to be subsumed under the heading "everything is right with the world". For up to a maximum of one third of one's funds intended for hoarding, one can follow the recommendations of local bankers in this case – depending on personal affinity and trust. Due to low interest rates, the incentive for such investments is however not particularly high currently, after fees there will probably not remain a significant enough return to justify the loss in sovereignty.

Hoarding is part of the "Austrian" investment strategy, because it is a very slow and long-term oriented strategy. Anyone who has made five good investment decisions throughout his life has already been blessed with a lot of luck. "Austrian investing" therefore requires patience and a strong stomach. Today's currencies are unfortunately not really designed for this. The art of "Austrian" investment in practical terms consists of being able to seize good opportunities and try not to despair in view of all the "lesser evils" and pounce on one out of impatience, as small as that evil may appear. Good investors must avoid ever facing pressure to sell or to feel under greedy pressure to buy. Only by keeping an eye on liquidity, will one possess the steady hand that is necessary for good investment decisions.

Investing

Once one has repaid one's debts and hoarded a sufficient amount of liquid funds, investment becomes more interesting, but at the same time more challenging. Investment-oriented saving is equivalent to capital accumulation from the point of view of the Austrian School. Capital is quite distinct from money – indeed, money must be spent in order to accumulate capital. From the perspective of the Austrian

School, the only way to sustainable capital accumulation and thus wealth accumulation, is thrift, value preservation, and responsible risk taking by employing liquid funds in roundabout ways on assets offering higher value creation potential. Consumption is not the cause, but the consequence of higher prosperity and thus the ultimate goal of value creation.

Capital is a complex latticework of goods, knowledge, decisions, labor and expectations. Unfortunately, the capital structure has been distorted globally as a result of the artificial boom. This means that a great many investments are not congruent with the actual preferences of consumers and their willingness and ability to pay in the long term. The necessary corrective process is politically postponed ever further, which keeps making the situation worse. In such an environment, investment becomes ever more akin to gambling, even more than it would already be on account of ever-present uncertainty: the artificial uncertainty due to political decisions (regime uncertainty) becomes an additional factor. Due to monetary inflation, companies routinely overestimate their profits and as a result the foundation of real capital declines.

Capital accumulation is in any event most likely to succeed in an area into which one personally has better insight than the broad masses, and that is one's own value creation. Focusing solely on bloated stock exchanges with their artificial volatility is misguided. Investment means to lengthen the capital structure in order to achieve higher value creation. This is most likely to succeed in one's own value creation process, one's own profession. Most successful companies are established in sectors in which the founder is already experienced, or is even able to bring a customer base along with him.

Even if one is not self-employed, one can still invest in one's own value creation potential. Investments are expenditures that can raise one's income at a later stage, such as an investment in further education. Unfortunately, the education sector is among the sectors displaying the largest distortions, therefore diplomas, certificates, government incentives and accredited programs do not offer sufficient guidance. Much more sensible, but also more difficult, is the classical path: searching for someone who is a master in his field and make an attractive offer for the time during which one can look over his shoulder, ask him questions and have him examine one's own efforts.

Investment is also a forgoing of income, for instance if it corresponds to the buying of time that can be used intensively for advanced training, reflection, experiments, or unpaid or lower-paid work that helps one with developing new skills. 10,000 hours of work without perspective dictated by someone else seem like a never-ending hardship, 10,000 hours of purposeful work with a perspective are the necessary precondition for true mastery. In light of today's horrendous tax progression, it often makes sense to ask oneself the following question: what offers a greater chance of success – finding profitable investments in distorted markets for 10,000 dollars one has saved in the course of one year, or rather using the time one had to spend for earning this net amount for developing a profitable undertaking on the side? Of course there are no answers to this that are applicable to everybody – the task is rather to ask the right questions. The idea that if one only knew how, one could comfortably, simply and with acceptable risk build a fortune by means of good investment decisions made on the side with a few mouse clicks – without any responsible entrepreneurial effort – is definitely an element of the prosperity illusion. Those who cannot disengage from it, are likely to be disappointed by this book.

Investment is always an entrepreneurial activity. It consists of taking uncertain risks with the aim of future value creation for the benefit of other people. From the Austrian School's subjectivist perspective, four preconditions need to be fulfilled so that a good or a service represents value to other people which they are prepared to pay for: 1. it needs to address a human want or goal, 2. it must be useful in satisfying this want, respectively in helping people to attain their goals, 3. people need to be informed of the offer, 4. the good or service must be made available to people at the proper place and point in time. Greater value can also be created by: 1. the recognition of unsatisfied or poorly served needs, respectively of solutions for human problems and better ways for the attainment of human ends, 2. the improvement of existing solutions, 3. teaching about existing solutions, 4. improving the availability of such solutions.

It can easily be seen from this itemization that only a relatively small part of value creation actually consists of technological innovation. Most people do not trust themselves to become entrepreneurs, because they do not believe they are sufficiently ingenious to come up with completely new ideas no-one has thought of previously. This is a significant misconception of the economy, which can be rectified by reading the works of "Austrians" on the topic of entrepreneurship. There is no lack of ideas or means in our time. What is lacking are the addressing of relevant ends, guidance amid an abundance of offers, and overcoming laziness and conformism, which lead to better solutions being overlooked.

The decisive question for entrepreneurs is this: what will people need tomorrow? One's own needs, wants and ends in conjunction with the circumstances one is most familiar with due to one's own professional and life experience, are the logical starting point of new entrepreneurial approaches. The biggest gaps must be expected to exist in those areas in which distortions are most pronounced nowadays, because they are ruled by subsidized irresponsibility and favoritism instead of by personal responsibility: security, education and media, health, money production, retirement provision and not least, the preservation of wealth.

The two most obvious investment opportunities aimed at increasing one's own value creation potential are the division of labor and better tools. Due to the law of comparative advantage (also known as the law of association), it is often advantageous to outsource simple tasks, even if one can perform them better oneself. As a rule, about 20 percent of one's own activities produce 80% of one's income. By means of suitable structuring, the remaining activities can possibly be transferred to others, although this requires quite a bit of entrepreneurial effort. The absurd tax burden on labor is a big obstacle to a large part of these opportunities, which is why such personal outsourcing investments are most prevalent in low-wage sectors or the shadow economy. An extreme example that illustrates the possibilities is that of a programmer in the US, who outsourced his entire work to Chinese programmers for a fifth of his salary. With his results, he at times even achieved the best evaluation scores in the company he worked for. Unfortunately, he did not use the time he gained in an investment-related manner, but rather to senselessly surf the internet and watch videos at his place of work.[105]

Investments in capital goods, such as for instance better tools, have the goal to increase one's own productivity with the aid of better means. Unfortunately, most work places provide disincentives for better productivity, as faster working employees have to spend the same amount of time at work as their less productive colleagues. This is a result of the erroneous cost theory of value, which the Austrian School refuted a long time ago. In our short-term oriented times, many underestimate the long-term gains in productivity better tools can provide: for today's work, which often takes place in front of computer screens, this can consist of better software or ergonomic improvements. Instead of wrestling with the question of where to invest 5,000 dollars one has saved, why not examine if outsourcing the development of a few customized macros could create a lot of time and quietude for new projects, which might either offer the prospect of advancement in one's place of work, or create new sources of income on the side?

The biggest problem for entrepreneurial activity today, apart from the excesses of taxation, which lead to ever more sources of real value creation drying up, is the difficulty of economic calculation in the face of monetary instability. Since companies lack policy-independent calculation inputs, they are again and again driven to commit errors that are then discovered during crises. Entrepreneurial solutions for this problem promise to produce large returns. In its stressing of such calculation problems, the Austrian School overlaps with value investing, which we will still discuss in more detail, but actually reaches beyond it. Investment in companies is always investment in future value creation. Of course participating in value creation structures one has not built up oneself is also legitimate and important. The decision in which company one should invest is an entrepreneurial decision as well – this is to say a risk one must take responsibility for, which no "recommendation" can relieve one from.

In times of devaluation, there is widespread focus on price increases. This is the wrong perspective in the long term, in spite of the fact that it is possible to be among the inflation winners. A dollar invested in stocks in 1950 would have produced eight times more in terms of dividend yields than capital gains. Dividends represent 70 percent of all long-term stock market returns.

Only investment in profitable companies conforms to the narrower economic meaning of investment. Striving for profit is of course not everything, the Austrian School always stresses this point. It is, however, not reprehensible either, but a necessary precondition of the best possible employment of capital according to human value scales and judgment.

Investment means the accumulation of assets, this is to say income producing wealth. Things that generate no income are either hoards, consumption or non-economic projects, which we will still discuss. One of the biggest problems in investing is that contrary to hoarding, it is not possible to divide up one's capital into infinitesimally small units. This is additionally aggravated by regulations. Analogous to the problem with micro-loans, which require creative ways of lowering transaction costs, most small investors are faced with a "micro capital" problem. Magnificent institutional solutions for the denomination of capital in smaller units exist, namely in stock corporations, but the largest portion of the illusory values created by the monetary revolution tends to flow into them, so that it is rarely possible to purchase shares in these entrepreneurial income sources at acceptable prices. If the purchase of shares is solely motivated by the expectation of price increases, it cannot be called an investment in the narrower sense, but should more legitimately be seen as equivalent to speculation.

8. Austrian Investment Philosophy

Unfortunately the picture is more complicated due to today's distortions: on the one hand, income is punished by taxes, on the other hand, short-termism is artificially boosted. As a result, not even recurring income from an investment is a sufficient basis for investment decisions anymore. In this environment, there is often no other choice but to bet on growth stocks. However, this requires that one differentiate between actual growth as opposed to mere growth in the share price. Growth companies are those that are highly profitable, but instead of distributing their profits, reinvest them into their business. As long as growth is possible, the return of such investments can be tilted toward price increases that can be monetized by partial sales, rather than dividend returns. Eternal growth is however neither possible in nature, nor in any entrepreneurial sector.

A proper investment strategy always proceeds step by step. Up to a certain threshold amount of savings, there are in any case barely any good opportunities to sensibly invest in other companies than one's own. For the typical small investor, who is part of the mass demand on the stock exchange and is generally scorned as the *dumb money* by professional traders, stocks are as a rule a rip-off. Bill and Will Bonner get to the heart of this scam:

> The idea is to sell people parts of companies about which they know nothing, at prices which the people who do know something about these companies consider too high. Why else would they want to sell their shares?[106]

Investment in other companies is especially interesting if one can afford to buy shareholdings beyond what the typical small investor can buy and is realistically able to buy shares in companies that are not listed. "Austrian" investing in this case equates to value investing with great patience – characterized by a long-term entrepreneurial approach. We will still discuss this concept further.

Much of what we call investment today has nothing to do with investment in the narrower "Austrian" sense. Often it amounts to consumption decisions, which – as we will see just now – are just as legitimate and difficult, such as owner-occupied real estate. Often it concerns attempts at hoarding in order to beat debasement. For instance, gold and silver are certainly not investments. There once was a time, the "golden age", when everybody was still able to undertake investment in terms of gold. Even today, gold contracts exist, but they are financial instruments used by a small minority in distorted markets. Something that does not or cannot produce productive returns, does not represent capital in the economic sense. The return does not have to necessarily consist of money, but a return, this is to say a certain value added, has to be there, otherwise taking the detour of investing would make no sense. Investment is putting liquidity at risk for the discovery of more productive roundabout processes.

Consumption

With the effort involved in wealth accumulation, one must not lose sight of its goal. This is a frequent mistake of otherwise successful investors: making the safeguarding and expansion of wealth an end in itself. This mistake leads to relative impoverishment amid rising nominal wealth. The prosperity illusion strikes, and action is stood on its head – means determine ends. These are adjusted to the rising means and the prosperity effect evaporates. According to subjectivist value theory, real added value is only created if one can employ lesser valued means to achieve higher valued ends. If one attaches too much value to the means (such as one's bank deposits), one can no longer keep up with one's goals. Being rich is quite expensive. Three quarters of all lottery winners are materially worse off and less happy than before they won after just three years. In this sense, one would almost have to hope for failing in one's investment endeavors.

This danger of confusing means and ends can be mitigated by giving as much room and time to thinking about one's goals as one gives to thinking about the means – the area of traditional investing. Consumption is a major area in which one's goals are expressed through one's priorities. Today's distorted consumerism threatens to lead to a reaction that condemns consumption as such. This can express itself in a form of misanthropy, which castigates every impact man has on his environment. The largest part of "nature", which is often used to argue against human influence consists however of cultural landscapes. On the heels of politically boosted consumerism with its incredible destruction of nature and culture then follows politically regimented and limited consumption, which ultimately means that politics decides over the life and survival of human beings.

Consumption is an interaction with nature in which a benefit is generated for an individual by employing scarce means and using them up either immediately or over the long term. Since time has a direction for human beings and things decay and disorder increases without continual attempts to impose order, we are forced to make decisions. Every moment we fail to use to make subsequent moments possible and make better use of them, is consumed merely by means of passing by.

Consumption has two dimensions: on the one hand, the acquisition and using up of non-durable consumer goods, and on the other hand, the acquisition and use of durable consumer goods. A notable portion of consumption of both types consists of what Thorsten Veblen called "conspicuous consumption", whereby consumption by itself becomes a means to achieve social standing. Veblen writes:

> The basis on which good repute in any highly organized industrial community ultimately rests is pecuniary strength; and the means of showing pecuniary strength, and so of gaining or retaining a good name, are leisure and a conspicuous consumption of goods.[107]

The human desire to impress others is one of the major drivers that has made consumerism and paradoxically, also confiscatory levels of taxes, possible. Many would otherwise rather forego additional income, if it does not stand in an acceptable relation to the additional effort. The problem of conspicuous consumption is that the effect quickly reverses: bought prestige is rarely permanent and if one is unable to maintain the level of conspicuous consumption, contempt is the result. All the friends one suddenly gains after a lottery win quickly disappear as soon as the money has been spent.

The "Austrian" approach to consumption is a long-term one, one of appreciative slowness. Achieving a good ratio between price and value is just as important and difficult in the case of consumer goods as in investments. The cheapest products rarely exhibit a good ratio, and the most expensive ones do so even more rarely. As a rule, one is best served with quality products the prices of which have not yet been driven up by fashions, media attention and conspicuous consumption.

Life is short. The wrong conclusion from this fact is to give in to high time preference and attempt to get as much as possible out of the present moment. This is the worst use of a limited time span. A consequence of high time preference is a "stingy is cool" mentality, the combination of miserliness and wastefulness that has become a mass phenomenon today. It is a yearning for as many as possible, immediately available and as strong as possible feelings of obtaining a benefit, which makes the willingness to pay for the individual "kick" very small. This results in the accumulation of especially illiquid products – those for which the purchase itself is part of the kick, and which are especially short-lived. The spread between new purchase price and resale price is so large in these products that they ultimately end up in the garbage bin. In his book about impoverishment, Alexander von Schoenburg analyzes the astonishing worthlessness of the household goods found on average in apartments:

> While society today has hundreds of possessions, across all social strata, only a vanishingly small and ever more dwindling social class is actually in possession of real values. Incomes can be immense, even for someone in the lower middle class – a skilled laborer can earn far more than a million euros in the course of his life – but his personal, permanent possessions will as a rule amount to only a fraction of what he has earned,

8. Austrian Investment Philosophy

as he has wasted his income on worthless junk or the senseless killing of time: traveling to the Seychelles, bottle shelves made from badly screwed together softwood, fondue tableware, waffle irons, club memberships, ice and yoghurt machines, gel sandals, activity backpacks, combi jackets, travel onion choppers, body fat scales, meat shredders in "burnished chrome finish", lint shavers with a detachable bin, electrical massaging devices, thermal sealers for plastic bags, two juice presses, one Chi machine, designer pans and a magnetic memory foam pillow.[108]

The difference between consumptive and lasting consumption can be well described by the difference between fun and joy. Psychologist Erich Fromm defines fun as a passive satisfaction of a desire, which creates a thrill, but not sustained joy. The thereby steadily increasing joylessness of life makes people greedy for ever more new fun, ever more distractions and vicarious satisfaction. Joy on the other hand is tied to activity:

> Joy is the concomitant of productive activity. It is not a "peak experience", which culminates and ends suddenly, but rather a plateau, a feeling state, that accompanies the productive expression of one's essential human faculties. Joy is not the ecstatic fire of the moment. Joy is the glow that accompanies being. Pleasure and thrill are conducive to sadness after the so-called peak has been reached; for the thrill has been experienced, but the vessel has not grown. One's inner powers have not increased. [109]

The more durable, qualitative, timeless and sustainably joy creating consumer goods are, the closer consumption is to investment. A part of one's consumption can prove to be a store of value, another as a form of investment. Consumption becomes an investment in four different ways: long-term savings is one means – the opposite of the saying "penny-wise, pound foolish". This only represents an investment if one can actually lower long-term costs in this manner. Consumer goods can turn out to be investments if they open up potential uses that generate an income in the long term by creating value for one's fellow men. In our supposedly affluent society, this rarely happens, but that could change. The third way in which consumption can become an investment is by caring for improving one's health in order to improve one's long-term creative powers. One's diet and environment play a role in this that should not be underestimated. Sustainable consumption harms one's body as little as possible, but on the contrary, strengthens it. The fourth way is long-term and should perhaps rather be assigned to creation than consumption. The world as we experience it, with all its distortions, traps, and illusions that impinge on our wealth, is a result of many individual decisions – among which there are primarily consumption decisions. After all, our consumption decisions are ultimately decisive for the economic structure that surrounds us, and for that reason alone is part of every "investment strategy". Victor Mataja, another economist of the Austrian School, describes this moral aspect of consumption as follows:

> In order to obtain competent performance, in whatever field, one must search for it, prize it, and pay for it.[110]

With every consumption decision, we feed certain entrepreneurs, structures, sectors, politicians, classes, ideas, behaviors and ways of life. More than any other economic tradition, the Austrian School stresses the responsibility of the individual. Ludwig von Mises regards the consumer as the sovereign of the economy:

> Mankind does not drink alcohol because there are breweries, distilleries, and vineyards; men brew beer, distil spirits, and grow grapes because of the demand for alcoholic drinks. "Alcohol-capital" has not created drinking habits any more than it has created drinking songs. The capitalists who own shares in breweries and distilleries would have preferred shares in publishing firms for devotional books, had the demand been for spiritual and not spirituous substance. "Armament capital" did not create wars; wars created "armament capital."[111]

Due to massive market distortions and the decoupling of currency from real values, this is unfortunately no longer entirely true today. American "Austrian" Frank Fetter still called every penny a ballot.[112] These ballots are however barely worth anything anymore, the pennies of the little guy are outweighed by the flood of virtual dollars. Nevertheless, a considerable amount of responsibility remains with consumers: on the one hand, many overestimate the number of customers necessary to cause changes in the market – how many businesses must close because ten regular customers die, how many get started with just one good customer! On the other hand, consumption consists not only of purchasing decisions, but also decisions about what we focus our time, attention and appreciation on.

The Austrian School stresses human action, because it knows that true responsibility can only be expressed through action – whenever there is actually something to take responsibility for, because a scarce good must be employed. Economists speak in this context of the obvious contradiction between merely expressed and actually demonstrated preferences. As it is almost without cost, it is easy to bemoan circumstances, make conversation about alternatives and criticize the actions of others. In contrast to the passive consumerism of today, active consumption requires at least as much brains, will power and creativity as investment.

Endowment

Some investments are of such a long-term nature, that we ourselves will barely see a return on them. These are often the most fruitful and most important investments, as they enable especially long, complex and thus especially profitable detours. The more long-term oriented an investment, the more difficult it is to foresee who its beneficiary will be one day. In old families, which have accumulated and preserved wealth over many generations, such investments are often especially important. The term "sustainability", which has today degenerated into an empty phrase of political mountebanks, comes from the forestry of the nobility. Its cultural economy in turn is not measured solely in the far-away profits of descendants, but goes beyond the purely economical: long-term efforts of this type create the sphere which lies between the inaccessible jungle of nature and the eroding deserts of over-exploiting civilization – islands of rich biodiversity in which culture and nature interact.

Friedrich A. Hayek spoke of spontaneous orders, which are magnificent results of human action, without obeying a single plan alone. Human society, which is sustainable because it is based on voluntary cooperation, belongs to this organic sphere, which lies between organization and chaos, between cultural plans and natural limits and laws. Human beings are unable to survive on their own, they can compensate their physical weakness only with their civilization. The quality of our life strongly depends on the capital that is available for us to employ – and in most cases only the tiniest part thereof is a result of our own efforts. The fact that this is an important aspect of investing, is shown by the maxim: better to be poor in a rich country, than rich in a poor one. Of course the individual appears to have barely any influence on these framework conditions. However, complaining about politics is not enough: ultimately, every country has the politicians it deserves. Of course "democracy" is a farce, governments directly represent only minorities, and approval rates are at historical lows. However, other structures are a result of human decisions as well. As French philosopher Etienne de la Boetie – another antecedent of the Austrian School – recognized, even violent structures consist of countless actions of going along, keeping quiet, legitimizing, even more still of the exploitation of small advantages and avoiding possible disadvantages:

> I do not ask that you place hands upon the tyrant to topple him over, but simply that you support him no longer; then you will behold him, like a great Colossus whose pedestal has been pulled away, fall of his own weight and break into pieces. [...]

> This does not seem credible on first thought, but it is nevertheless true that there are only four or five who maintain the dictator, four or five who keep the country in bondage to him. Five or six have always had

access to his ear, and have either gone to him of their own accord, or else have been summoned by him, to be accomplices in his cruelties, companions in his pleasures, panderers to his lusts, and sharers in his plunders.[...] These six have six hundred who profit under them, and [...] the six hundred maintain under them six thousand, whom they promote in rank [...]. And whoever is pleased to unwind the skein will observe that not the six thousand but a hundred thousand, and even millions, cling to the tyrant [...].

In short, when the point is reached, through big favors or little ones, that large profits or small are obtained under a tyrant, there are found almost as many people to whom tyranny seems advantageous as those to whom liberty would seem desirable.[113]

The ancient Greeks called man the *zoon politikon*. This expression has since become widely misunderstood, as today's politics has nothing in common with the Greek term, it is in many respects the complete opposite. *Zoon politikon* means that man is a communal being, i.e., that the unlocking of his full potential and a good life requires other human beings living in stable structures of non-violent cooperation and peaceful competition. These structures are by no means a matter of course, as in his striving for community, man is often too eager to gain recognition, which causes groupthink and makes majorities prone to manipulation. The ancient Greeks thus considered politics the most difficult art, namely the opposition to the ongoing destruction of human societies by violence, stupidity, peer pressure, ideologies and other delusions. Every commonwealth in which men find sufficient freedom and stability to give expression to their potential, needs very long-term oriented citizens who are prepared to bear costs which do not promise them an immediate return.

Such efforts must under no circumstances be confined to tax payments or donations. Taxes have always primarily fed structures of violence and political group interests. The gravest danger of the tax state is the complete absorption of the public spirit and dedication of citizens on the grounds that "one is paying taxes anyway". Donations on the other hand are as a rule not given to profit-oriented organizations. Unfortunately, a lack of profits is by no means necessarily an indication of sustainable value creation, rather the opposite. Often profits are simply hidden: they exist in the form of salaries and commissions. Solicitation of donations is a big business, which consists of selling a good conscience. Good intentions however are not necessarily a guarantee of positive results. The effect of donations is often paltry – the farther away and alien the goals of the effort, the lower the donations that arrive. The NGO sector is massively distorted by subsidies, ideologies and an academic proletariat, which is produced by universities, bypassing the needs of the real world.

Therefore this sector of extremely long-term investment in the framework of a good life in community should rather be called "endowment". Taxes and donations are used up, while endowment in the original sense of the term refers to the accumulation of capital. As a result of tax policies, today's legal forms of endowments such as trusts have unfortunately become a refuge for people who dispossess themselves as a precaution, in order to escape the grasp of the State. Rarely does this tool still have anything to do with sustainable capital accumulation, even though it would be suitable for the purpose. The watering down of property in trusts however leads to recklessness, this is to say to feeding lawyers and boards, as well as the waste and misuse of funds contrary to the founder's intentions. After the founder's death, most large foundations or trusts distance themselves from his values, they are basically the equivalent of blocked accounts which one must ultimately leave to the disposal of agents.

Accumulation of capital that sustainably supports good framework conditions is a difficult task. It is ultimately similar to developing a company, with the difference that the purpose is not immediate income through value creation, but value creation in areas that cannot be monetized directly or completely. These areas include all those whose beneficiaries lack the ability to pay, or where the willingness to pay is lacking because one is too far ahead of one's time, or the beneficiaries cannot be directly identified. Returns will always play a role, as one could otherwise not speak of capital. However, a large part of human culture was created by such foundations: monasteries, schools, universities, sacred or other magnificent buildings, libraries, orders, settlements and towns, prizes, academies, festivals, sports facilities, sports associations and competitions, orphanages and hospitals, soup kitchens and homeless shelters.

All of this can in principle also be accomplished by means of a profit-oriented company or by a tax-funded authority (as is the rule today). However, in the status quo, markets and politics can exhibit too much of a short-term orientation due to the extant distortions, so that the efforts of companies and authorities do not suffice to hold back the community's destruction – rather, the destruction of culture and community may even be accelerated. For instance, the great cultural institution of the university is today almost completely destroyed; it has been usurped by tax-funded political institutions and debt-funded private producers of degrees. The same applies to nearly all the areas mentioned above. Whether the producers of things that are ugly, wrong and detrimental to the community are financed by banks or the state makes no big difference.

An endowment is thus the attempt to create sustainable structures, which give rise to values that go beyond immediate personal benefit. As a rule, it is more sensible in this context to focus on one or only a few endeavors and bear a shared entrepreneurial responsibility in the process. Charitable engagement does not exclude ownership responsibility from a legal perspective either, after all, charitable corporations exist as well. Only the arbitrary statist definition of the "common good", which similarly to the "public interest" is a term easily abused by ideological blinders, and the possible discrimination against such legal forms are arguing against this. In this area too, there are no recommendations that will be right for everybody, the task is first of all to correctly identify the problems. Profit orientation is not in conflict with endowment as it is understood here. Only, the focus is not on dividends, as profits are either not achieved for some time or are reinvested.

Speculation

In times of a bubble economy, all attention is focused on speculation. Today, many regard investment merely as the purchase of suitable financial instruments in order to sell them at a higher price once they have rallied. Speculation differs from investment insofar as the former seeks to profit from price changes, while the latter seeks a return on capital.

There is nothing illegitimate or damaging about speculation as such, contrary to what is nowadays often insinuated. The Austrian School is one of the few economic traditions that appreciate and defend speculation: all action is uncertain and thus necessarily speculative. Successful speculators level price differences by arbitrage, and help to better distribute dispersed knowledge in the economy by uncovering mistakes. The fact that speculation has become ubiquitous to such an extent and is attracting the broad masses to the stock exchanges is not the result of an immoral temptation, but of the artificial bloating of all asset prices. The expansion in fiduciary media sets a process in motion that is akin to a pyramid scheme: assets are no longer bought for their productive return, but in the expectation that one will find even greater fools whom one can sell them to at a higher price.

Speculation with one's own means is an important and honorable activity, if it is pursued earnestly. Earnest speculation consists of the attempt to discover errors in the markets. Mass buying after "information" has been received from the mass media can only be successful by sheer coincidence. It is like a lottery with conditions absurdly skewed in favor of the bank. Who would otherwise buy a lottery ticket for $100,000, promising a jackpot of e.g. $1,000,000 (and that would be the much yearned-for, but extremely rare ten-bagger, which everybody dreams of)? The artificial environment of continual devaluation and therefore recurring price explosions leads to "casino capitalism", which has relatively little to do with capital.

8. Austrian Investment Philosophy

Speculation fulfills an economically sensible function and brings on average positive returns to speculators, if they bring with them special knowledge, experience, intuition or talent – as in every other occupation. It is naive to believe that it is possible to find a short-cut on this path through investment tips. Today's flood of information certainly contains more than enough "tips", but speculation is about correct decisions with respect to the timing of one's buying and selling. Potential capital gains are correlated with risk: if a positive trend were certain, higher future prices would after all already be fully priced in, apart from the minimal discounting due to the low interest rate environment.

Employing hard-earned savings in speculation on a large scale as a hobby borders on willful negligence. However, it is not only greed that is a driver in this context, but rather panic due to the pressure created by monetary debasement. Indeed, even hoarding resembles speculation nowadays. The difference is only in intent. Speculation demands constant watching of prices, in order not to miss opportune points in time. Hoarding is a long-term accumulation activity and investing a long-term constructive activity, whereby both activities require one to ignore current nominal prices if possible, so as to keep one's wits about oneself.

Small degree speculation can however also be a hedge, a small additional insurance policy for hoards and capital. Laymen will tend to employ investment funds for this purpose though, as active management is essential. If one's own calling lies elsewhere, the effort bears as a rule no relationship to the return. The time one needs to invest in watching the markets, one can usually invest in one's own undertakings at a higher return.

One of its major functions makes speculation interesting for the typical saver as well though: namely, its educational value. Involvement in markets can be quite instructive, however, only if one does not get carried away by overconfidence based on short-term experiences, but instead if one approaches the markets with great humility. Trying to be smarter than the market rarely works. However, taking one's measure in the markets can give one an idea of the volatility of our age, and some may well discover that they have an extraordinary talent and with that a new calling. For purely pedagogical speculation, numerous simulations are available free of charge, i.e., virtual securities accounts. However, ventures that involve neither pain nor gain are rarely taken sufficiently seriously, and result in different behavior. In the worst case, these games end up feeding an overinflated self-confidence, which drives one to take fateful risks in the real world. Thus, if one wishes to make real bets, one should set aside a limited amount of speculative capital. Speculation must not take the place of saving and investing, but should be funded from one's consumption budget. After all, even well chosen consumer goods can achieve higher selling prices at a later point in time, if one finds an opportune moment to sell. In most cases, higher nominal prices are however a consequence of devaluation.

In an inflationary environment, especially good opportunities are offered to investors if they suspect hypes before they appear. Hypes are probable in sectors that are part of "big narratives". In the post-modern age, the yearning for such "narratives" is especially pronounced. These are narratives that link the mood of the present to promises about the future. Currently, especially dominant moods include: fears of scarcity (impoverishment), loneliness, lack of orientation, information overload, a void of meaning, a bad conscience, cognitive dissonance between reality and political correctness. Technologies and products that allow for narratives that address these concerns and wants, are predestined to become hypes. A hype, however, does not relate to the actual usefulness of a product or service, but to the narrative's suitability for dissemination.

Two concrete examples: a recent investment hype was provided by the 3-D printing sector. The printers can be integrated in Utopias of the end of scarcity, which are part of modern-day popular myths (such as the TV series *Star Trek*). Apart from simplifying the production of prototypes, 3-D printers however do not really offer anything akin to the abolition of scarcity, as the printed products are as a rule more expensive (i.e., require the employment of more means) than elements mass-produced by injection molding or other methods. Compared to mass-produced parts, the "printed" parts merely offer more and more individual variation of forms, but no qualitative advantage.

The second example concerns corporate hype: a female entrepreneur offered engineering toys for girls, which in terms of coloring and motives corresponded to typical toys for girls. As a product, it offers an atrocious price/performance ratio, and the whole concept is absurd. However, the media eagerly threw themselves at the narrative, namely that differences between the sexes that are perceived as negative could be offset by the purchase of toys. A high volume of orders was the result. More and more business formations are oriented toward this short-termism: translating mass-media attention into sales and thus attracting venture capital. Speculators who recognize the patterns of these attention bubbles can definitely achieve short-term profits. However, attention spans, and with them the cycles of such undertakings, are continually declining. Nevertheless, one piece of advice for investors can be deduced from this: do not underestimate the importance of narratives, i.e., the outward appearance and philosophy of an enterprise. A lot of value creation potential is contained in properly smartening up the meaningfulness and value of small, already existing companies and products, which the masses have not yet noticed.

A Philosophical Portfolio

The philosophical deliberations up to this point offer certain guidelines for weightings in wealth accumulation. As speculation in the narrower sense can either be a calling and with that a normal source of income (even though not a regular, but an entrepreneurial one), or can otherwise as a trial, entertainment and educational outlay be subsumed under consumption, four areas remain. These equate to four strategies, which are mutually dependent and conditional. Endowment, the long-term set-up of communal structures without a direct expectation of return, is the smallest of these areas. Traditional experience and religious recommendations prescribe a maximum of ten percent to this strategy. This is equivalent to the historical tithe, which was later, in conflict with biblical recommendations, usurped by compulsory levies. A tithe is an amount that respects the priority of the individual and his family relative to larger social units.

This allows one to deduce a rough formula, which can naturally only describe approximate ratios. Wealth is sustainably invested, if it is roughly distributed as follows: 30 percent in liquid hoards, 30 percent in capital (machines, tools, shares in companies, rented out real estate,...), 30 percent in durable consumer goods (owner-occupied real estate, art, high-value appliances...) and 10 percent in endowments (shares in enterprises for charitable, scientific, peace-promoting, cultural and environmental purposes).

What is the purpose of such guidelines? They prevent exaggeration, if one does not exaggerate the guidelines themselves nor take them too seriously – as in for instance breaking up successful enterprises merely in order to fulfill a quota. Division into small units is after all only possible with hoards, which is why they represent the first stage of investment. On the other hand, such guidelines should definitely provide an incentive to dissolve positions if relative prices are changing significantly. Fixed portfolio ratios have the advantage that they automatically lead one to strike a balance. Over a long period of time, this results in additional purchases at relatively low prices and sales at relatively high prices. This represents a good hedge against today's volatility. If one accumulates wealth over long time periods, one does not have to worry too much about opportune timing and can focus on more important things than erratic market movements.

The recommended division can also be used for the process of wealth accumulation and not only for keeping an eye on the weighting of assets. If one enjoys a regular income, such a piecemeal division is easier to implement. In this sense, 30 percent of the monthly difference between ones income and expenditures would initially be withdrawn

8. Austrian Investment Philosophy

in the form of cash and be exchanged for liquid hoards (for instance a one ounce gold coin). Such piecemeal purchases normalize price fluctuations over a longer time period. A further 30 percent remain in one's account for investment purposes, e.g. to increase selected shareholdings in companies (buying of stocks) or to increase one's own value creation efforts. Investments in securities in the capital markets can be complemented by hedges (funds), to an extent that bears a reasonable relationship to the capital employed. If no investment opportunities arise in the course of a year, hoards are increased and dissolved when favorable opportunities are discerned. A further 30 percent of one's monthly available savings are spent on increasing one's quality of life and the value of one's household and residence. If there is no better use for them, a portion of these funds can be used for instructive speculation, bearing in mind the basic rule that one should never expand speculative positions beyond a predetermined budget, even (or especially) after a lucky streak. The remaining ten percent are invested progressively in setting up and developing better communal framework conditions. In the best case, wealth accumulation will become a long-term habit, which allows one to sleep well, because it no longer consists of big and panicky decisions after which one has to worry daily about market prices, but rather of many small drops that are filling a reservoir.

Such a "formula" is naturally not sufficient, it is merely a beginning. We live in a time that is extremely unfavorable for the accumulation of wealth. However, we are still forced to make decisions against this backdrop of growing uncertainty. The best investment decisions can encompass an incredible range: 50,000 dollars in cash, which one can have at one's disposal within a day when someone else needs to sell urgently, can be worth more than 1,000,000 dollars in shares; 1,000 dollars for a Chinese language course can be worth more than a life insurance policy; 100 dollars for software plus the time needed to learn how to operate it can be worth more than a property; coins buried a decade ago and forgotten can be worth more than a savings account filled to the brim. One needs to go through life with one's eyes open, be active, full of zest for life, value-oriented and adopt a long-term perspective, while paying attention to liquidity, entrepreneurial opportunities, the quality of life and possible problems in one's environment and the opportunities to fix them.

In the following pages, we want to take a look at which traditional vehicles for hoarding, investments and speculation investors can choose from. Hoards include cash currency and foreign exchange, precious metals, bank deposits and money market positions, investments include stocks and bonds under certain preconditions, most other financial instruments should be considered speculation.

9. Austrian Investment Practice

Investors who want to invest money according to the tenets of the Austrian School are in spite of – or even because of – being more knowledgeable in terms of economic theory, subject to certain risks and dangers; these should definitely be taken into account when making investment decisions. Thus knowledge about the nature of the currency and fractional reserve banking system as well as Austrian business cycle, interest and capital theory can in certain situations prove to be dangerous: whether consciously or unconsciously, one tends to be prejudiced with regard to investment decisions. Due to their critical examination of markets and framework conditions, many "Austrians" exhibit a bearish bias: trends are judged too pessimistically.

Closely tied to this bearish bias is the problem of correct timing, which can lead to being wrongly positioned at certain junctures. The following figures illustrate this problem. When William Anderson warned about the dot-com bubble in 1999, the Nasdaq had not even reached half of its subsequent year 2000 peak. If one had bet on falling prices in 1999, one would not only have missed the biggest part of the artificial rally, but suffered losses instead. A similar picture emerges in the subsequent real estate bubble. After Mark Thornton warned in 2004 that bailouts would eventually occur, US real estate stocks continued to rise for almost three years.

9. Austrian Investment Practice

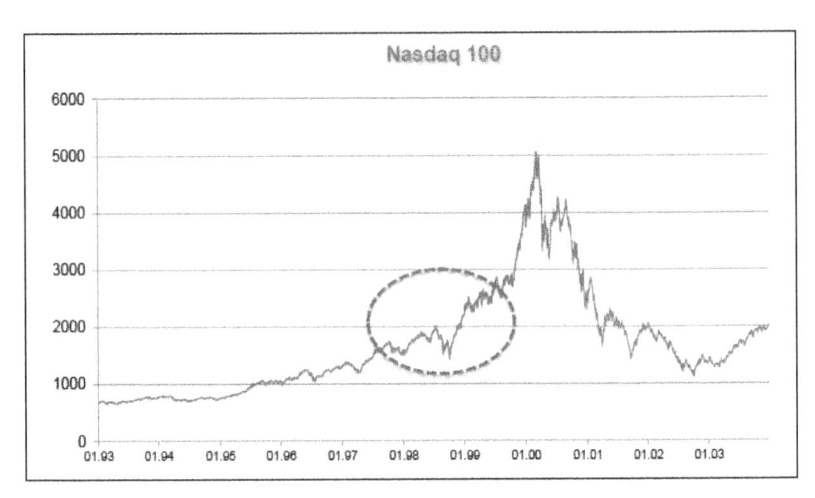

Figure 9.1.: Nasdaq 100 (Source: Federal Reserve St. Louis)

William Anderson: "While we may be currently celebrating a record boom, we have not overturned the laws of economics. No doubt when it happens, the usual Keynesians in the halls of academe and in the media will blame high interest rates and the Fed's refusal to expand credit."[114]

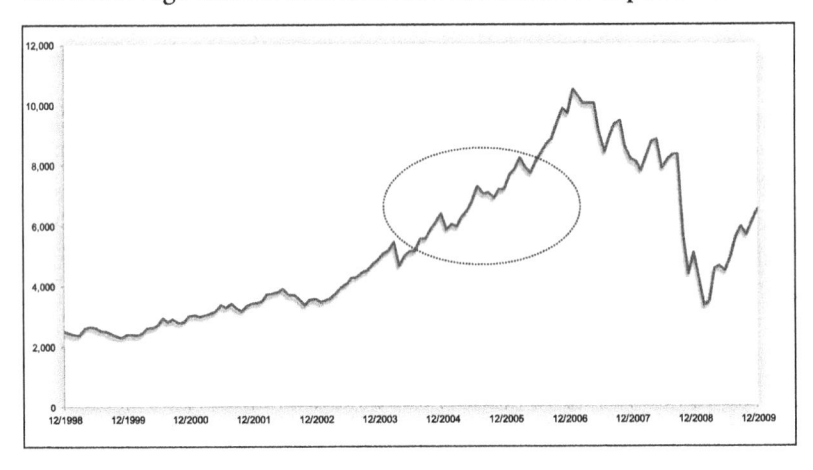

Figure 9.2: US real estate stocks (FTSE NAREIT) (Source: Bloomberg)

9. Austrian Investment Practice

Mark Thornton: "Given the government's encouragement of lax lending practices, home prices could crash, bankruptcies could increase, and financial companies, including the government-sponsored mortgage companies, might require another taxpayer bailout."[115]

Another danger for "Austrian investors" could arise from the risk allocation problem. Due to widespread mispricing in the market during an artificial boom, the discovery process of the crisis tends to go hand in hand with significant market reactions. One consequence of the bubble economy is an artificial increase in volatility. Choosing too extreme a portfolio, which some "Austrians" may be tempted to do due to their apodictic views, leads to the possibility of being unable to withstand strong fluctuations. An "Austrian" investor's strong convictions can lead to stubborn positioning, while the rest of the market acts differently due to ignorance.

We do not believe that there is such a thing as the correct Austrian investment process. Austrian Investing in our minds could be defined as "the utilization of guiding principles of the Austrian School of Economics for investment decisions". Below we want to discuss different forms and aspects of investment from an "Austrian" perspective. In common parlance, "traditional" and "alternative" forms of investments are differentiated. Among traditional forms of investment are securities in the widest sense, which contribute to the financing of companies and governments. Titles to equity capital are called stocks, titles to external capital bonds. Securities are offered as a bundle in funds (including ETFs). Among alternative investment classes are e.g. hedge funds, direct stakes in companies and art.

It is a widely held erroneous belief that the capital markets represent a zero sum game. Investors buy stocks (respectively bonds) in order to obtain a claim on a company's future returns. These are either distributed as dividends, or reinvested in the business. Companies use external financing because they need additional resources, in order to fund research and development projects and acquire productive capital. These investments are aimed at increasing productivity, respectively

9. Austrian Investment Practice

sales. The exchange is regarded as advantageous by both sides (in advance) and in the event of a successful investment represents a positive sum game, since additional value could be created. Contrary to the capital markets, derivatives markets can indeed be regarded as a zero sum game. Hedges on future price trends of financial assets (or commodities) are traded in these markets. In this case, the rule that always applies is: one man's joy is another man's sorrow.

	type of investment	liquidity	cashflow	counterparty / entrepreneurial risk	taxation / expropriation risk
money market investment	traditional	high	yes	yes	high
Bonds	traditional	high	yes	yes	high
Stocks	traditional	high	yes	yes	high
securities fund	traditional	high	yes (pay-out)	yes	high
derivatives (listed)	alternative	high	no	yes (clearing house)	high
hedge funds	alternative	medium	no	yes	high
company shares	alternative	low	yes	yes	high
private equity funds	alternative	low	yes	yes	high
real estate	alternative	low	yes	yes	medium
precious metals	alternative	high	no	no	low
Art	alternative	low	no	no	low
Jewelry	alternative	medium	no	no	low

Figure 9.3: Forms of investments and their specific characteristics (Source: Incrementum AG)

9. Austrian Investment Practice

Another popular misconception is cemented by regularly repeated headlines in the financial press. After unusually negative price trends in the stock market, it is often reported that within the recent trading period, a certain – often impressively large – amount of money has been destroyed on the stock exchange. However, money is neither created nor destroyed on the stock exchange. Traded prices merely reflect expected returns in the respective local currency. A plunge in stock prices can happen even if not a single stock changes hands. John Mills has already formulated this quite trenchantly:

> Panics do not destroy capital; they merely reveal the extent to which it has been destroyed by its betrayal into hopelessly unproductive works.[116]

Sources of Information

The internet offers private investors a wide universe of possibilities for price data, securities selection, technical and fundamental analysis, news, exchange of opinions in forums, and of course online brokerages. The following sites lend themselves to general information that is helpful for investment and speculation:

- In the English-speaking world, *Yahoo Finance, Bloomberg.com, investing.com, Money.MSN.com, marketwatch.com, financialsense.com* and *seekingalpha.com* are excellent and extremely comprehensive sources of information.
- For technical analysis, there are among others *stockcharts.com, bigcharts.com, Google Finance, Zignals.com* or *TradingView.com.*
- At *Investopedia.com* one can improve one's financial knowledge.
- A neat and above all comprehensive calendar for the release of market-relevant macro data and statistics can be found at *mam.econoday.com.*
- Some useful blogs commentating current developments from the Austrian perspective include *acting-man.com* and *viennacapitalist.com.*

- A lot of interesting information is provided by the so-called alternative media. Interesting financial news especially regarding financial repression is provided for instance by *gordontlong.com*.
- Probably the most interesting financial market research from an Austrian perspective for institutional investors is provided by Dr. Frank Shostak's *AAS Economics*.

Screening

Screening refers to the selection of securities according to certain criteria. One of the best tools for this purpose is provided by *finviz.com*. The site provides more than 50 screens using a plethora of descriptive (stock exchange, sector, country of origin, analyst consensus, trading volume), fundamental (P/E ratio, price/cash, debt and growth metrics, etc.) as well as technical (volatility, RSI, candlestick formations) criteria. In addition, trading activities of insiders and company descriptions can be screened. A disadvantage is the site's sole focus on the North American markets (approximately 6,500 US and Canadian stocks).

A much larger universe of stocks is offered by *ft.com/marketsdata*. All in all, 40,000 securities from all over the world can be compared with the help of 50 screens. Especially interesting are the predetermined search criteria based on well-known "guru" strategies, such as those of Warren Buffett, Benjamin Graham, or Martin Zweig. Even more comprehensive is the Google screener *(google.com/finance/stockscreener)*, which comprises nearly 50,000 stocks and 60 screening criteria.

Brokerage Firms

For better or for worse, banking services are indispensable for the implementation of speculative, but also many productive investments. As a general rule, securities custody accounts at banks in most cases involve higher fees and offer fewer possibilities than those at online brokerage firms. The specific selection depends among other things on the frequency of orders, the asset classes traded and the size of one's portfolio. A good overview of the best brokerage firms (ordered by instruments, e.g. brokers for options, difference contracts, structured products, foreign exchange, stocks, etc.) is offered by *stockbrokers.com/compare* and *fool.com/how-to-invest/broker/*.

The Permanent Portfolio

One of the possibilities to transpose the "Austrian" investment philosophy as we have described it above into an actual portfolio is the so-called "permanent portfolio". It was developed by Harry Browne, a famous US investment analyst, in the early 1970s.[117] Browne was strongly influenced by the Austrian School. It is one of the most simple investment concepts, which, while it can of course also not truly resolve the problem of concrete allocation in distorted markets, is impressive due to its simplicity and consequently easy implementation. At the core of its approach is the humble (and very "Austrian") insight that the future cannot be foreseen, and investors should therefore diversify their funds in such a manner that they are equally well prepared for any possible economic environment (economic prosperity, recession, inflation, deflation). The individual asset classes it comprises tend to be non-correlated in different economic scenarios. For this reason, the permanent portfolio consists of gold, cash, stocks and bonds, with a weighting of 25% for each. The four economic scenarios that are covered in this manner are:

- Inflationary growth (favorable for stocks and gold)
- Disinflationary growth (favorable for stocks and bonds)
- Deflationary stagnation (favorable for cash and bonds)
- Inflationary stagnation (favorable for gold and cash)

9. Austrian Investment Practice

Figure 9.4. shows in some more detail which economic environment affects the examined asset classes positively respectively negatively. The combination of the four building blocks results in long-term stable returns with significantly reduced volatility. In this respect, the permanent portfolio is not a get-rich-quick approach. Significantly higher returns can only be achieved with highly concentrated portfolios, which entail significantly greater risks:

asset class	positive environment	negative environment
Stocks	• economic boom • rising investor confidence	• strongly increasing inflation rates • deflation • periods of great anxiety and loss of confidence
Bonds	• economic downswing • (slightly) deflationary environment	• strongly increasing inflation rates • increased credit risk • rising interest rates
Cash	• strained credit environment • deflation • rising interest rates	• strong inflation • economic boom
Gold	• rising inflation rates • deflation • diminishing of investor confidence	• rising investor confidence • clearly positive (or rising) real interest rates

Figure 9.4: Positive vs. negative environment for different asset classes (Source: Incrementum AG)

The notion that stocks become less risky the longer they are held is a fallacy. The "fallacy of temporal diversification" was unmasked by John Norstad, when he discovered that the S&P 500 Index had lost

4.62% of its inflation-adjusted value in the 15 years from 1968 to 1982. The probability that investors can sit out such long periods of time is vanishingly small. The permanent portfolio exhibits far more stable returns than for instance traditional balanced growth portfolios, which in most cases consist of 70% bonds and 30% stocks. Figure 9.5 shows the nominal and real returns of the permanent portfolio from 1972 to 2010. At closer inspection, three characteristics are especially noteworthy. Firstly: the portfolio has generated respectable growth. The average return of 9.2% per year equals that of far more risky investment portfolios. Indeed, the return is almost identical to the 9.8% generated by a portfolio 100% invested in stocks, whereby this return would only have been achieved with far greater volatility.

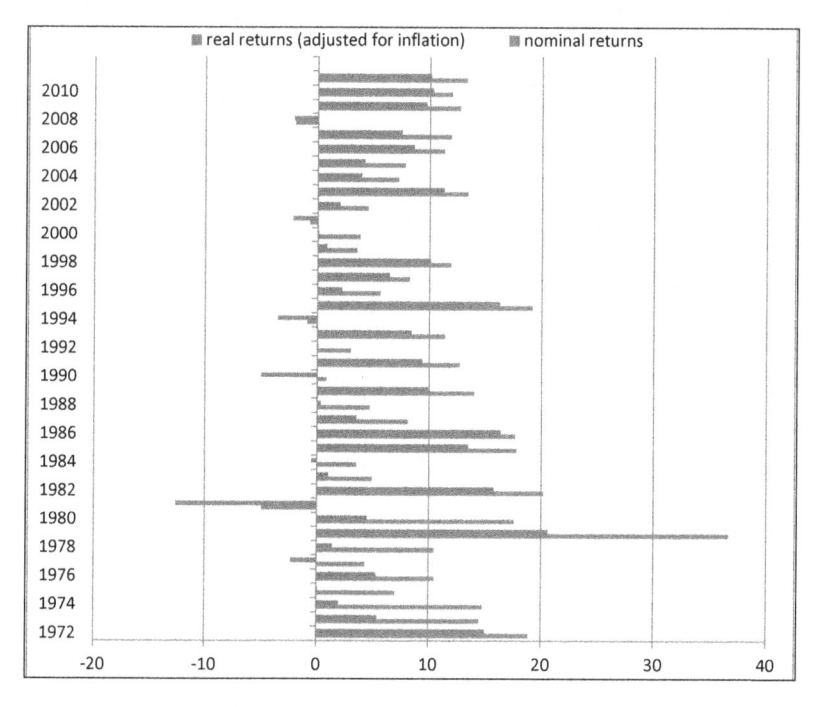

Figure 9.5: Annual return of the permanent portfolio, 1972-2010: nominal and real performance (Source: Datastream)

The second characteristic is that the portfolio exhibited no large losses. The number of loss-making years is very small. Moreover, the losses in those years were quite modest. In its worst year, the portfolio recorded a nominal loss of 4.9%, respectively 12.6% adjusted for inflation (in 1981). This is a moderate loss compared to pure stock portfolios. Furthermore, the permanent portfolio recouped the loss the following year with a real gain of 16%.

Thirdly, the real return column displays mainly positive values over the time period examined. This means that the permanent portfolio was able to generate returns for investors that were significantly above the rate of inflation, irrespective of market trends. In short: the portfolio generated real returns. Inflation adjusted returns are extremely important for the evaluation and comparison of investment strategies, a fact that is often overlooked.

An additional important characteristic is the requirement to balance the weightings in the portfolio on a regular basis. As soon as the share of an asset class exceeds 35% or falls below 15%, it is balanced back to a 25% share. In practice, the component that stands at or above 35% is reduced until its share in the portfolio is back at 25%, and the component that stands below 15% is added to until its weighting is back at 25%. This concept takes the phenomenon of mean reversion into account, as well as the fact that markets tend to be prone to exaggerations, which are corrected again over time. In keeping with the saying: the higher they climb, the harder they fall – and vice versa. This rather rare re-weighting is based on the philosophy that the maintenance effort for the portfolio should be kept at a relatively low level and that one cannot foresee when an opportune time for shifts within the portfolio has arrived. As a result, the portfolio is indeed a relatively low-maintenance one, as no specific timing decisions need to be made and costs are kept in check due to the low frequency of transactions. How important transaction costs are for the long-term performance of a portfolio can be seen in figure 9.6, which depicts the hypothetical effect of different fees on an investment with a 10% gross return per year:

initial value	expenses	earnings after expenses	years	final value	expenses
$10,000	0%	10%	20	$67,275	$0
$10,000	0.1%	9.9%	20	$66,062	$1,213
$10,000	0.2%	9.8%	20	$64,870	$2,405
$10,000	1%	9%	20	$56,044	$11,231
$10,000	2%	8%	20	$46,609	$21,116
$10,000	3%	7%	20	$38,696	$28,579

Figure 9.6: Fee percentage: important for investment success in the long term (Source: Incrementum AG)

Additional rules for investors include not leaving one's own decisions to others, not investing in companies or instruments one does not understand, and to include a portion of investment outside of one's country of residence. The latter is known as geographical diversification. It protects investors from risks ranging from natural catastrophes to government decrees. The point is not to hide money from the tax authority, but solely to hedge against extreme developments. Emotions including greed, envy or fear often play a major role in investment decisions and are often responsible for failures. The rules of the permanent portfolio – many of which are simply based on common sense – help to protect one's savings by taking these dangers into account.

The overall development of the portfolio is based on three principles. The first is that a good growth rate can increase the value of the investment over a long time period, without taking undue risks. The second principle is avoiding large losses. It is difficult to recover from such losses without taking high risks (which can make the situation even worse), having a lot of luck, or simply waiting for a long time (which is usually not an acceptable alternative for investors close to retirement). The third decisive principle is the focus on real returns. Inflation must never be ignored when evaluating returns.

There are currently two funds that are managed according to the principles of the permanent portfolio: The Permanent Portfolio Fund (ticker: PRPFX) was launched in 1982 and currently manages approximately $16 billion, and the permanent ETF (ticker: PERM) that was launched in 2012. Figure 9.7 illustrates however that the actual investment strategy of the two funds diverges somewhat from Harry Browne's original recommendation.

asset class	Harry Browne	Permanent Portfolio Fund	Permanent Portfolio ETF
stocks	25% - stocks of US enterprises with a high market capitalization	15% - strongly increasing stocks 15% - non-U.S. real estate and commodity stocks	9% - stocks of U.S. enterprises with a high market capitalization 3% - stocks of U.S. enterprises with a low market capitalization 3% - stocks of international companies 5% - U.S. real estate stocks 5% - U.S. and foreign commodity stocks
bonds	25% - long-term U.S. treasuries (>25 years time to maturity)	35% - U.S. treasury bills and other investments based on the U.S. dollar (about 7%)	25% - long-term U.S. treasuries (<20 years time to maturity)
gold	25% - physical gold	20% - gold coins and gold bullions	20% - exchange-traded gold funds and securities 5% - exchange-traded silver funds and securities
liquid assets	25% - liquid assets in U.S. dollar	10% - investments based on the Swiss franc	25% - U.S. treasury bonds and short-term U.S. government bonds (<3 years time to maturity)

Figure 9.7: Implementation of the principles of the permanent portfolio (Source: Incrementum AG)

Precious Metals

We have already discussed in previous chapters why the monetary experiments of our time are likely to lead to extreme distortions in financial markets. There exists no instruction manual for the current financial era. We believe that this period of uncertainty will be followed by a harking back to traditional monetary virtues. In the current environment, gold plays the role of a monetary insurance policy. Antony Sutton describes the counter-cyclical character of an investment in gold as follows:

> Those entrapped by the herd instinct are drowned in the deluges of history. But there are always the few who observe, reason, and take precautions, and thus escape the flood. For these few, gold has been the asset of last resort.[118]

As noted above, precious metals are characterized by their high marketability. The monetary importance of a good is all the more pronounced the easier it can be exchanged for other goods. The marginal utility of gold declines at a slower rate than that of other goods. It is owing to this superior characteristic that gold and silver enjoy their monetary status, and not their supposed scarcity. Their high marketability represents also their decisive advantage over other stores of value, such as real estate or works of art. In crisis situations, these are very difficult to liquidate at acceptable prices, especially in the short term. For this reason, central banks hold gold as a currency reserve, and not real estate, artworks or commodities.

9. Austrian Investment Practice

Gold and Inflation

Most analysts assert that gold has the characteristics of an inflation hedge. There are, however, also critical voices. They opine that there is no statistical correlation between gold prices and price inflation rates, and conclude that the inflation hedge notion is thus a myth. We examined this question and drew the following conclusion: gold does not correlate with the rate of inflation as such, but with the rate of change of the inflation rate. In order to buttress this hypothesis, we calculated the regression depicted in figure 9.8.[119]

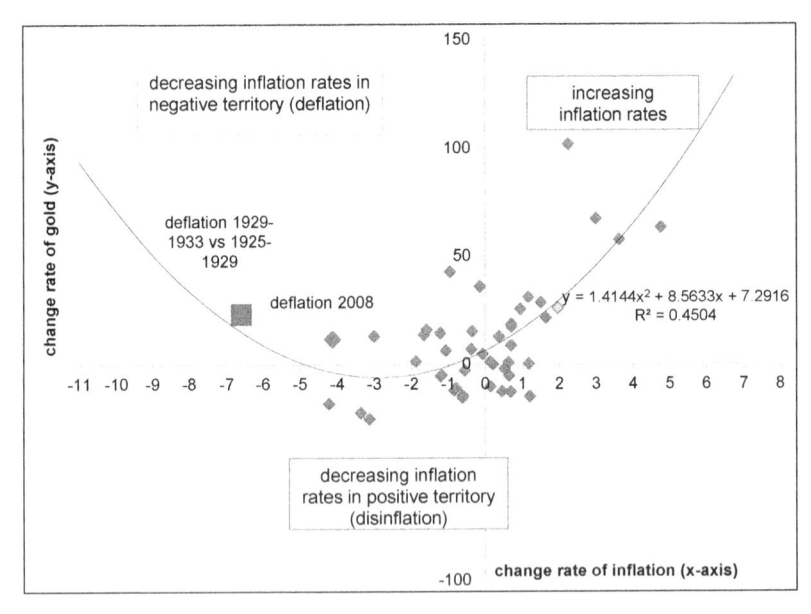

Figure 9.8: Change in the rate of price inflation vs. change in the gold price (Sources: Federal Reserve St. Louis, Incrementum AG)

Explanation: the data were collected on an annual basis since the end of the Bretton Woods agreement. The data point in red is not included in the calculation of the regression. It serves to support the hypothesis,

258

since this was the only time period in which there was a notable move in the gold price prior to 1971. The data point fits astonishingly well with the regression curve and confirms that gold exhibits a positive trend both in real and nominal terms during price deflation. Periods of disinflation, this is to say declining inflation rates that are still in positive territory, such as were observed in 2012 and 2013, thus represent the most unfavorable environment for the gold price.

Gold and Deflation

Positive attributes are only ascribed to gold in periods of high, respectively rising price inflation. This view can probably be traced back to the 20 year long bear market during the period of disinflation of the 1980s and 1990s. By means of a simple extrapolation, it was concluded that if gold is already weakening in a period of disinflation, it must be even weaker in a period of deflation. This is however a fallacy. The trend of gold in a deflationary environment has barely been analyzed, not least because there exist only very few examples of deflationary periods. The Great Depression of the 1930s is certainly relevant in this context. However, during this period, there was a gold standard in the US and practically the whole world, and gold prices were therefore fixed. Thus it can be estimated what the gold price would have done by examining the devaluation of various currencies after the abandonment of the gold standard. For instance, Great Britain devalued the pound by 51% in 1931, and the US followed suit revaluing gold upward by 60% (an increase from $20.67 to $35 per troy ounce).

9. Austrian Investment Practice

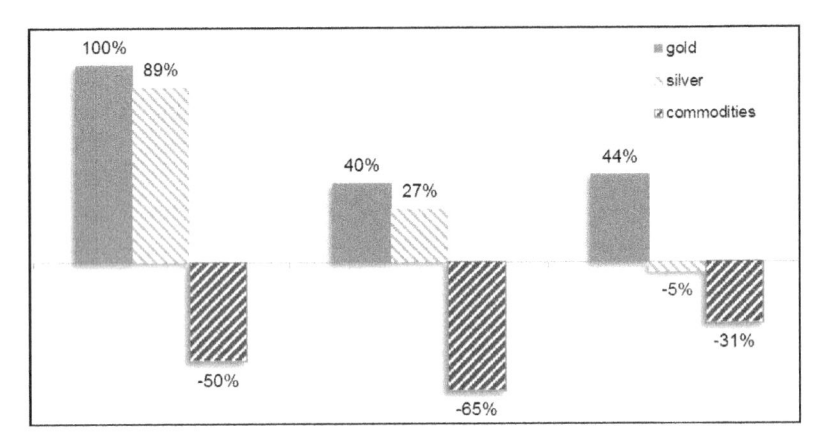

Figure 9.9: Gold, silver, and commodities in deflation
(Sources: Roy Jastram, *The Golden Constant*, resp. *Silver, the Restless Metal*, Erste Group Research)

This could be a hint that during the period of fixed gold prices, enormous buying pressure was building up. In 1933, gold reserves had already declined to a level close to the minimum requirement, which is why president Roosevelt ordered the confiscation of private gold reserves. As a result of the gold expropriation, the black market flourished and very considerable funds flowed into the gold mining sector. According to the US Bureau of Mines, there were 9,000 producing gold mines in the US in 1940. The stocks of the majority of listed gold companies rallied during this time, not only in relative, but also in absolute terms. For instance, the price of Homestake Mining, at the time the most important gold producer, rose within a few years from $75 (1929) to $500 (1935). In addition, dividends totaling $130 were paid out over this time period. Since the price of gold was fixed and the most important input costs (e.g. energy and labor) were exhibiting a deflationary trend, the profit margins of gold miners increased sharply.

In a period of pronounced deflation, government budgets become overstretched, the financial sector is faced with systemic problems, and currencies are devalued in order to reflate the system. Credit quality gradually declines, and the creditworthiness of companies and governments comes into doubt. A change in thinking takes place, with capital maintenance becoming more important than capital growth. Trust in the financial system and paper currencies declines, while gold gains in importance due its top-notch credit quality, and a rediscovery of its monetary significance.

In modern times, a good example for this was provided by the sovereign debt crisis in the euro area between 2010 and 2012. The European banking system suddenly found itself in dire straits: a major part of its capital held in the form of sovereign bonds was under threat, and short-term funding in the capital markets dried up. This made it increasingly difficult to finance long-term assets on the balance sheets of banks. The overall effect of these developments was deflationary: banks ceased to extend new credit and instead attempted to call in outstanding loans wherever possible. Money supply growth rates began to decline precipitously, and even went sharply negative in the peripheral countries that were hardest hit by the crisis. Depositors began to fear for their deposits. Large depositors fled from the euro area to the US, where unlimited deposit insurance temporarily granted by the FDIC in the wake of the mortgage credit crisis of 2008 was still in force.

All over Europe, the demand for gold increased substantially, as people sought to insure themselves against a possible break-up of the euro and the possibility of the banking crisis spiraling out of control. The gold holdings of bullion ETFs soared as well, and while the amounts involved were small relative to the entire gold market, they did serve as a good indicator for sentiment towards gold at the time. What this demonstrated was that people are well aware that genuine deflation represents a grave risk for a fractionally reserved banking system and that the fiduciary media held in demand deposits are in danger of losing their otherwise assumed monetary character. As was later seen in Cyprus, such deposits are no longer money when banks become insolvent and the government lacks the means to bail depositors out. Instead, they are suddenly revealed as just another claim of creditors that can no longer be serviced. By accumulating gold held outside of the banking system, people were able to mitigate both this danger and the danger inherent in a potential reconversion from the euro to the previous domestic currency.

The most famous schematic illustration of a deflationary downward spiral is by US economist and vice president of the New York Fed, John Exeter. Akin to an hourglass, liquidity in the financial system gradually flows downward as the willingness to take risks declines. At the top are speculative investments, from which liquidity is increasingly removed due to the loss of confidence, which exerts price pressure on them. A sellers' market becomes a buyers' market. As is well known, credit is "suspicion asleep", and as a result, creditors attempt to steadily sell more illiquid asset classes and move their funds to asset classes at lower levels as risk aversion increases. At the very bottom is gold. Due to general skepticism, the circulation of gold declines as it is increasingly hoarded. The degree of hoarding is always proportional to the confidence in government and its currency. Gold is never scarce, except if it is hoarded – for good reasons – and hidden away on purpose. Since no promises to pay are associated with gold, it is the only alternative to paper currencies and is therefore at the very bottom of the inverted pyramid.

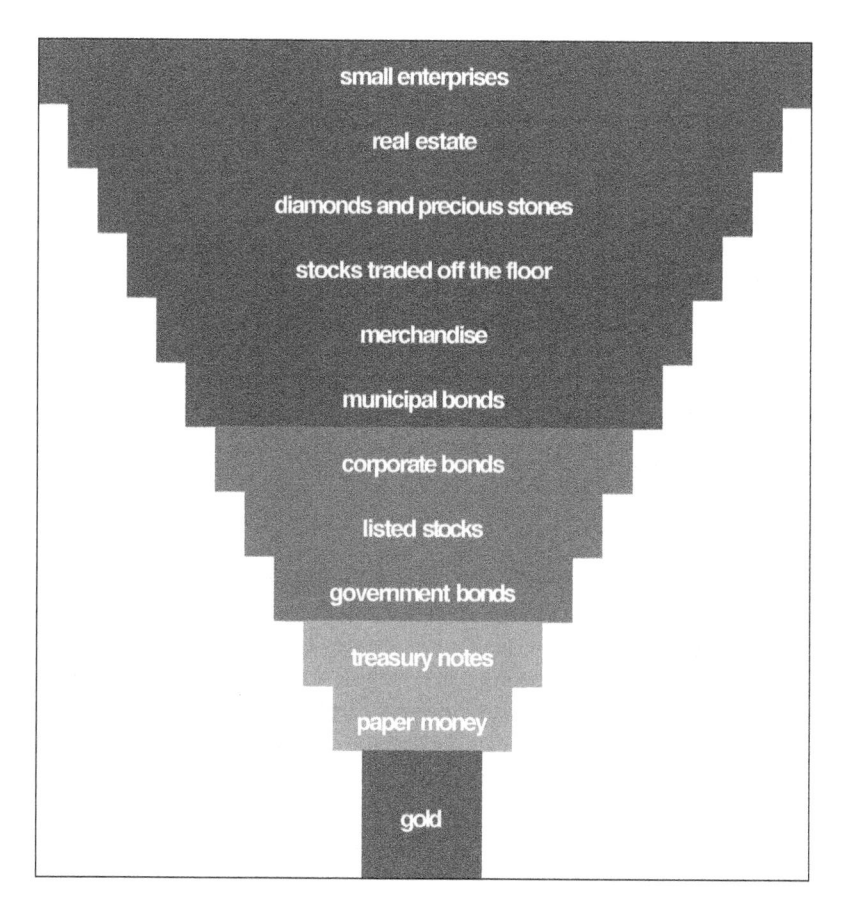

[Inverted pyramid diagram, from top (widest) to bottom (narrowest):
- small enterprises
- real estate
- diamonds and precious stones
- stocks traded off the floor
- merchandise
- municipal bonds
- corporate bonds
- listed stocks
- government bonds
- treasury notes
- paper money
- gold]

Figure 9.10: Exeter's pyramid

In the event of increasing prosperity and growing confidence, risk appetites increase again and liquidity begins to once again gradually flow from the gold sector into segments of the pyramid above it. A new cycle begins. Deflation thus means that the quality of money improves, while inflation means that its quantity increases.

9. Austrian Investment Practice

Gold and Real Interest Rates

One of the most important metrics for the gold price is the level, respectively the trend of real interest rates. There has always been a strong correlation between negative real interest rates and a rising gold price. Why is this the case? The renunciation of interest returns equals the opportunity cost of holding gold. Thus, when real interest rates rise, opportunity costs for gold owners increase, which most often has a negative effect on its price. The lower yields are, the less attractive bonds are relative to gold. Negative real interest rates are therefore a primary driver of gold bull markets. Additional important factors are the growth rate of monetary aggregates, political risks, the volume and quality of outstanding debt, as well as the attractiveness of competing asset classes.

Negative real interest rates are continually mentioned as a supposed solution to the problem of over-indebtedness. In figure 9.11, one can discern that negative real interest rates have provided the perfect foundation for positive gold price trends. In the previous great gold bull market of the 1970s, real interest rates were in negative territory most of the time. After Paul Volcker hiked short-term rates massively and implemented his strong dollar policy, he also ended gold's bull market. In the 1980s and 1990s, real interest rates were negative only 5.9% of the time. This was a bearish environment for gold investments, as opportunity costs were too high and stocks and bonds were more attractive. However, in the year 2000, the environment changed in favor of gold again. Since then, real interest rates have once again spent most of the time in negative territory.

Figure 9.12 confirms this as well. The first column shows the percentage of all months during which the real yield of US treasuries stood below 1%. The second column shows the nominal return of gold for the respective time period and the third column shows gold's real return.

Precious Metals

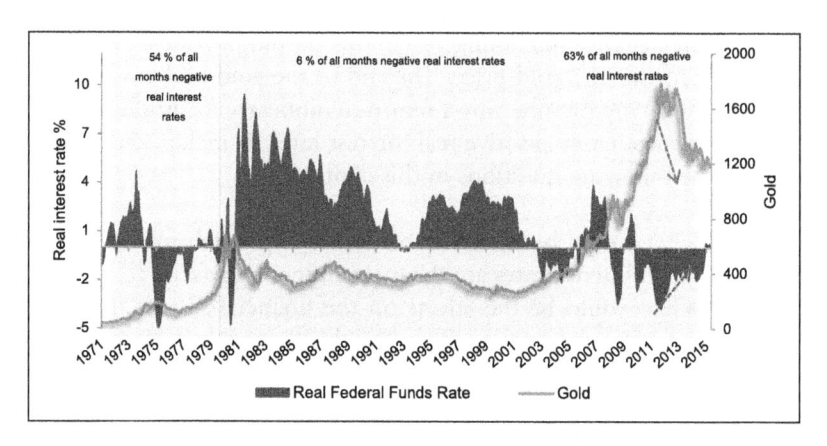

Figure 9.11: Real interest rates vs. the gold price since 1971 (Source: Federal Reserve St. Louis)

decade	percent of all months with real interest rates under 1%	nominal returns per decade	real returns per decade
1970s	50%	1356%	627%
1980s	11%	−22%	−53%
1990s	25%	−28%	−46%
2000s	60%	281%	196%
2010-2013	64%	26%	20%

Figure 9.12: Real yields of US treasuries vs. nominal and real return of gold (Source: Erste Group Research)

Due to the over-indebtedness problem and the pseudo-solution of "financial repression", we expect that real interest rates will remain low,

265

respectively negative in coming years. This should provide an excellent environment for the gold price. The end of the gold bull market thus would have to involve not only a return to monetary rectitude, but also rising and sustainably positive real interest rates. It makes sense to ask oneself the following questions in this context:

1. What would be the effect on valuation models for stocks, for which interest rates are the main influencing factor?
2. What would be the effects on the financial sector, and especially the short-term effects on the economy, if interest rates were to rise significantly?
3. What would be the effect on the bond market, especially the junk bond sector and emerging market bonds?

Gold as a Portfolio Hedge

Gold has numerous qualities that make it a major pillar of a balanced and long-term oriented investment strategy. Gold exhibits a very low correlation with most other asset classes, especially stocks and bonds. Since 1970, its correlation with the S&P 500 Index stands at -0.18 and at -0.04 with 10-year treasury notes. Gold as a non-correlated asset class therefore represents a means of portfolio diversification. Similar correlations are also evident over shorter time periods. Figure 9.13 shows gold's 5-year correlation coefficient to commodities, stocks and bonds.

Figure 9.14 shows quite impressively why gold is also often referred to as an event hedge. It shows the annual price moves in gold and the S&P 500, ordered by the worst years for the S&P 500 (i.e., crash years are listed on the left hand side). One can see that gold has not only exhibited a better trend on a relative basis, but also in absolute terms during these terrible dark-red years. However, the same also applies vice versa.

Precious Metals

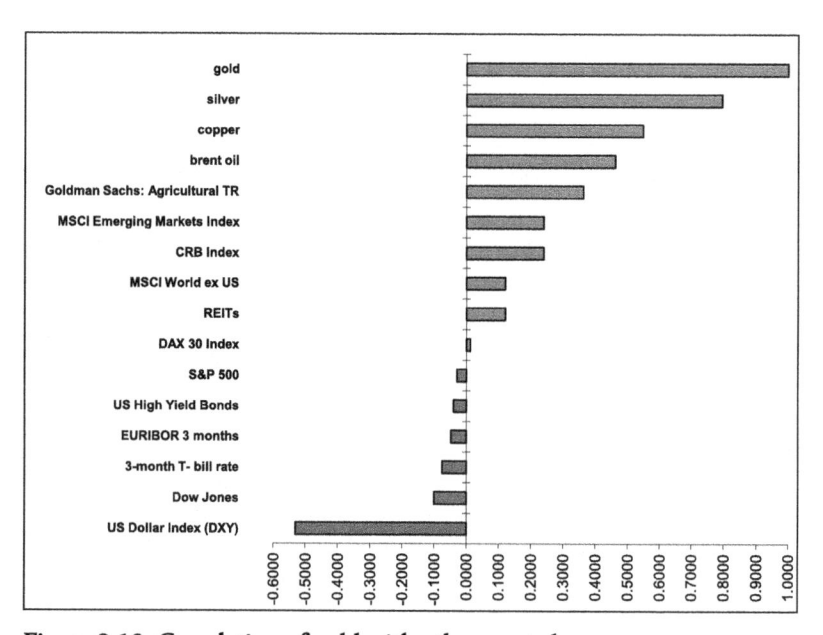

**Figure 9.13: Correlation of gold with other asset classes
(Sources: Datastream, Erste Group Research)**

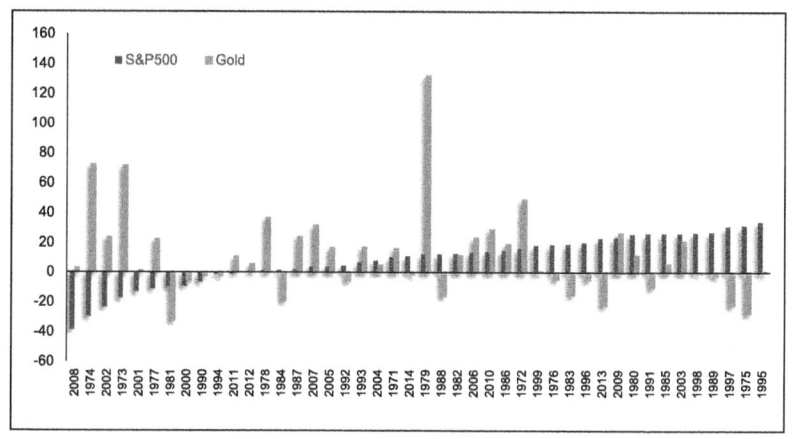

Figure 9.14: Annual performance of gold vs. S&P 500, ordered by weakest years for the S&P 500 (Sources: Datastream, Erste Group Research)

267

Numerous academic studies[120] on the performance characteristics of gold exist. The majority of them conclude that gold lowers a portfolio's overall risk and decreases its fluctuations, especially in periods of extremely high volatility. Most studies recommend a gold allocation of between 5% and 10% of one's total wealth. In light of the monetary experiments currently under way, we would employ a significantly higher percentage. A rule of thumb with respect to this is that the proportion of gold should be roughly equivalent to the expected probability of the occurrence of extreme scenarios. If one assumes that the probability of hyperinflation or a currency reform stands at 50%, the share of gold in one's portfolio should accordingly stand at 50%.

Due to its unique characteristics, gold is one of the few sensible hedging instruments in the current period of monetary ruination and excessive indebtedness. It is presumably the only liquid asset that is not subject to some creditor relationship. It is independent of governments, and a means of payment that is accepted and recognized on every continent, and has hitherto survived every government bankruptcy and every war. We expect that the current crisis period will eventually bring about a return to sound money and that the monetary importance of gold, which has established itself over the past several centuries, will be rediscovered.

Precious Metals

	type of investment	transaction costs	counterparty risk / entrepreneurial risk	correlation with gold/silver	storage
physical investment	numismatic coins	very high	none	medium	storage costs / risk of theft
	bullion coins gold	low	none	1	storage costs / risk of theft
	gold bullions	low	none	1	storage costs / risk of theft
	bullion coins silver	medium	none	1	low value density!
	silver bullions	medium	none	1	low value density!
securities on precious metals	ETFs, ETCs	low	conceivably (prospect)	very high	custody account
	futures / options	very low	conceivably (stock exchange)	very high	custody account
	certificates / warrants	high	issuer	very high	custody account
Stocks	silver mining stocks	low	entrepreneurial risk	medium (stock risk)	custody account
	gold mining stocks	low	entrepreneurial risk	medium (stock risk)	custody account
	mining funds	high	entrepreneurial risk	medium (stock risk)	custody account

Figure 9.15: Comparison of different types of precious metal investments (source: Incrementum AG)

9. Austrian Investment Practice

The Stock-to-Flow Ratio

The probably most important characteristic that distinguishes gold from its peers and explains its monetary significance is its high stock-to-flow ratio. The total gold mined in the course of history currently amounts to approximately 175,000 tons. This is the extant stock of gold. Annual mine production amounted to approx. 2,700 tons in 2012. This is the annual flow. If one divides the stock through the flow, one gets a stock-to-flow ratio of 64.8. Philip Barton explains the historical background of this relatively large stock of gold:

> There is a start to everything. A stock of 174,000 tonnes does not just suddenly appear; it is the end result of a long, process of incremental accumulation. At a moment in time, way back at the dawn of human history, the fateful decision was made to begin to accumulate Gold. One person made that decision. Others followed this first unknown and unsung hero. Yet no one would put aside a dozen eggs or some iron bars and expect them to have value sixty years later, let alone sixty centuries later. […] [F]rom the moment the first unrefined nugget was set aside, Gold was already considered a store of stable value. If not, the decision to hoard it would not have been made. Something with an unstable value would not be widely stored.[121]

The worldwide stock of gold therefore grows only by about 1.5% per year. This growth rate is approximately equivalent to the growth rate of the global population and is significantly lower than that of global monetary aggregates. A simple example shows how the high stock-to-flow ratio provides a natural inflation hedge. In the extremely unlikely event of a 50% increase in mine production, the total stock of gold would only rise by 2.3% per year. Compared to the current rate of monetary inflation by central banks, this increase is rather inconsequential. Moreover, a complete interruption in mine production for an entire year would have very little effect as well. If such a scenario were to occur with copper, inventories would be used up within 30 days. Furthermore, should a large new copper mine be brought online, the impact on the price of copper would be significant. The same does however not apply to the gold price. This difference creates confidence in the stability of the precious metals gold and silver and is the reason why substantial monetary importance is accorded to them.

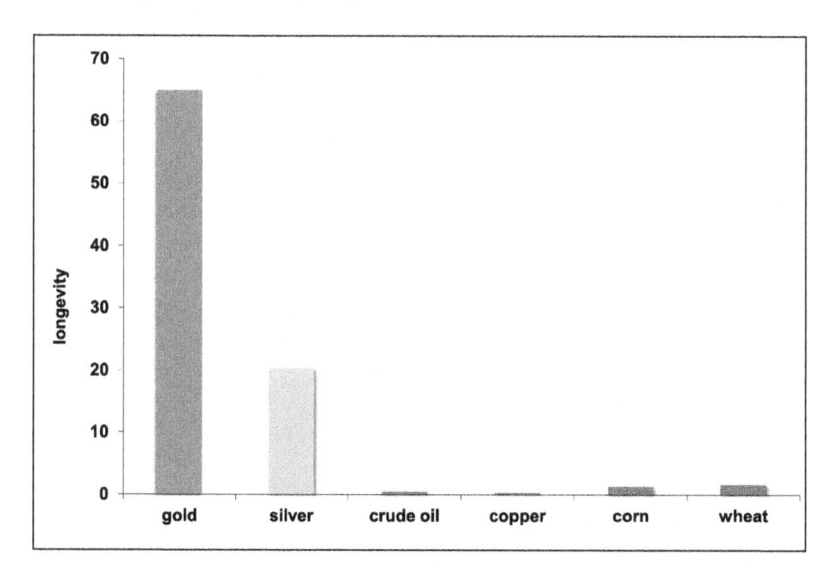

Figure 9.16: Stock-to-flow ratio of gold, silver, and other commodities (Sources: Erste Group Research, Incrementum AG)

"Experts" often announce sotto voce that the price of gold can never decline below its cost of production (which is currently around $ 1,200 on an "all in" basis). This is a fundamental misconception, which is due to the fact that many still analyze gold as though it were an industrial commodity. Since such commodities are used up, while gold is hoarded, conventional supply and demand models are not valid in the case of the gold market. Consequently, production costs are rather immaterial for the determination of the gold price. They are, however, highly important for the trend of gold mining stocks.

On the demand side of the gold market are central banks, the jewelry industry and investors. The largest part of demand is, however, so-called reservation demand. This refers to owners of gold who are not prepared to sell their gold at the current price and are thereby responsible for keeping the level of prices stable. As a result, the decision not to sell gold at the current price is of similar importance as the decision to buy it. The net effect is the same. In summary, the supply of gold is always large, and the often cited "gold deficit" is a myth.

It is important to examine the gold market in a holistic manner and not to disassociate the annual growth in supply from the total stock, as this leads to erroneous conclusions. Irrespective of whether gold has been mined recently or a thousand years ago, or if it is recently recycled dental gold: all sources of supply are equal. Thus annual mine production and its ups and downs are relatively unimportant for gold's price formation.

Gold Stocks

While gold is a means of hoarding, gold stocks are instruments of investment or speculation. At present, gold stocks essentially represent an extremely anti-cyclical speculation that is strongly leveraged to the gold price. There is no sector that is currently more strongly underweighted by institutional investors. It appears as though gold mining shares are being punished by frustrated investors for capital-intensive development projects, risky takeovers and strongly rising production costs. This can also be gleaned from looking at the ratio between gold stocks and gold: the oldest available gold index, the Barron's Gold Mining Index (BGMI) is currently trading at the lowest level relative to gold in more than 70 years, as figure 9.17 shows.

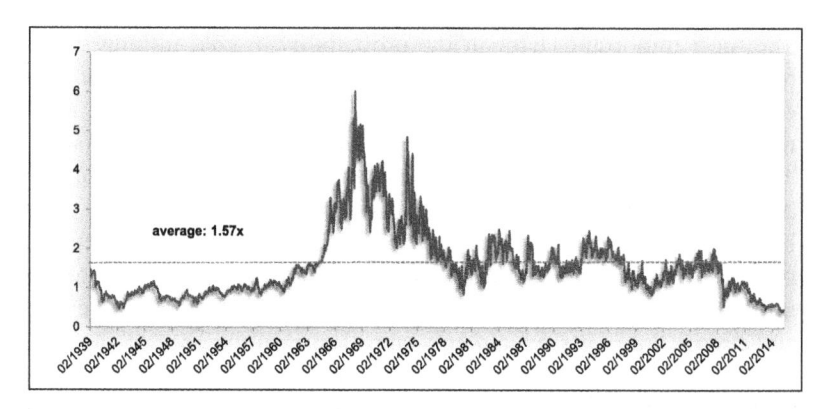

Figure 9.17: BGMI/gold ratio
(Sources: Barron's, Sharelynx, Incrementum AG)

The gold industry is currently experiencing a sea change. It appears as though the sector is finally in the process of changing its priorities. Profitability, capital discipline and stable returns per ounce seem in the meantime to be preferred over maximizing production. Numerous projects have been sold or mothballed over the past two years, and many senior managers have been replaced. The new commitment to cost transparency, greater financial discipline and shareholder value is an important – albeit late – insight. Whether this new focus will turn out to be more than mere lip service will become evident in coming quarters.

The extrapolation of forever rising production costs still appears to represent the current consensus opinion. We are skeptical. In light of anemic economic growth and falling commodity prices, many input costs have stopped rising, and some have even begun to decline. Thus prices for energy, industrial tires, explosives, and labor costs have already declined in the course of the brutal market adjustment that has recently occurred. We believe therefore that the mantra of "forever rising production costs" is erroneous and expect an end to the increase, respectively even a decline of production costs.

9. Austrian Investment Practice

The most important factor in the profitability of gold mining stocks remains the spread between the gold price and production costs. At a certain price threshold, mining would become unprofitable for most mine operators, but already mined gold would continue to be traded. Thus, while mine production has little impact on the gold price, the gold price conversely has an enormous impact on mining and its profitability. Since there is no uniform production cost for all mines, the profitability of different mines diverges substantially. It is therefore not unusual for non-viable reserves to become viable if the gold price rises and production costs remain constant. The absolute level of the gold price is relatively unimportant in this. For instance, gold is a beneficiary of times of declining economic confidence and recessions. As a result, gold stocks are one of the few sectors exhibiting a long-term negative correlation with the stock market. This could for instance also be observed in the 1970s. The S&P 500 moved essentially sideways between January 1973 (level: 118 points) and January 1981 (level: 135 points). Over the same time period, the Datastream World Gold Index rallied from 100 to 407 points.

In our opinion, the "6 big Ps" represent essential challenges that every investor in mining stocks should thoroughly investigate:

- People: a shortage of skilled expert workers, geologists and engineers leads to strongly rising labor costs
- Procurement: rising costs in goods and services needed for mining
- Power: rising costs of energy, e.g. due to declining ore grades
- Permits: stricter conditions and higher costs for mining licenses
- Projects: it becomes ever more difficult to replace mined out reserves
- Politics: an increase in government interference in the market, e.g. for environmental and labor protection, as well as rising taxation (such as "windfall" taxes, royalties, etc.)

Especially the last point is an ever more important consideration for successful investment in the mining sector. The trend toward nationalization and higher taxation of the mining industry has grown significantly in recent years. Chronic budget deficits around the world are giving rise to covetousness. Numerous new taxes and license fees have been proposed and introduced in recent years. The following represent the political risks faced by miners:

- Mining reforms, new legislation, new negotiation of existing license agreements (Mongolia, Guinea, Brazil, Zimbabwe)
- Expropriations, nationalizations (Argentina, Venezuela, South Africa, Zimbabwe, Uzbekistan, Kyrgyzstan, Kazakhstan)
- National champions (South Africa, Brazil, Russia)
- Security (Cote d'Ivoire, Mail, Niger, Mexico)
- New taxes and levies (Tanzania, Zambia, Peru, Brazil, Australia)
- Environmental legislation (US, Canada, Chile, Europe)

One reason why gold and oil stocks are currently valued so cheaply is that these sectors are especially strongly exposed to political risk: as soon as one has invested billions of dollars in a mine or an oil production facility, one is a potential captive of politicians, who can raise taxes arbitrarily or even confiscate one's assets. As these assets cannot be simply moved elsewhere, they are essentially sitting ducks. Hence, the choice of jurisdiction is now one of the most important decision criteria for investment in gold stocks.

Sound mining companies in politically stable regions currently represent a speculative opportunity with great leverage and an attractive risk/reward profile. Since gold stocks are de facto the only stock market sector that exhibits a negative correlation with the broader stock market, they can also be regarded as a hedge against a decline in the stock market. This is especially true in times when the sector is extremely oversold relative to the broad market, as is currently the case. Investigating political risk as well as the "6 Ps" are major criteria investors should employ in selecting individual gold mining stocks suitable for investment.

9. Austrian Investment Practice

Silver

Similar to gold, silver is a monetary metal, however, its industrial importance is far greater than that of gold. Silver therefore tends to rally more strongly during economic expansions, while gold as a rule performs better in periods of economic stress. For this reason, silver is also an excellent inflation indicator. Silver tends to rise markedly stronger than gold in times of rising price inflation rates (i.e., the gold/silver ratio declines) and it loses more ground in times of disinflation (i.e., the gold/silver ratio rises). It should also be noted that silver tends to rally more strongly than gold in periods of intense speculation in the precious metals sector. Figure 9.18 shows the gold/silver ratio since 1971.

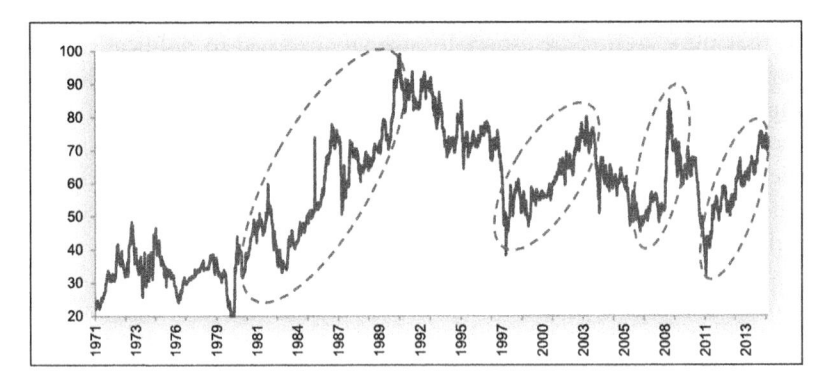

Figure 9.18: Gold/silver ratio
(Sources: Federal Reserve St. Louis, Incrementum AG)

Currently, the ratio stands at about 75, considerably higher than the median level of 55. Over a 40-year time horizon, silver is therefore relatively undervalued at present. The trough in the ratio was achieved in 1980, when one ounce of gold could be exchanged for only 14 ounces of silver. The historical peak was reached in 1940, at the time one ounce of gold could be exchanged for 100 ounces of silver. Similarly high levels were also recorded in 1990. We expect that silver will exhibit significant relative strength in the final phase of the gold bull market. This is buttressed by the trend in the ratio at the end of the 1970s (circled in the chart above).

Looking at the trend over a timespan of several centuries, it becomes evident that gold's purchasing power has increased strongly relative to that of silver since the beginning of the 20th century. The ratio's long-term median (since 1688) is 15. This is also approximately in line with physical stocks. Silver is approximately 17 times more abundant in the earth's crust than gold. According to the USGS, measured and inferred silver resources are even only 6 times higher than those of gold.

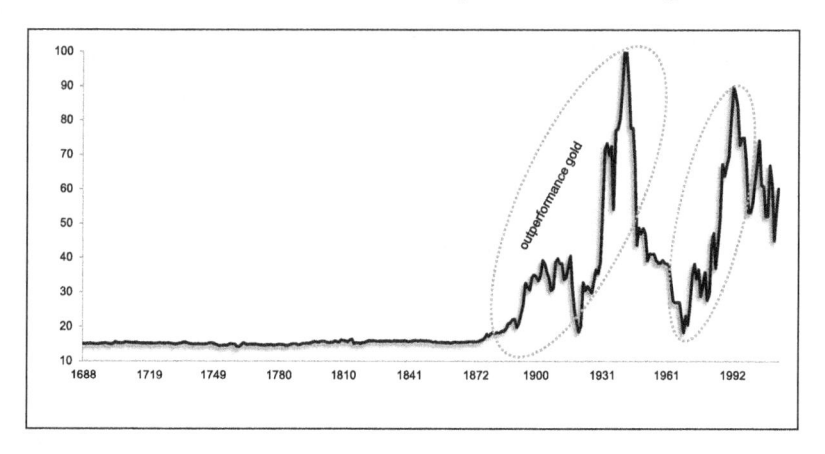

Figure 9.19: Gold/silver ratio since 1688
(Sources: Measuringworth.com, Incrementum AG)

In antiquity, gold was approximately 12 to 13 times more valuable than silver. This ratio was based on astronomical calculations (since the silver-colored moon moves about as many times faster through the zodiac than the golden sun) and this ratio was maintained for more than 800 years, until the age of the Lydians. In times of bimetallism, the ratio was held between 10 and 15 most of the time. This was, however, not a market-determined ratio, but one decreed by governments.

9. Austrian Investment Practice

Since 1870, the ratio has increased, which may be an indication that the market regards gold as the primary monetary metal.

year	France	England	Venice	Germany	average
1300		9.29	10.84	10	10.04
1350	11.1	11.57	14.44	11.33	12.11
1400	10.74	11.15	11.69	11.37	11.24
1450	11.44	10.33	12.1	11.12	11.25
1500	11.83	11.15	10.97	11.12	11.27
1550	12.07	12.23	11.07	11.38	11.69
1600	11.68	10.9	12.34	11.5	11.61
1650	13.5	13.34	15.37	11.64	13.46
1700				14.81	14.81
1750				14.53	14.53
1800				15.68	15.68
1850		15.7			15.7
1990		26.49			26.49

Figure 9.20: Gold/silver ratio in the times of bimetallism
(Source: The Prudent Investor, John F. Chown, *A History of Money*)

However, the strongest rally could be observed after the 1929-1932 deflationary period and the sudden onset of inflation from 1932 to 1935. We can easily imagine a similar scenario in the future. The stability of gold stocks during the collapse in stock prices in this time period can probably be explained by the fact that the gold price was fixed and the revenues of gold producers therefore remained stable, whereas all other commodity prices collapsed.

Purchase of Bullion

One should only purchase physical bullion from recognized and reputable merchants, who have successfully established themselves in the marketplace over many years. Merchants specialized in precious metals in most cases offer a much larger range of products in terms of investable gold and silver than commercial banks. Moreover, their prices are often lower and their advice is more competent.

Both bullion coins and bars are suitable for investing in gold. Smaller coins (e.g. 1/10 of an ounce, and 1/4 ounce coins) and bars usually have a relatively high mintage premium. The rule of thumb is that the larger the unit, i.e., the greater the weight, the more gold or silver one receives for one's money. Two bars weighing 50 grams each always cost more than one bar weighing 100 grams.

Among bullion coins, Krugerrand, Lunar, American Eagle, American Buffalo, Kookaburra, Maple Leaf, Panda and the Philharmonic are the most important brands. When purchasing bars, one should focus exclusively on LBMA certified suppliers such as e.g. Umicore or Heraeus. One should only trust 'reputable mints and refineries when investing in physical gold and silver. Among those are the Austrian Mint, Valcambi, Umicore, Argor-Heraeus and the Royal Canadian Mint.

In order to address the important problem of storage, one should know the answers to a number of questions beforehand. How long is one's investment horizon? Which persons should have access? What costs is one prepared to incur in order to store one's precious metals safely, respectively insure them? Apart from one's own residence (disadvantage: security risk, advantage: ready access), vaults and safe deposit boxes independent of banks, as well as bonded warehouses are most suitable for storage. The traditional bank deposit box is usually acceptable in terms of cost. However, a significant disadvantage is that one is dependent on the opening hours of the bank branch office – which could be especially disadvantageous in the event of a major banking crisis. Moreover, in most cases one is forced to prove one's identity, since anonymous rentals are generally no longer possible. Furthermore, seizures by the government can not categorically be ruled out; there already exist a number of historical precedents.

By contrast, discreet and anonymous solutions are offered by companies independent of banks (often precious metals merchants) and specialized safe storage suppliers. Storage in a foreign bonded warehouse can also represent an interesting alternative. While the costs are usually relatively high, the advantages predominate. Especially if the share of white metals (platinum, silver, palladium) is relatively high, one should consider this possibility, as the white metals are subject to value added tax in a number of countries. In a bonded warehouse, this tax does not have to be paid, as long as purchase and sale are effected through the warehouse and no delivery is undertaken. Moreover, bonded warehouses in most cases offer full insurance protection and are regularly audited by certified accountants.

Stocks

"An act of entrepreneurial discovery occurs when a market participant searches for and finds what others have overlooked."[122] This is how Israel Kirzner, a student of Ludwig von Mises, describes the process of entrepreneurial discovery by stressing the essential talent of an entrepreneur in a market economy, namely to discover unexploited opportunities. In line with this approach, a value investor, who applies Benjamin Graham's fundamental method of analysis and systematically invests in undervalued assets and later sells them at a profit can be regarded as an "Austrian entrepreneur" as well.

Warren Buffett is regarded as the most famous and successful value investor in the world. He says of himself that he is a better investor because he is a businessman, and a better businessman because he is an investor. In his opinion, the most important insight about investing is Benjamin Graham's statement that investing was more intelligent the more business-oriented it was. Benjamin Graham was convinced that mathematical models for the valuation of stocks should be as simple as possible. In his 44 years on Wall Street, he never came across a reliable model that employed more than elementary algebra or simple arithmetic. The use of higher mathematics was in his opinion merely a warning sign that indicated that the user attempted to replace experience with theories and make speculation appear to be akin to investment. This is clearly in line with the premises of the Austrian School.[123]

Generally, it can be stated that the approach of value investing is largely congruent with the Austrian School's approach, both with respect to the emphasis on the divergence between price and value, as well as with respect to the role of interest rates, capital and time preference in investment decisions and the employment of alternative risk assessments. In his probably most famous work, *The Intelligent Investor* (1949), Graham vehemently rejects the notion championed by modern portfolio theory that a security's price volatility is to be equated with its risk. This is mainly justified by the fact that cyclically induced price fluctuations lead to temporally limited divergences between price and value, which value investors systematically exploit as buying or selling opportunities. Considering that Graham and Mises lived in Manhattan only a few blocks apart from each other for a time period of 16 years, but that in all this time no verifiable direct exchange of ideas and opinions took place, the many commonalities between value investing and the theoretical concepts of the "Austrians" is quite remarkable.

At the core of value investing is the determination of a company's fundamental (or "intrinsic") value, which is examined independent of the stock price. Only various corporate metrics as well as generally accepted company evaluation methods are used for the calculation (DCF method, discounted earnings and net asset value calculation method, multiples approach). The weighting of individual metrics, respectively the choice of one or several valuation approaches, can vary greatly from investor to investor, so that naturally no generally valid method exists.

9. Austrian Investment Practice

The concept of intrinsic value implies a strict separation of "price" and "value". It should be noted here that the term "intrinsic value" in this context is not meant to deny the fundamental subjectivity of value judgments. Rather, it is in the words of Robert Blumen, "the entrepreneur's appraised price, based on assumptions about the future". The probably most famous quote of Benjamin Graham gets right to the point: "Price is what is paid, (while) value is what is received".[124] It can therefore be stated that while stock prices and fundamental values tend to converge over time, divergences between them can occur at any time, which allows for systematic excess returns to be achieved. The efficient market hypothesis of Eugene Fama, a Nobel laureate for economics, is rejected both by value investors and the Austrian School as divorced from the real world. In recent decades, the value investing thesis has successfully withstood countless empirical tests and studies.[125]

Another important criterion is the presence of a sufficiently large margin of error, which is defined by the difference between the observed market price and the fundamental value calculated by the investor. The margin serves mainly as a safety buffer against the inevitable occurrence of erroneous valuation assumptions or other calculation errors in the evaluation of a business model. Although no generally valid number can be stated in this case either, many conservative value investors only invest if the discount to the calculated intrinsic value is above 30%.

Aside from well-known traditional characteristics such as a low price-to-book ratio, as well as a low price-to-earnings ratio (according to Graham and Dodd adjusted for seasonal extremes, whereby the current stock price is divided by the 10-year moving average of earnings) and a high dividend yield, Benjamin Graham developed the following criteria shortly before he passed away in order to identify whether a stock offered especially good value:

1. The earnings yield is at least twice as high as the yield on an AAA rated bond.
2. The current P/E ratio amounts to at most 40% of the maximum recorded over the past five years.

3. The dividend yield amounts to at least two thirds of the yield of an AAA rated bond.
4. The stock's market price amounts to at most two thirds of the company's tangible book value.
5. The market price amounts to at most two thirds of net current assets (current assets minus short-term liabilities).
6. The sum of all liabilities amounts to a maximum of two thirds of tangible book value.
7. Third grade liquidity (current assets divided by short-term liabilities) is greater than 2.
8. The sum of all liabilities is smaller or at most equal to twice net current assets.
9. The annualized earnings growth rate over the past 10 years amounts to at least 7%.
10. Over the past ten years, a company may exhibit negative earnings growth greater than 5% in only two years.

There are, of course, barely any stocks in the investment universe that fulfill all ten criteria. However, these are to be seen as benchmarks to be aimed for, whereby Graham's guidelines ensure that the chosen investment is valued favorably, earns stable returns for the investor and that the company one invests in has a sustainable level of debt. Especially during recessionary periods, low debt levels are one of the most important preconditions for a company's survival, as this makes it possible to obtain new capital even under difficult circumstances. Graham favored the fifth criterion in this evaluation, as it reflects the idea of intrinsic value and the associated price-value divergence especially well.

Value Investing in the Paper Money Era

In spite of the sound theoretical basis and the empirical confirmation by studies showing the long-term increase in value achieved by value investing techniques described above, a historical analysis of value investor portfolios reveals extraordinarily negative trends during

9. Austrian Investment Practice

recessionary periods. Value stocks exhibited significant underperformance in all economic downturns of the past few decades. A pertinent example was the dramatic decline in the Templeton Growth Fund (of approx. 60% peak-to-trough) during the last big financial crisis in 2008. It seems that there are regularly recurring periods during which the otherwise highly successful criteria of value investing fail.

Adherents of the Austrian School assert that this negative performance is due to the fact that value investors do not take sufficient account of the macroeconomic environment. At the core of the critique is that value investors almost completely dismiss questions of monetary policy and economic theory in their decision making process. A quote by Warren Buffett, the probably most famous and successful value investor, illustrates this:

> If [former] Fed Chairman Alan Greenspan were to whisper to me what his monetary policy was going to be over the next two years, it would not change one thing I do.[126]

Since the complete abandonment of gold cover following the end of the Bretton Woods system in 1971, many value investors time and again fall prey to fateful calculation errors, which lead to painful losses at regular intervals. The key to understanding these mistakes is provided by the Austrian business cycle theory developed by Ludwig von Mises, which we described above. Numerous classical value investors who ignore developments on the monetary policy front and the associated economic dynamics, become victims of the falsification of economic calculation caused by credit expansion.

If one looks at the excessive[127] monetary policy interventions of the globally most important central banks in reaction to the financial crisis of 2008, it should be obvious that central banks are increasingly distorting interest rates and prices by means of indirect and direct monetization of government debt. Apart from influencing short-term interest rates by setting policy rates at historic lows near a level of zero percent, the "guardians of the currency" are also attempting to manipulate the long end of the yield curve by purchases of government bonds (see further below). The new money created from thin air initially flows primarily into financial markets, where it creates speculative bubbles, which are sooner or later rectified by a strong correction.

There is a noteworthy technical difference between the boom since the end of the 2008 crisis and the "normal" booms of preceding post war boom-bust cycles. Previously, central banks primarily accommodated credit and money supply expansion initiated by commercial banks. This largely private sector-driven monetary inflation tended to enter the real economy at specific points (technology companies and consumer credit in the late 1990s, real estate development and mortgage credit in the 2000s) and concurrently spread to the markets in which titles to capital are traded (stocks and corporate bonds) in a feedback loop.

Private sector credit demand was high and commercial banks did their best to satisfy it and egg it on further. They devised financial innovations allowing them to extend credit to less and less creditworthy borrowers. The banks achieved this by continually freeing up capital for new lending by selling securitized loans to yield-chasing investors. The major credit rating agencies supported these efforts by assigning very high ratings to the senior tranches of the structured credit products banks had created. These ratings were based on historical default rates in the sub-prime credit sector and assumptions regarding the risk buffers supposedly provided by subordinated tranches.

The crisis revealed that the analysis of historical data was insufficient to properly judge the risks, as a bigger and more pervasive mortgage credit bubble had never before occurred. The bust unmasked the fact that many of the profits reported during the boom had been an illusion: in reality, enormous amounts of capital had been consumed. This left households, the financial sector, as well as other industries near the center of the boom in dire straits. Their balance sheets were thoroughly ravaged. Since then, commercial banks have no longer acted as the main drivers of monetary inflation that is passively accommodated by central banks. Instead, central banks have actively driven monetary inflation by monetizing debt. Newly created money has therefore first and foremost entered financial markets, with relatively little of it being devoted to funding activities in the real economy. As a result, there is now an unprecedented disconnect between financial market trends and valuations and the real economy they are supposed to mirror.

This has created new challenges for investors. Inter alia, it appears that extremes in valuations as well as sentiment and positioning data can be sustained for longer time periods and driven to greater heights than in previous bubbles. It seems likely that the eventual downturn will as a consequence turn out to be especially large and painful.

Adherents of the Austrian School ascribe every ongoing stock market boom to the preceding expansion of circulation credit. This is inter alia substantiated by the fact that asset prices in both the consumer and producer sector can only rally at the same time if there is an artificial expansion of the money supply, as only additionally created money can replace demand that would otherwise not exist. Since neither merchants nor speculators know for how long and to what extent expansionary monetary policy will be pursued, positions that have been entered into tend not to be liquidated for some time. As a result, even clearly overvalued securities can remain at irrationally high price levels for quite protracted time periods.

Another characteristic of an artificial boom is growth in sectors far removed from the consumption stage, combined with a concurrently declining savings rate.[128] Since artificially low interest rates lower the incentive to save and negative real interest rates result in a gradual devaluation of savings, consumption tends to increase, which ultimately means that scarce capital will be consumed in the economy concerned. If investment in production processes far removed from final consumption takes place in spite of a lack of investable resources (as these are flowing into consumption), it is definitely attributable to the supply of additional monetary means artificially created by the financial sector. Expansionary monetary policy also results in otherwise unprofitable and risky business models obtaining financing. Only when the "money spigot is turned off" and a recession ensues, does it become possible to redirect misallocated capital into proper channels again. However, this means that investors who have failed to recognize the unprofitable nature of bubble activities will suffer large losses.

Every investor needs to be aware of the causal relations described above when observing a rally in financial markets. In the early stages of a rally, when an increasingly expansionary, or at least a continuation of expansionary monetary policy is expected, the following metrics (momentum criteria) are recommended for successful investment in stocks:

• Strong growth in earnings per share (EPS) compared to the same quarter of the previous year. The EPS sequence should exhibit a clear growth trend. Based on empirical observation of the strongest stocks of the past century, investor William J. O'Neil recommends investing in stocks with EPS growth of 25% or more. However, even slower growth rates (if an upward trend exists) are usually a good buy signal.

• A clear growth trend should also be visible in EBIT (earnings before interest and tax) and the return on equity (earnings/equity capital). Ideally these growth metrics should be supported by the company reporting rising sales and be accompanied by increasing trading volume in the stock concerned. According to O'Neil, the higher the growth rates in these metrics, the better.

• Another very important and reliable metric is the return on invested capital (ROIC). ROIC is calculated by dividing net operating earnings after tax by capital invested (equity capital plus interest-bearing external capital plus long-term provisions). With respect to this datum, the important point is that ROIC should always be greater than the company's cost of capital. As companies in cyclical sectors or companies domiciled in economies that are considered unstable as a rule are subject to higher capital costs, they must exhibit a commensurately high ROIC. ROIC is thus a relative metric, and indispensable for estimating a company's profitability.

9. Austrian Investment Practice

One should always keep in mind that an artificial boom in the markets across all kinds of different sectors can only be of limited duration. It is therefore essential to take one's profits before the expansionary monetary policy ends. The critical signs that a rally is close to ending include rising risk premiums for credit default swaps, rising interest rates on loans due to an increase in defaults and private sector bankruptcies, as well as interest rate hikes by the central bank. All these factors reduce the ability of commercial banks to issue additional circulation credit, which sooner or later leads to the unmasking of unprofitable business models and the beginning of a recessionary corrective process. In addition to the traditional value criteria discussed at the beginning of this chapter, it is therefore necessary in the long term to keep an eye on the following two characteristics when choosing investments:

• Sound debt metrics: in recessionary periods, companies with strong credit ratings that have room to maneuver independent of external capital providers are especially valuable. Indicators that reflect a sound capital structure are a strong equity ratio, as well as a current ratio of 200% or more. In order to calculate the current ratio, one divides current assets by short-term liabilities. If the current ratio stands below 100%, short-term debt cannot be covered by current assets. As a result, the company concerned could quickly face an existential threat, namely whenever its short-term debt comes due. At manufacturing companies, the ratio of fixed to current assets should be high. A low ratio can be interpreted as a sign that the company being analyzed employs technology that is out of date, as it operates with fixed assets that have already been greatly depreciated.

• A strong value orientation: a high dividend yield (see Graham's third criterion) provides substantial cash flows and reflects the direct return from the associated investment. Investors should also focus on companies that have valuable patents, brands and production techniques, as well as fixed assets of great long-term value. In line with the tenets of the classical value investment approach, a low price to book ratio is regarded as a good indicator for a favorably valued company.

In keeping with business cycle theory, it is furthermore recommended that investors reallocate their funds into companies in the consumer goods sector at the end of a stock market boom, as they tend to be less affected by corrections in the capital markets. Moreover, allocations to stocks should be generally significantly reduced and allocations to cash and bonds increased until the bear market ends.

Family-Owned Companies

Contrary to large listed corporations, the boards of which are prone to thinking in quarters rather than years due to short-term performance pressures and frequent management changes, family-owned companies are more likely to pursue long-term oriented and sustainable business strategies. As a result, management decisions are taken with far greater clear-sightedness, and business processes are planned and implemented with greater consistency. This is mainly due to the fact that in view of tradition and family ownership, management has much stronger ties to the company, which makes family-owned companies a lot less susceptible to conflicts of interest than large listed corporations. From the perspective of investors, this is reflected in more stable long-term returns. Family companies that pursue a niche strategy and thus exhibit exceptional expert competence in a clearly defined market segment are especially suitable for investment. As described in the previous section, the business model should have a strong equity base and should have produced stable returns over several preceding years.

The characteristics of family-managed companies are at the same time their greatest advantages. The fact that management as a rule represents the majority of shareholders prevents conflicts of interest between the two parties. As a result, CEOs of family companies tend to be in charge for much longer time periods. Moreover, these managers tend to act more responsibly, as a considerable portion of their own wealth is employed as risk capital. In this context, risk can be regarded as an opportunity to increase the company's value further. Family companies also exhibit stronger relative financial stability, as their equity capital is on average greater than that of peers. Another advantage this type of company harbors, is greater entrepreneurial freedom, which in turn provides more flexibility, as in most cases capital is invested for the long term. Consequently, more sustainable value accretion can be achieved, as management is not solely focused on short-term targets like increases in the share price or profit maximization. Goals including high product quality, development of the brand and above all, good personal relationships with customers and suppliers are prioritized. The happiness of employees is also a key to success. An additional advantage is the lean and efficient structures of family companies, which simplify processes like cost control, shorten decision-making channels and create clear power relations.

The disadvantages of this type of company management include a certain dependence on the owner, who in most cases acts as a figurehead and on whom the company often crucially depends. If the owner retires and a change of generations take place, tensions between family members over succession planning often ensue, which in turn reflect negatively on the company's development. A small number of free-floating shares can impair tradability, resulting in greater volatility of the security. In addition, in certain market periods a small public float can lead to unfavorable market valuations.

All in all, however, the advantages of family-managed companies predominate. Figure 9.21 shows the performance of family-managed companies worldwide, represented by the CS Family TR Index, compared to the MSCI World Index NTR. Clearly, the former exhibits a significant increase in value, which is additionally confirmed by the chart of the cumulative performance differential. A study by the University of St. Gallen of March 2013[129] comes to similar conclusions, and among other things, points out that there is a positive correlation between family ownership and business performance, which is all the more pronounced if a company's founder is actively involved in its management.

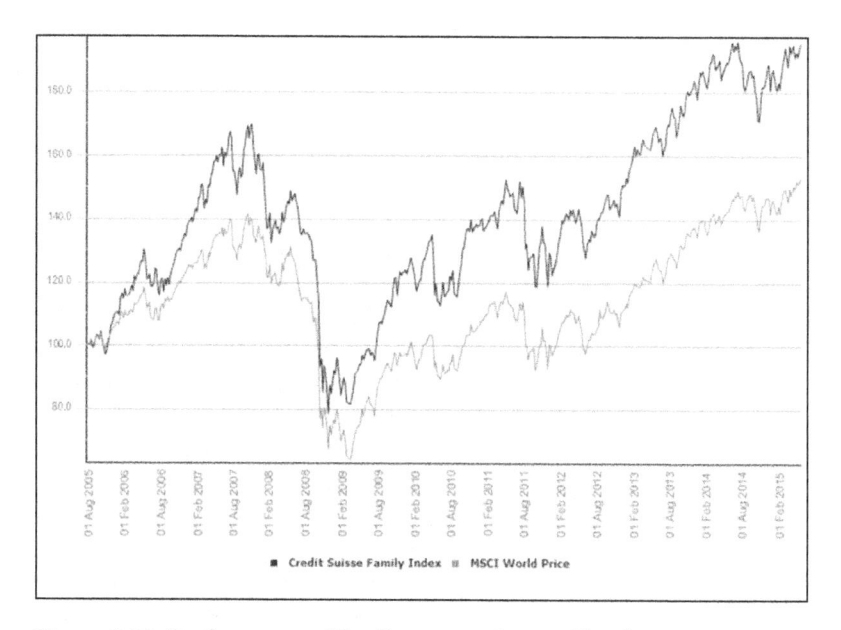

**Figure 9.21: Performance of family companies worldwide
(Source: Bellevue Asset Management)**

Numerous statements from studies confirm this assessment: "Our results indicate that there is a significantly positive relationship between insider ownership and firm performance as measured by stock price performance over a five year period."[130] Or: "[F]amily firms perform better than nonfamily firms [...]. [F]amily ownership is an effective organizational structure."[131] Or: "The value of family companies increases further if a family member holds the position of CEO."[132]

Analysis

Tobin's Q

In order to be able to make use of Austrian business cycle theory as an investor, it is helpful to make a quantify the effects of monetary policy. In investment decisions – the assessment of the likely success or failure of individual investments – one depends on experience. Thus one requires tools that can be used to measure the phenomena that are of decisive importance in investment selection.

One of these tools is Tobin's Q. This metric can – with certain limitations – measure the effects of an artificial monetary expansion. It is named after the economist and Nobel prize winner James Tobin, who introduced the concept in an article published in 1969.[133] Tobin is definitely not a member of the Austrian School, however, one can detect a few elements in his work that can be regarded as an application of Austrian theories. Hedge fund manager Mark Spitznagel describes his practically identical proprietary metric, the Misesian Stationary Index (MS Index), as follows:

> A natural extension of the understanding of the time structure of capital, roundabout production and time preference according to Menger and Boehm-Bawerk – as well as Mises' insight into economic distortions due to monetary interventions.[134]

An index of this type can be helpful in performing a kind of measurement of the level of misallocations as they are described by business cycle theory, and thereby enable one to make forecasts regarding future economic developments. Before an economic cycle starts, one can compare the economic situation with an equilibrium model for the purpose of illustration, so as to contrast it with later phases. Ludwig von Mises and Murray Rothbard referred to this model as the *evenly rotating economy* (ERE). There is no room for entrepreneurial action in this model, as there are no price changes and no uncertainty - therefore there are also no capital misallocations. In order to recognize at which stage of the business cycle one happens to be in a specific situation, one can observe how big the deviations from this equilibrium model are.

This fictive model has of course no counterpart in reality, which is why Spitznagel employs an altered model, which he refers to as an "aggregated ERE". While there is entrepreneurial action in this model, its aggregated profits and losses still amount to zero. If aggregated capital yields are suddenly permanently higher or lower than the cost of capital replacement, the reason has to be monetary policy. A change in time preferences of market participants would only lead to temporary deviations. This relationship is informative, as it cannot be expected that the aggregated return on invested capital (ROIC) will deviate in the long term from the weighted average cost of capital (WACC). Periods of high Q ratios are phases when malinvestment is especially pronounced. Periods of declining Q ratios are periods when these malinvestments are liquidated. Tobin concluded:

> When Q Is High, Large Losses Are No Longer a Tail Event, But Become an Expected Event.[135]

Figure 9.22 depicts the trend of Tobin's Q in the US economy since 1950. Interestingly, the median since 1900 stands at approximately 0.7 and not 1. Spitznagel concludes from this, that the fair value of the companies included in the calculation stands at 0.7 as well.[136] Exceeding this value thus indicates overvaluation and with that a high risk that the value of stocks will decline strongly. Since 2009 (0.59), a rise in Tobin's Q can be observed. It has in the meantime increased to 1.15. The further it rises, the higher the probability of a comprehensive correction or even an economic collapse. It therefore pays for investors to keep a close eye on Tobin's Q.

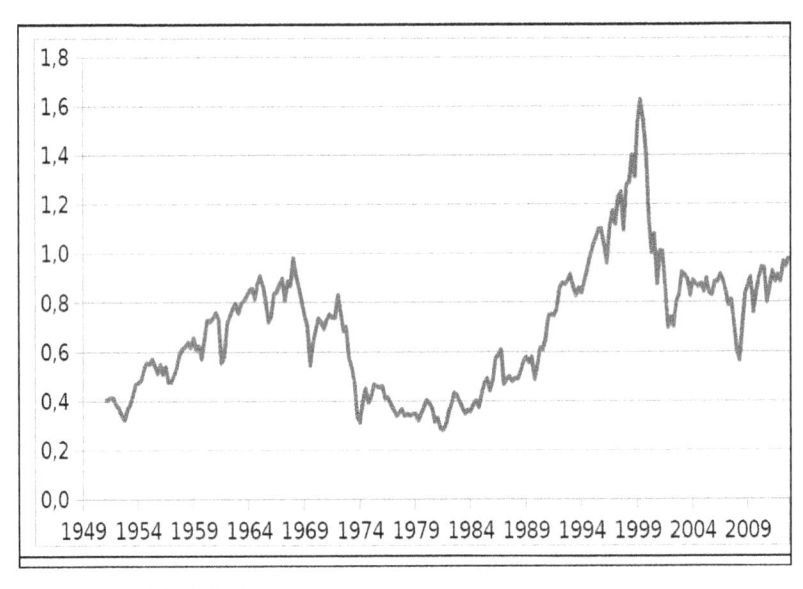

Figure 9.22: Tobin's Q
(Sources: Federal Reserve St. Louis, Incrementum AG)

The Yield Curve

The term structure of interest rates (yield curve) reflects market participants' expectations of future interest rates. It compares the interest rates of bonds of the same type, but with different maturities. Usually, one looks at the government bonds of a specific country, as these are generally still regarded as risk-free. Interest rates of maturities of a few months up to interest rates of maturities of two to three decades are thereby charted. The result is broken down into four different patterns: a normal, flat, humped and inverted yield curve. The actual curve does not have to be precisely similar to any of these types. They merely represent schematic simplifications.

Analysis

A normal yield curve exhibits an initially strongly, but later less pronounced, rising shape. It is called "normal" because it has usually exhibited this or a similar pattern in the course of the 20th and 21st century. The reason for this shape is that a risk premium is attached to long-term bonds, as well as a price premium, i.e. they reflect the expectation of higher inflation rates in the future as well as the restrictive monetary policy associated with them. Future economic growth is anticipated, and attendant with it an increase of short-term interest rates by the central bank. The monetary policy tactic on which such rate increases are based is intended to prevent the "overheating" of the economy.

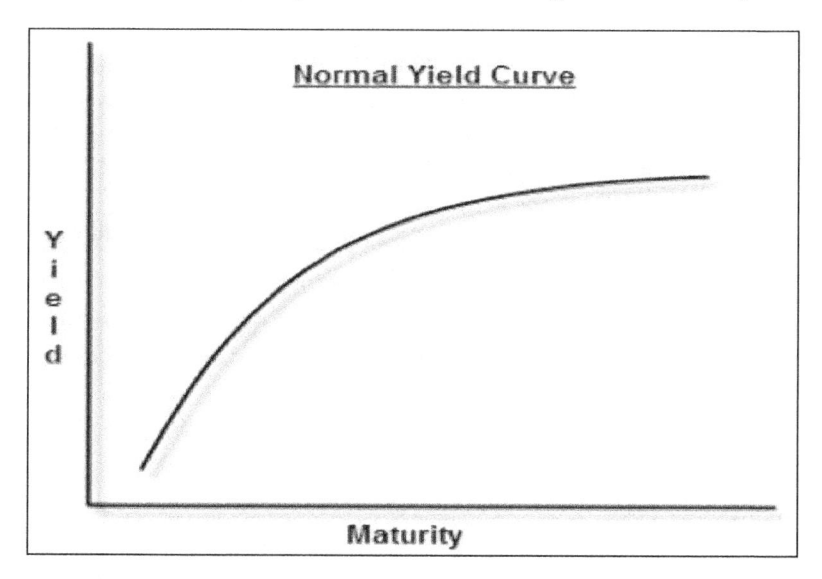

Figure 9.23: Normal yield curve

A flat yield curve by contrast reflects expectations of declining interest rates. As a result, interest rates on bonds of different maturities are at a similar level. One is no longer rewarded for taking the higher risk inherent in longer-term bond maturities, thus an investor who has to invest in bonds has no incentive anymore to prefer long-dated bonds over shorter-dated ones. The implications of a humped (or bell-shaped)

9. Austrian Investment Practice

yield curve are similar to those of a flat one. Both patterns can be observed at the – for investors – decisive transition from a normal to an inverted term structure. The two are also similar because the most important bond prices – those with the shortest and longest maturities – are at approximately the same level.

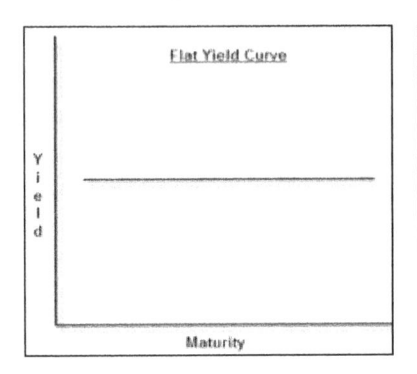

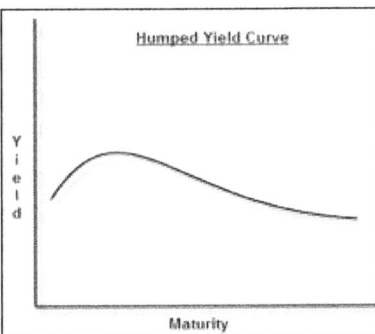

Figure 9.24: flat yield curve

Figure 9.25: humped yield curve

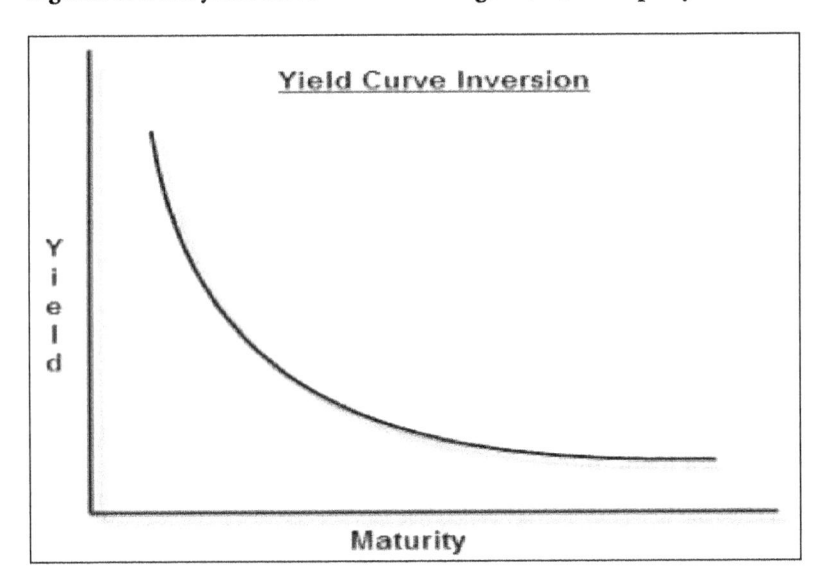

Figure 9.26: Inverted yield curve

Analysis

An inverted yield curve expresses the expectation that the normally high rate of money supply expansion is coming to an end. Contrary to a normal yield curve, it is usually not as steep as shown in the schematic depiction below.

In order to illustrate this point, we examine the shape of the US treasury yield curve shortly before the bursting of the dot-com and real estate bubbles. These curves shift every trading day. One can get a good impression of the changing shapes in animated videos on the internet. For this book, we selected specific days on which the different types of curves could be easily discerned.

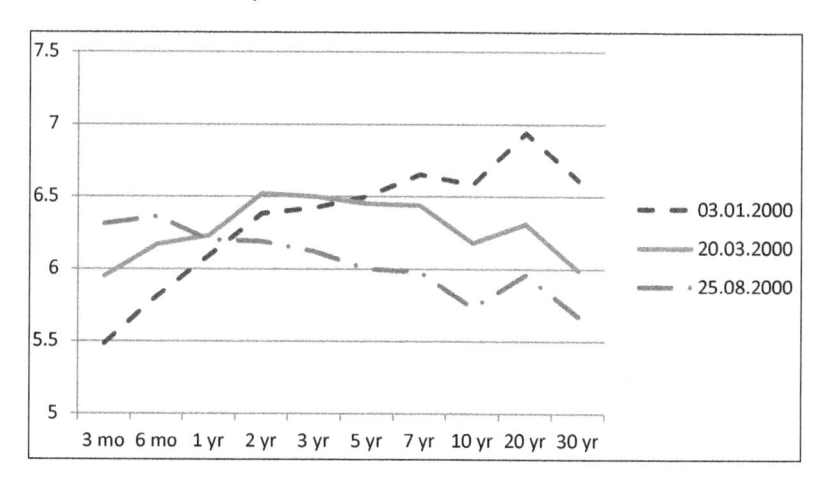

Figure 9.27: Shape of the US treasury yield curve in 2000 (Source: Incrementum AG)

At the beginning of January, the shape was still quite normal, in March it became humped and in August it inverted. The implicit warning given by the yield curve about the impending bursting of the real estate bubble in the US in 2007 can also be seen quite well. Until February 2006, the yield curve was still of rather normal shape. Thereafter, it flattened out for a while, until it clearly inverted at the end of the year.

9. Austrian Investment Practice

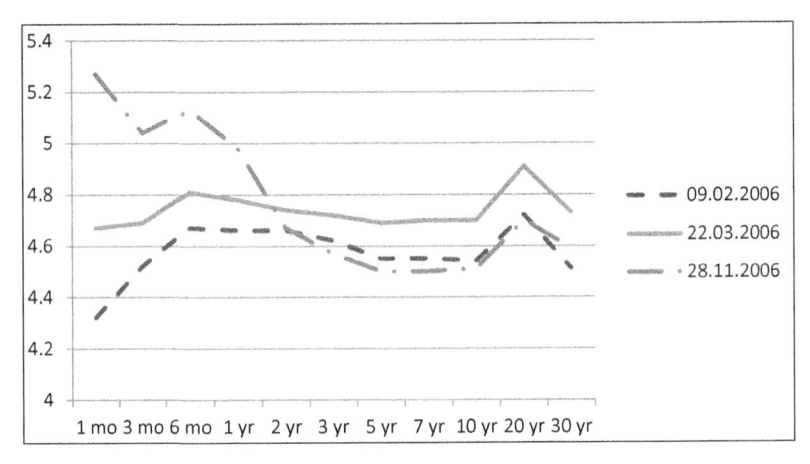

Figure 9.28: Shape of the US treasury yield curve in 2006 (Source: Incrementum AG)

In order to emerge from recessions without damage, or in the best case even in a stronger position as an investor, one must be able to time their occurrence with as much precision as possible. "Austrian" economist Paul Cwik writes on this:

> The malinvestment boom is an unsustainable state. There is an insufficient supply of savings to support the malinvestments built up during the boom. The resulting crunch comes about as a credit crunch, a real resource crunch, or a combination of the two. Each of these scenarios leads to an inverted yield curve approximately one year before the economic downturn.[137]

According to economist Gary North, an inverted yield curve almost always signals a decline in stock prices shortly after its occurrence, as well as a recession that begins approximately six months later:

> It was on the basis of this indicator that in the November 2006 issue of my Remnant Review newsletter, I predicted a recession in 2007.

It arrived in December 2007, according to the National Bureau of Economic Research.[138]

Currently, the situation must be judged stable. The yield curve is clearly of normal shape, which is however also a result of the Fed's unprecedented interventions in both the short and the long end of the yield curve.

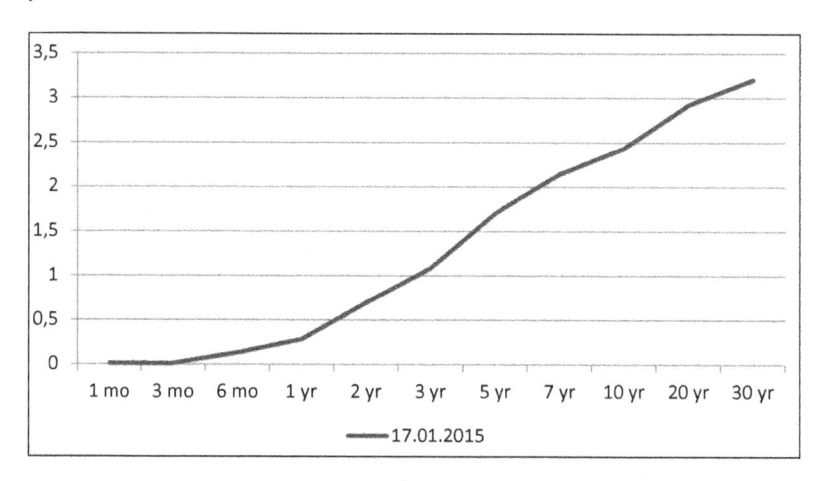

Figure 9.29: Shape of the US treasury yield curve in 2014 (Source: Incrementum AG)

Technical Analysis

Technical analysis (also known as chart analysis) attempts to forecast future market trends based on historical price trends and certain price patterns. This method is a tempting, but dubious attempt to derive future prices from historical data. Not only prices and price trends, but also trading volume, data on the market structure and psychological factors (various sentiment indicators) are studied. There are numerous tools technical analysts employ to come to their conclusions. Among them are:

- trend lines
- moving averages
- price patterns (e.g. head and shoulders pattern, triangles)
- indicators, resp. oscillators (e.g. RSI, MACD, Williams %R)
- cycles (e.g. Elliott waves)
- sentiment indicators
- Fibonacci relationships
- data on market structure/positioning (commitments of traders)
- intermarket analysis

With the help of these tools, technical analysis tries to determine points in time that are relatively favorable for buying and selling. Its primary goal is therefore not the choice of asset classes, but the timing of purchases and sales. While in fundamental analysis, securities are carefully evaluated and chosen and often held for an extended time period after purchase, technical analysis is mainly oriented toward short-term trading. Often the underlying business does not matter at all, instead only price trends are examined. Fundamental analysis by contrast comprises selection criteria such as those discussed in the context of value investing. While fundamental analysis deals with the question of *what* to buy, technical analysis deals with *when* to buy it.

Technical analysis can be traced back to Charles Henry Dow (1851-1902), who founded the *Wall Street Journal* in 1889 after publishing the first US stock market index five years earlier. The Dow Jones Railroad Average initially contained eleven, later fourteen stocks (mainly of railroad companies). In 1896, Dow developed the famous Dow Jones Industrial Average. The "Dow Theory" was later derived from his 255 editorials in the Wall Street Journal. The theory is today regarded as the precursor to technical analysis.

While fundamental analysis assumes that there is no connection between historical data (prices and trading volumes) and future events or prices (returns and losses), technical analysis assumes this to be the case. From the perspective of fundamental analysis, market errors lead to the over- or undervaluation of asset classes, whereby erroneous assessments will sooner or later be recognized and corrected. From the perspective of technical analysis, the market is always right. Possible errors are consequently not the market's fault, but the analyst's.

fundamental analysis	technical analysis
a causal relationship between historical price and revenue data and future returns is commonly ruled out (future cash flow)	causal relationships between historical prices and future returns are assumed
"the market" is prone to fallacies, which leads to over- or undervaluations	"the market is always right", share prices incorporate all relevant information
misjudgments of the markets are corrected with time	the analyst can be wrong, not the market

Figure 9.30 Fundamental vs. technical analysis
(Source: Incrementum AG)

Adherents of the Austrian technical analysis with skepticism, which is shared by mainstream economists. Adherents of classical financial market theory consider the efficient market hypothesis, respectively the random walk hypothesis, as the standard model for the analysis of financial markets. The efficient market hypothesis assumes that the markets are as such efficient. Efficient, in this context, implies that the entirety of already existing information that could potentially influence the price of a security is already "priced in" at all times.

A well-known joke about the efficient market hypothesis runs as follows: a professor of finance and his doctoral candidate are walking around on campus. The candidate discovers a $100 note lying on the ground and stoops to pick it up. The professor says to him: "Save yourself the effort; if the banknote were really there, someone else would have picked it up already."

An important point is the segmentation into weak efficiency, medium-strong efficiency and strong efficiency. Weak efficiency asserts that based on already priced in information, a forecast of future prices is not possible. The best forecast is the current price. Technical analysis therefore cannot deliver better results (since the current price would be the best forecast). Medium-strong efficiency asserts that apart from past price trends, publicly available and market-relevant information has been priced in additionally. This makes not only technical analysis useless, but fundamental analysis as well. All information that could be gathered by thoroughly analyzing a company is already contained in the share price. The strong efficiency hypothesis even goes as far as asserting that insider knowledge is priced in as well. In such a model, it is even impossible to make profits with insider trading, as stock prices are plainly regarded as unforeseeable.

The random walk theory represents yet another approach that is based on the efficient market hypothesis. It assumes that the prices of securities fluctuate randomly around their fair value. Information about historical price levels or price structures is therefore irrelevant, as these cannot reveal anything about future random prices.

The Austrian School's criticism of technical analysis is based on a different angle. Due to the continual change in the means-ends relationships of economic actors, the future is uncertain. No-one can say today, what items consumers will most urgently demand tomorrow. More precisely: no-one is able to gather and evaluate the value judgments of individuals. The weakest point (from the Austrian School's perspective) of technical analysis is that it is not based on any economic theory. The study of moving averages, trend sequences and price patterns has no relation to the theory of human action. The main reason for the price fluctuations however is human action. Prices rise and fall as a consequence of actions. They do not change because certain indicators have broken. Technical analysis is too focused on mathematical and statistical processes and marginalizes the influence of human action. Mark Thornton summarizes this aspect as follows:

> The Austrian School teaches that understanding the "economy" can only be undertaken with the aid of economic theory. There is no formula or equation for understanding the economy. It cannot be measured in any meaningful scientific way. Only the logical construction of cause and effect aid us.[139]

Technical analysis nevertheless has a certain degree of justification in the financial world. The Austrian School does not allow for any forecasts of suitable timing. For investors this is its weakest point, since it is a top priority for investors to catch the "correct" point in time. What point is there in knowing that a crisis is on its way, without knowing when it will happen? Technical analysis can, in a limited manner, provide indicators of prevailing market psychology. With that, a certain usefulness for investment decisions cannot be ruled out – after all, it also tells us something about what makes the typical investor tick. Moving averages for instance reflect a market's general trend. Are we still in a strong or a weak trend? From a sober perspective, the breaking of a trend line does not necessarily signal the end of a trend. However, the fact that use of technical analysis is widespread among speculators cannot be ignored. Breaking significant lines or structures can become a "self-fulfilling prophecy", as such events receive a lot of attention amongst traders.

Sentiment indicators can also provide useful support for the decisions of the "Austrian" investor. They show the extent of optimism or pessimism prevailing in a market. This gives an investor the opportunity to determine whether a stock is potentially overvalued or undervalued. If the majority of investors are optimistic, this can be interpreted as a warning that a stock may be overvalued. If there is great pessimism, undervaluation of a stock may potentially exist. Information about market sentiment is essential for an investor, who in the best case buys assets when they are undervalued and sells them when they are overvalued (i.e., acts in an anti-cyclical manner), in order to be successful.

The commitments of traders (CoT) report can also prove a useful tool. It depicts the positions of large merchants (commercial traders), large speculators (non-commercial traders) and small speculators (non-reportable positions). With its help, it is possible to observe and analyze the positioning of individual groups of market participants. Especially important in this context are historical extremes in the net speculative position (long or short), as well as differences in the positioning of large vs. small speculators (large speculators tend to be better informed) and divergences between the net speculative position and prices or price trends. Commercial hedgers often take positions that do not depend on price trends, because they either hedge inventories in the actual underlying financial instruments or commodities, or hold offsetting over-the-counter derivatives. In the futures markets, they should mainly be seen as liquidity providers, whose activities make the position-taking of speculators possible.

Although technical analysis is not based on economic theory and is therefore regarded with skepticism by adherents of the Austrian School, it can be a useful timing tool for investors. Taking its weaknesses into account, it can provide important information about the current market situation and especially about market psychology.

The Wicksellian Differential

One method of analysis that is quite close to the approach of the Austrian School was developed by Thomas Aubrey in 2012.[140] His strategy is based on the theory of Swedish economist Knut Wicksell (1851-1926). Aubrey attempts to integrate Wicksell's differentiation between the natural and the money rate of interest in an investment strategy that anticipates important turning points (peaks and troughs) in the economy's trend at an early stage. This is supposed to give investors a tool for positioning themselves in line with the business cycle. For this purpose, Aubrey defines the "Wicksellian Differential" as the difference between the natural and the money interest rate.

Certain market indexes are employed as gauges of the natural and the market interest rate. The return on equity and external capital serves as a measure of the natural interest rate. The five-year moving average of government bond yields is used as the money interest rate.

If the differential increases, it indicates a bull market according to Aubrey (investment in government bonds), if it shrinks, a bear market (investment in commodities). Historically, Aubrey managed to achieve an average annual return of 8.7% between 1986 and 2011 with this method. The self-defined goal (anticipation of peaks and troughs) is, however, only partially possible with this investment strategy. In the 2007 crisis, Aubrey's Wicksellian differential was a useful tool to exit the market in a timely fashion, in the dot-com bubble from 1996 to 2001 it proved less successful. One inherent difficulty is that the natural interest rate cannot really be observed or measured, as it simply represents the society-wide expression of time preference, i.e., the discount of future goods against present goods. It would only become observable in an economy in "equilibrium", i.e., an evenly rotating, unchanging economy. In such an economy it would correspond precisely to the interest rate differential prevailing between the stages of production. However, since the evenly rotating economy is merely a mental construct and can never come into existence in the real world, the natural interest rate will never become truly measurable or observable. Proxies like that employed by Aubrey can at best be viewed as approximations.

Bonds

Bonds are fixed interest securities that are issued by companies or governments to finance themselves. The issuer borrows external capital from the bond buyer (creditor). For this reason, bonds are also referred to as debentures or debt certificates. Special types of bonds include zero coupon bonds, amortizing bonds, annuities, convertible bonds.

9. Austrian Investment Practice

We will focus on standard bonds here, most of which are fixed interest rate securities.

Credit conditions such as yield, maturity and redemption are agreed in advance. Interest payments can be made, depending on the agreement, in regular intervals such as annually or bi-annually, or only at the end of the term. Maturities can range from one to thirty years. At the time the bond matures, the creditor (buyer) is entitled to a repayment of 100% of the bond's face value.

During the bond's term, its price is variable, this is to say it changes over time. Apart from the borrower's creditworthiness, the price depends essentially on market interest rates. As the time to maturity draws closer, the bond's price will converge towards its face value. This change in price that is independent of a change in the structure of interest rates is also called the "rolling down the yield curve" effect.

The advantage for an issuer in issuing a bond is the possibility to obtain external capital without having to post collateral. Collateral is as a rule demanded in bank lending, and if one issues shares, shareholders will have a say in decisions. The purchase of a bond does not make the buyer a shareholder, but a creditor. The advantage for the buyer are regular interest payments agreed upon in advance, as well as the repayment of 100% of the capital invested at the end of the term. Moreover, it is possible to sell the bond in the securities markets before it matures and thereby benefit from price gains. In addition, in case of insolvency, the claims of bondholders are senior to those of shareholders.

However, bonds also harbor enormous risks. The main risk that needs to be highlighted is credit risk. In the market economy, every company is subjected to the market test. Companies that are able to fulfill the wants of consumers best and most efficiently will remain established in the market. Companies that fail in this endeavor will be forced out of the market. It is therefore possible that a bond issuer will delay payments or will become insolvent. Both interest payments and the return of the principal amount are endangered in such cases. The ratings of international credit rating agencies are helpful in enabling one to better judge this risk. Although rating agencies are experts in the area of company evaluation, one still needs to take into account the possibility of human error, political pressure and other factors. Investors tend to lose more money in the category of bonds sporting triple A (AAA) ratings than in any other – as unpleasant surprises are often lurking in this segment.

Another risk is interest rate risk. This is the uncertainty associated with changes in market interest rates while one is holding a bond. As already mentioned, the price of a bond fluctuates with changes in market interest rates. Declining interest rates lead to rising bond prices, rising interest rates to falling bond prices. Interest rate risk is an important factor if one plans to sell a bond before it matures. If market interest rates move above the bond's yield, this entails a loss, if market interest rates move below the bond's yield, a profit can be made. This risk can be minimized with floating rate bonds. Market interest rates depend on monetary and government policy, as well as economic trends. Signals and trends that can influence market interest rates therefore need to be carefully analyzed if a sale prior to redemption is intended.

In addition, there can possibly be foreign exchange risk. As the denomination currency (the currency in which redemption takes place) and the coupon currency (the currency in which interest is paid) are usually identical, the purchase of a foreign currency denominated bond entails the additional risk of exchange rate fluctuations. Future exchange rate fluctuations can exceed the return believed to be certain, and lead to a nominal loss. On the other hand, a profit due to exchange rate fluctuations cannot be ruled out either.

Bonds are moreover subject to inflation risk – the uncertainty with respect to the real value of future interest payments. Rising inflation rates will increasingly diminish the real return and can even exceed it. In small markets and exotic investments, there is liquidity risk. This risk describes the possibility that the price received for a bond upon selling it can turn out to be lower than expected due to low trading volume.

Government Bonds

Government bonds are considered a "conservative" investment and appear to offer low, but safe yields. These are interest-bearing securities that are differentiated by maturity. In Germany: "Schatz" notes (one to two year maturities), federal notes, a.k.a. "Bobls" (from "Bundesobligationen" - five year maturity), and federal bonds, a.k.a. "Bunds" (from "Bundesanleihen", ten year maturities and higher); in the US: treasury bills (maturities of less than one year), treasury notes (one to ten year maturities), and treasury bonds (maturities exceeding 10 years). Government bonds are backed by the power to levy taxes, i.e., the government's ability to service principal and interest payments from tax revenues. Since coercive taxation is currently regarded as legitimate at any arbitrary level, the creditworthiness of most Western industrialized nations is still deemed to be very high by international rating agencies. However, this only means that government insolvencies are held to be improbable.

Government bonds differ from other types of bonds in that their proceeds are not used for the accumulation of capital, but to finance consumption. Even when politicians speak about "investments", these must clearly be regarded as consumption from an economic perspective. On the one hand, the goal is to be reelected, which results in extending favors to certain population groups. Government expenditures are a direct means to this end and not a value-adding roundabout method, which requires temporary sacrifices. Instead, they immediately and directly benefit certain people, especially politicians themselves (as they gain power and popularity).

On the other hand, even the return on long-term projects cannot be determined by government officials, due to the socialist calculation problem (which Ludwig von Mises first recognized and analyzed); thus there is no responsibility for losses. At best, government expenses can lead to higher tax revenues at a later stage; but on account of the problem that opportunity costs cannot be calculated by bureaucrats, it can be practically ruled out that these additional revenues will be higher than the associated expenditures plus interest expenses. This problem is that spending financed by taxes merely replaces private spending and does not add anything to it. "Austrians" regard private budgeting decisions in favor of saving as a form of legitimate, potentially economically fruitful spending as well, in comparison to which government consumption should by no means be preferred from an economic standpoint.

Every purchase of government bonds is therefore a speculation on higher tax ratios, as a result of which tax revenue must however ultimately decline in the long term, as a result of negative incentives, tax avoidance and income avoidance. This makes the whole affair a kind of pyramid scheme, which is unsustainable in the long run. Either the government becomes insolvent, or it avoids insolvency by debasing the currency. Government bonds are of course only "guaranteed" in nominal terms, their supposed safety thus depends directly on the underlying currency's stability.

However, in an inflationary environment, the prices of government bonds initially tend to rise. Especially for those who are able to "refinance" themselves at favorable terms at the central bank, government bonds indeed temporarily provide a risk-free yield. The higher the interest rate differential between government bonds and the yields on alternative assets that are declining due to a low interest rate policy, the more the prices of government bonds will increase, which makes them a popular object of speculation in inflationary periods. However, this is not the fault of speculators, whose actions merely demonstrate that there are distortions that they cannot be held responsible for.

Due to the long-term, historical perspective of the Austrian School, the risk of government bonds is deemed to be far greater than according to conventional wisdom. As objects of speculation, bonds can form the core of bubbles – and we are certainly experiencing a giant government bond bubble at present. In conjunction with Austrian capital theory, this leads to a critical assessment: the tax revenues to be distributed must first be produced by the private sector, and this becomes ever more difficult in high tax countries. There seems to be little upside potential left, but a great deal of downside potential.

From a purely economic perspective, government bonds can form part of a portfolio; the lower the tax burden and total public debt, and the less belligerence and willingness to devalue its currency a government displays, the more sensible this is. As a result, adherents of the Austrian School have occasionally recommended the purchase of Scandinavian or Swiss government bonds during the 19th and 20th century. In today's world, the choices are far more limited. To buy government bonds of countries in which one is obliged to pay tax, or one's offspring are obliged to do so, is a dubious proposition both from an investment perspective and one's perspective as a citizen: one is essentially betting on a rising tax burden. Over the long term, this so to speak amounts to an act of self-expropriation.

The current situation in government bonds paints an extremely distorted picture. Normally, low interest payments are an indication that investments are safe and government indebtedness is low. However today, the extent of public debt is at record highs, while bond yields are at historic lows. A number of examples: the federal Republic of Germany issued a federal Schatz note with a 6 month maturity in December 2011 that yielded 0.0005%. The interest cost of this bond with a principal amount of 2.675 billion euro amounted to a mere 6,687.50 euro. In the course of the past few years, yields for 6 month and two year notes fell to new all-time lows, and for the first time ever, their yields to maturity even turned negative. At the time of writing, some two trillion euro worth of European government bonds were displaying negative yields to maturity, and several governments have been able to sell bonds at primary market auctions with a negative yield.

As figure 9.31 shows, that the US government was never able to finance itself more cheaply. Without institutionalized interest rate manipulation, this would be an indication that the government's creditworthiness is greater than ever. However, looking at the trend in US federal debt makes one doubt its creditworthiness. Since 1971 alone, the public debt has risen more than forty-fold. Due to this extreme level of over-indebtedness, it seems obvious that there is very little leeway for significant rate hikes, and that the Fed's remaining room to maneuver is gradually decreasing over time. Since 1870, the average yield of US treasury notes amounted to 4.65%. Were the US government for instance be forced to refinance itself at 7%, over an extended time period, debt service costs would rise from the current 300 billion dollars per year to 2 trillion dollars, respectively 80% of tax revenues.

Even more extraordinary is the over-indebtedness of Japan. Due to a zero interest rate policy that has now been in place for eighteen years, the government has already refinanced the bulk of its debt burden at the lowest possible interest rate levels. In spite of these favorable refinancing conditions, debt service costs amount to 25% of government revenues. If the average yield were to increase by three percentage points (to 4.4%), debt service costs would devour the government's entire tax revenue. This alone makes it quite clear that higher levels of interest rates cannot possibly be reconciled with the budgetary situation.

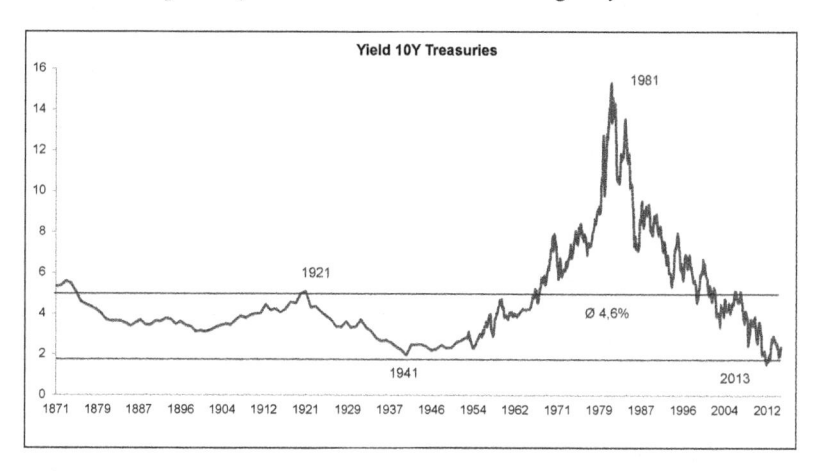

Figure 9.31: US government bond yields since 1870
(Sources: Prof. Robert Shiller, Incrementum AG)

9. Austrian Investment Practice

The term risk should be redefined for investors in an environment of zero interest rates, since nominally "safe" investments will lead to losses in real terms. This means, however, that even asset classes exhibiting low volatility by no means represent low risk or even risk-free assets. The difference between saving and investment is that savers attempt to *preserve* their purchasing power, while investors attempt to *increase* their purchasing power. In an environment of negative real interest rates, it is however necessary to take risks merely to preserve one's capital. The hunt for yield, combined with loose monetary policy and financial repression, already shows the effects associated with this today. Since supposedly safe investments like money market funds, CDs or government bonds no longer provide any yield to speak of, investors are increasingly embracing riskier asset classes.

The hunger for yield is in fact producing quite worrisome effects. According to Bank of America, yields on bonds with a total face value of 20 billion US dollars are below 1%. As a result, the hunt for yield leads to irrational exuberance in the high yield bond sector and emerging market bonds. Thus the Barclay's US High Yield Index fell below 5% for the first time ever in 2014. Not too long ago, a 5% yield was regarded as low even for US treasuries. Even nations that are not regarded as paragons of stability, such as Mongolia or Rwanda, have been able to issue bonds without problems in recent years. Mongolia's government issued bonds with a principal amount of 1.5 billion dollars (equivalent to approximately 20% of the country's economic output) at just 5.125%, while Rwanda's government was able to finance itself at 6.62%.

Currently, many asset classes are exhibiting negative real yields. "Risk-free" government bonds are sporting historically low yields. At present, one gets the impression that market participants are like a herd of Pavlovian dogs, which have been conditioned to expect ever more monetary stimulus. It is otherwise impossible to explain the ever-present hysteria over central bank policies, with market experts and investors poring over the nuances of every word uttered by central bankers. Whenever these monetary "coups de whiskey" are not provided, flight into liquid and seemingly safe US treasury bonds or German Bunds ensues, which continue to regularly make new all time highs in price. This "risk on, risk off" game is reminiscent of manic-depressive mood swings.

In the current environment, the stability that was once provided by gold bonds is sorely missed. Demand for gold-backed bonds could well grow in the future. There are a number of precedents for the use of gold in crisis situations. For instance, in the 1970s, Italy and Portugal used their gold reserves as collateral for loans by the German Bundesbank and the Bank for International Settlements. In 1991, India used its gold as collateral for a loan from the Bank of Japan.

Even a study on behalf of the European Parliament recommends gold-backed bonds. Its author, Ansgar Belke, arrived at the conclusion that gold-backed bonds would be far more transparent, attractive and fair for investors than a central bank government bond purchasing program. Gold-backed bonds would at least serve to decrease the pressures of the sovereign debt crises in the short term. Even the World Gold Council is moving in this direction and has advised Italy to issue gold-backed bonds. A part of its 2,400 ton gold reserve should be used as collateral. This would lower financing costs and restore the damaged confidence in Italy's creditworthiness. As the study noted:

> Simply speaking, a gold based solution would be less inflation-prone. Those arguing that the gold-backing solution would decouple the money supply and hard currency potentially leading to hyperinflation neglect the current non-role of gold for backing a currency. But above all, the use of gold as collateral avoids or lessens in importance, the reduction of incentives for reform of the beneficiary countries under the SMP (Securities Markets Program, targeted bond purchases by the ECB) and the OMT (Outright Monetary Transactions, theoretically unlimited bond purchases by the ECB).[141]

Economist Antal Fekete, who is an adherent of the Mengerian tradition, also recommends that crisis countries should issue gold-backed bonds in order to strengthen their creditworthiness and prevent insolvency. With that they would provide an example to other countries showing how gold bonds can be usefully employed as well. Fekete enumerates additional advantages of such bonds, as well as of a gold currency in general:[142]

1. Government gold is rendered liquid.
2. This would encourage privately held gold to be used for the backing of privately issued gold bonds.
3. Gold that is made useful is more valuable than gold that just gathers dust in vaults, just as developed land is more valuable than fallow land .
4. Circulating gold creates confidence; hoarded gold is an indication that confidence is lacking.
5. Contrary to fiat monies, gold regularly stabilizes currencies that are backed by it versus foreign currencies.
6. Market interest rates would also be stabilized. Contrary to other prices, the stabilization of which is not desirable as that would mask important price signals, interest rates should be stable to prevent capital outflows.
7. Gold was always used as money, directly and indirectly. The developments that followed in the wake of abandoning gold have led to today's crises.
8. Irredeemable currencies of course imply irredeemable bonds. With that the foundation that imparts real safety to a bond is lacking.

How would a gold bond, whether issued by governments or private parties, work? Essentially, principal and interest rates would be paid in gold or gold money at redemption. The market for gold bonds would be part of the wider capital markets, and investment bankers would act as intermediaries between issuers and buyers. An issuer of such bonds would of course strive to keep their market value as stable as possible. For this purpose, he could form sinking funds and if necessary buy back outstanding bonds early. In this manner, government gold bonds would become highly liquid and trade at low yields; these yields would in turn provide the yardstick for interest rates on bank loans and corporate bonds.[143]

Corporate Bonds

Corporate bonds normally trade at a spread over government bonds. This is primarily due to two factors. Firstly, defaults are historically more prevalent among corporations than states. Buyers thus have to be compensated for the potentially higher default risk, as they would otherwise invest in less risky assets. Secondly, government bonds are more liquid than corporate bonds, this is to say, they can be traded more easily, i.e., they have deeper market liquidity.

The recent sovereign debt crisis however led to a change in the traditional perception of corporate and government bonds. Government bonds that were previously regarded as risk-free were increasingly called into question. The background to this development is the ever-worsening budgetary situation of industrialized nations. Nowadays, debt-to-GDP ratios are already at unsustainable in several countries. Many companies are in comparatively better shape. As an investor, one must ask whether the traditional relationship between corporate and government bonds belongs to history. Will we see corporate bonds exhibit lower risk premiums and in extreme cases even lower yields than government bonds?

In the current situation, it is still difficult to imagine that an industrialized nation will go bankrupt, in spite of record high public debts. In case of emergency, governments that come under pressure can always shift their debt to third parties (the citizenry). The key words taxation, expropriation and inflation should be sufficiently descriptive. Moreover, there is of course always the possibility to service debt via the (virtual) printing press. Is the credit risk of corporations after all still higher because of this?

Corporations can so to speak defend themselves against domestic policies by establishing and hedging themselves internationally. Multinational corporations can skirt country-specific risks and instead drop anchor so to speak in safe havens. They are often managed more conservatively than many states. This is no contradiction, as corporations often exhibit a more long-term oriented decision-making horizon and are necessarily aiming for profitability. There is therefore a strong incentive to uncover possible inefficiencies and mistakes more quickly than is the case in the sluggish apparatus of the State.

During the recent sovereign debt crises, there were indications that corporate bonds can indeed be safer than government bonds. For instance, Greek telecommunications company OTE remained stable when the Greek government lost control over its budget. There are also dozens of examples of corporations with a better credit rating than the country they are domiciled in. How corporate bonds will actually fare in the event of a government debt restructuring, ultimately depends on a variety of factors.

The second reason why corporate bonds have traditionally traded at a higher spread is their liquidity. Government bonds used to benefit from large and liquid reference markets in the past. However, the further governments recede from AAA ratings, the more this liquidity premium tends to shrink. If a government has a very low credit rating, it can ultimately result in the corporate bond market becoming more liquid. The governments of Ireland and Portugal can tell us a thing or two about that.

However, corporate bonds are of course not immune to bubbles either. Since Mario Draghi has made more than a trillion euro available to private banks at extremely favorable conditions, the business with bonds of mid-size companies in Europe has flourished. This is no surprise, as yields between 5 to 8 percent are not only enticing for institutional, but also private investors. The currently very low yields on corporate bonds issued by borrowers of questionable creditworthiness certainly seem to be a typical bubble phenomenon.

Catastrophe Bonds (CAT-Bonds)

An interesting alternative in the bond sector are catastrophe bonds, also known as CAT bonds. This is a relatively new asset class, which is used to insure against natural catastrophes. The risk and return profile of a catastrophe bond has very little in common with traditional financial market products, but is rather comparable to the risk/return profile of a reinsurance contract. In order to properly categorize catastrophe bonds as an asset class, a brief historical review of the insurance business is required.

Insurance companies have been around for several centuries, with some historians even pointing out that insurance-like agreements were already made before the time of Christ. Due to its position as a maritime and global trading power, England served as an important "development volunteer" for the insurance business as we know it today. Shipping insurance, freight insurance and fire insurance were characteristic of the then most important insured risks. At the time, primary insurers were active in the market, and the insurance market Lloyd's of London developed rapidly. In 1842, the great fire of Hamburg led to grave capacity bottlenecks for the insurance industry, and in its wake the idea of overarching reinsurance originated. 1842 can thus be seen as marking the birth of the reinsurance business. The Reinsurance Company of Cologne, today General Re and owned by Warren Buffett (Berkshire Hathaway), is the oldest reinsurance company. Until 1992, this two-tiered system was sufficient for the insurance sector. However, the year 1992 left the insurance market shaken: hurricane "Andrew" caused massive damage in the US, and similar to 1842, the cry for more capacity went up. The idea to shift underwriting risk to an additional partner was hence developed. This partner needed to have large amounts of capital at its disposal and had to be interested in the risk/return profile of insurance premiums.

At the same time, it became evident that the global financial markets were searching for sources of uncorrelated returns, and thus they qualified as an ideal partner. The product, however, had to be designed in such a way as made it suitable for capital markets, and the catastrophe bond was the result: a bond that, instead of featuring a pure interest coupon and credit risk, is defined by insurance premium payments and by exhibiting insurance rather than issuer risk. The first catastrophe bond was issued in 1995. In 1997, the first ratings were assigned by credit rating agencies (BB on average) and the first catastrophe bond investment fund was established in the same year. In 2002, Swiss Re published the first CAT bond index. In 2013, the total market capitalization of catastrophe bonds reached the 20 billion dollar mark for the first time. Recent studies suggest that the volume of outstanding catastrophe bonds will more than double in coming years. Since catastrophe bonds represent a collateralized reinsurance policy, the sponsors of catastrophe bonds (as a rule primary and re-insurers), do not have to put up equity capital and as a result have a second avenue available to insure themselves against peak risks apart from traditional re-insurance contracts. On the other hand, investors in catastrophe bonds have an opportunity to generate returns and expose themselves to risks that are independent of traditional capital markets. Catastrophe bonds cover events like earthquakes and hurricanes, a small part also insures the risks of terrorism and pandemics. As a rule, they have a maturity of three years and a variable yield based on 3 month LIBOR plus the premiums written. They are usually issued with an expected loss rate of 2%, which is equivalent to one claim for damages every 50 years. Premiums differ depending on the type of risk covered, and range from 2% to 15% above 3 month LIBOR.

Mutual Funds

While collective investment products like mutual funds were established in the Anglo-Saxon world at the beginning of last century already, the first investment funds in Germany date from 1950. The mutual fund industry, however, only began to see strong growth in continental Europe in the 1990s and 2000s. With the 2008 financial crisis, the growth period in this asset class came to a halt. According to the European Fund and Asset Management Association (EFAMA), an impressive 9.7 billion euro was invested in mutual funds at the end of 2013 in the European Economic Area.[144]

Wealth is invested by mutual funds according to predefined investment principles in specific asset classes, such as stocks or bonds, but in some cases also in a mix of several asset classes. As a rule, these portfolios attempt to achieve a more or less pronounced degree of diversification. The main economic argument in favor of investing in a mutual fund is a better risk/reward profile due to the diversification across many different assets, in line with the principle that one should not put all one's eggs in one basket. The probably best-known studies regarding the advantageous characteristics of diversified portfolios are by Harry Markowitz, who worked on the topic in the 1950s. His "modern portfolio theory" later earned him a Nobel Prize in economics.

Due to transaction costs and minimum fees, private investors can often only achieve limited diversification over many different securities, hence broad diversification is one of the biggest advantages of investment funds. Diversified portfolios can be purchased at a relatively low cost, bundled as a security. The owner of units participates in the development of all assets held by the fund. Today, investment funds are a heavily regulated segment of the financial sector, with regulators issuing highly detailed prescriptions with respect to diversification and permitted investments.

Apart from considerations with regard to diversification, transferring asset management to specialized investment firms is an additional motive for investing in investment funds. In Germany and Austria, investment funds are legally defined as separate assets. The capital of investors is strictly segregated from the investment company's capital and is held by a deposit bank at arm's length from the investment management company. This legal and organizational segregation effectively eliminates counterparty risk from mutual funds. This is also the difference to so-called certificates (structured products), which are legally debentures and thus exposed to the counterparty risk of the issuer. Open-ended funds (contrary to closed-end funds, unless they are listed on an exchange) can be traded regularly. Investors can purchase or sell their units in intervals specified by the investment fund's terms. Investment funds can employ quite different investment strategies. A variety of investment philosophies, investment styles and various sub-categories are available. The Institute for Austrian Asset Management (*www.ifaam.de*), based in Germany, is a pioneer with respect to the selection of "Austrian funds" and is focused on investment vehicles in the areas of mining stocks, commodities and precious metals, family companies with a sound equity base, "deep value investing" and wealth management funds.

	fundamental analysis	technical analysis	portfolio optimization (asset allocation)
philosophy	active management	active management	passive management/ active management
goal	stocks selection	timing	risk-return optimization of the portfolio
investment styles	value / growth / garp	trend following / anti-cyclical	naive diversification vs optimized diversification
subcategory	bottom-up vs top-down	quantitative analysis / chart analysis	unlevered vs risk parity
trade philosophy	buy and hold	trading-oriented	buy and hold / tactical asset allocation
representatives	Kostolany, Buffett, Munger	Paul Tudor Jones, Charles Dow	Ray Dalio, US universities, Fama
asset class	esp. stocks	all liquid securities	combination of all asset classes

Figure 9.32: Fundamental vs. Technical Analysis (Source: Incrementum AG)

ETFs

ETFs or exchange traded funds, are as a rule passively invested funds and are characterized by relatively low fees (especially compared to actively managed funds). ETF assets are also segregated from the capital of the ETF manager, thus there is no issuer risk attached to these securities. Moreover, some ETFs are quite liquid and can – contrary to traditional mutual funds – also be traded intraday. In terms of their performance characteristics, ETFs are similar to so-called index certificates. Investors can achieve broad diversification with ETFs. Thus one can invest in individual sectors (such as gold stocks), countries (MSCI US), regions (Asia ex Japan) or styles (e.g. growth stocks), as well as betting either on rising (long) or falling (short) prices. In addition, there are also leveraged ETFs now available, which replicate the daily performance of the underlying benchmark multiplied by a factor of two or three.

Due to their tradability, ETFs are however also directly connected with the inflationary forces of the modern bubble economy. Instead of issuing a warning, Jim Rogers dispensed the following advice:

> While ETFs make the world simpler in some ways, they also open opportunities for those willing to scout and research the companies not contained in the ETFs and indexes. There are thousands of companies worldwide with little following because they are not included. An ambitious analyst can have a field day combing through them—with little competition.[145]

Absolute Return Funds

Most "traditional investment funds" are oriented toward benchmark indexes. This relative perspective is often disadvantageous for investors. While fund managers may be elated that they have "only" lost 25%

and thereby "outperformed" their benchmark because the benchmark index has declined by 30%, investors are unlikely to be bowled over with joy. Numerous studies confirm that actively managed funds rarely outperform their benchmarks.

Absolute return funds represent an alternative approach, as they are allowed to invest without any reference to benchmarks. This is basically the most prestigious asset management discipline. Its focus is absolute capital appreciation, regardless of the stock market climate. In most cases, this is achieved with a multi-asset investment strategy. More specifically, absolute return funds can flexibly invest in stocks, bonds, commodities and derivatives, both long and short. The main advantage of absolute return funds is the fact that one delegates asset management to a professional. The disadvantage of this type of investment fund is that absolute return funds often underperform pure equity funds during bull markets, since their main focus is on avoiding losses instead of generating "profits at any price". The success of such a fund is naturally always highly dependent on the quality of the fund's managers.

Costs and Fees

Financial services are often not very transparent for customers with respect to their fees and costs. Since recurring fees are charged to the fund and do not have to be paid directly, the cost burden is often underestimated. It is, however, a crucial aspect of profitable investment. The first cost burden investors must bear is usually incurred in the form of an upfront fee (also known as "load"). These sales charges are a premium on the fund's price and are as a rule pocketed by the distribution partner of the asset management company. It may be possible to minimize this upfront fee. Some online brokers recommend funds that are sold with a small load, resp. no load at all. If one has a specific fund in mind, it is sensible to compare the prices offered by different brokers. The load can sometimes also be reduced by negotiating with one's house bank or broker. The loads vary in size – as a rule of thumb, the more volatile the asset class, the higher the load.

Apart from this one-time upfront fee, there are numerous recurring fees, primarily administrative and custodian fees. These recurring fees are summarized in the so-called TER, the total expense ratio. Here too the costs as a rule depend on the volatility of the asset class, and in addition on whether the fund is an actively managed or a passive one.

	passive funds	active funds	active multi-asset funds	asset management funds	active stock funds
subscription fees	0–5%	1–3%	2–4%	2–4%	2.5–5%
TER	0.25%–0.75%	0.5%–1.25%	1.25%–2%	1.5%–2.5%	1.5%–2.5%

Figure 9.33: Comparison of fund fees (Source: Incrementum AG)

The term performance fee describes a fee that depends on the fund management's success; it is often also referred to as an outperformance fee. The argument for such performance-related fees is that they help to better align the interests of investors and fund managers.

However, performance fees can be an incentive for fund managers to engage in especially risky speculation, as substantial remuneration beckons in the event of success. So-called high water marks have been established in the meantime. The fund manager only receives a bonus if the fund achieves new all time highs. Another important feature for calculating performance fees is the so-called hurdle rate, a minimum return threshold. Only once the fund manager has achieved this hurdle rate, and the fund's net asset value exceeds its high-water mark, does the manager qualify for receiving a performance fee. As a result, fund managers have a strong incentive to manage their funds in such a manner that new highs are attained, while at the same time ensuring that the old high-water mark is not undercut too much. Regaining peak values is all the more difficult the further a fund's price has declined below the high-water mark.

Securities Lending

The market for securities lending (repo market), is a part of the capital markets the broader public is generally only tangentially or not at all aware of, and is generally little understood. For a variety of reasons, it can happen that market participants need to obtain delivery of a specific security. Fund managers can use the repo market to enter into lending transactions, in order to generate a small additional return. What is often not considered in this context is the fact that by lending out securities, one is exposed to counterparty risk. This risk can e.g. materialize during a banking crisis, when a counterparty runs into payment difficulties.

Many investment funds actively engage in securities lending, without investors being aware of the associated risks. A survey by fund analysis company Morningstar revealed that the average share of securities lending in (physically replicated) passive funds stands at more than 99% in some cases.[146] Often lending fees are not (or not fully) assigned to the fund. In this way, a favorable fee structure is cross-subsidized, but from an economic perspective, it is ultimately bought by taking a potentially fatal, largely hidden risk. Only if a fund's prospectus explicitly rules out the possibility of securities lending, can investors be certain that this risk is not incurred.

Alternative Investments

Alternative investments comprise all forms of investment that go beyond the usual investment techniques (i.e., investments with the goal of earning a return respectively of achieving price gains) in stocks, bonds and money market instruments. Alternative investments are primarily associated with hedge funds and private equity funds. In a broader sense, the definition however also encompasses real estate and precious metals investments, as well as investments in works of art, fine wines, and so forth. Typically, alternative investments exhibit one or more of the following characteristics:

- They often exhibit a low correlation with traditional investments
- The liquidity of the investment assets is often limited
- Unique risks are associated with these investments
- They often require a relatively high investment sum
- They are partly subject to fewer regulations

Options

One of the side effects of inflationism is that speculation gains in importance relative to investment. Due to financial repression, investors face the choice of accepting a guaranteed loss of purchasing power, or of dabbling in extraordinarily speculative investments. As a matter of principle, not every speculative investment necessarily has to be extremely risky, but nevertheless the risk of loss does rise in line with the potential return. Neither among retail investors, nor among institutional investors are there many people who are on average successful over the long term with speculative investments. Generally, the principle "cobbler, stick to thy last" is advisable in this context. Nowadays, an extremely broad range of speculative investment products is available. There are also various vehicles that small investors can use to invest with big leverage or to bet on falling prices. In Europe, derivatives for small investors are often issued as bank debentures and traded in the form of certificates (structured products), while in the US standardized options are more prevalent.

Options are often perceived as aggressive and highly speculative instruments. However, experienced investors can also use them as cheap hedging tools or for the creation of asymmetric payoff profiles. An option is a forward contract with which the buyer obtains the right to buy from or sell to the option seller (writer) an underlying asset (stock, index, commodity, currency) at a fixed price on or before a specific date in the future. In contrast to a futures contract, the option represents solely a right from the buyer's perspective and includes no obligation, thus it is also referred to as a conditional forward contract. In futures contracts, both parties to the contract are obliged to deliver or to pay for the underlying instrument, thus this type of transaction is called an unconditional forward contract.

Options transactions are normally not settled by physical delivery, but by cash settlement. The price of an option is called the option premium. There are two different types of options:

- *Call option*: the buyer of the option has the right to buy the underlying instrument from the option writer. The buyer of the option profits from a price increase in the underlying instrument. An example: the buyer purchases a call option with a strike price of $30 on a stock that currently trades at $30, because he expects its price to rise. The option gives him the right to purchase the stock from the option writer e.g. within one year for the price of $30.

- *Put option*: the buyer of the option has the right to sell the underlying instrument to the option writer at a specific strike price within a specified time period prior to the expiration date of the option.

One must take into account that the price of an option is not only influenced by the price of the underlying security, but also by factors such as the remaining time to expiration and volatility. Against this background, one can also speculate on changes in volatility by combining different options – independent of the price trend of the underlying security.

Options are traded on options and futures exchanges, such as the CBOT or Eurex, and are strictly standardized. Prices are determined by supply and demand. Option certificates are, however, placed by issuers (most often banks) and traded both on and off exchanges. The bid/ask prices of certificates are determined by the issuer and are therefore not a result of supply and demand. While the issuer uses the exchanges and the prices of comparable options for orientation, he can act in a far less transparent and arbitrary manner.

Important metrics for the valuation of options are the so-called "Greeks" (delta, gamma, vega, theta, rho, omega), however, we will not discuss them in detail here. We would only like to point out that the time premium (theta) as well as leverage (gamma) are in practice difficult to understand for private investors. Moreover, implied volatility is also an important factor in an option's valuation. The higher this implied volatility premium, the less attractive the option is for buyers.

Alternatives to options are index certificates and CFDs. Similar to other certificates, index certificates represent debentures (i.e., bonds). With the aid of index certificates, investors can participate in the performance of an index with ease. They represent a simple and cost-effective method compared to replicating an entire index (e.g. in order to replicate the DAX 30, 30 individual stocks would have to be bought in the appropriate weightings). The disadvantage consists of the associated issuer risk: should the issuer of the certificate become insolvent, the certificate becomes worthless. Index funds offer higher security, however, entail higher costs in most cases.

The abbreviation CFD stands for *contract for difference*. The buyer of a CFD does not purchase the financial instrument (stock, commodity, etc.), but merely becomes obliged to pay a price difference. The most obvious advantage of contracts for difference is that high leverage can be obtained with a very small capital outlay, as only margin need be posted. For example, with a leverage of 50, one can double the capital employed if the price of the underlying instrument changes by just 2%. However, leverage works in both directions; thus a loss of 2% in the underlying instrument amounts to a total loss for the CFD. Contrary to option certificates, price formation is transparent and easy to understand, as implied volatility or remaining time to expiration play no role. Since the purchase of a contract for difference is a credit-financed transaction, financing costs are incurred. These vary between brokers. If one trades with the high leverage inherent in contracts for difference, strict risk and money management is required.

Hedge Funds

Hedge funds are among the best known alternative investments: private investment vehicles for accredited investors, which often trade exchange-listed instruments with leverage, respectively in combination with derivatives. Short selling can also be employed, so as to profit from price declines. Hedge funds first appeared on the scene in the post WW2 era. A number of stock market investors realized that the returns of pure equity portfolios were negative in economic downturns, even if they succeeded in selecting the relatively best performing stocks. In order to mitigate this "economic risk", traditional equity portfolios were combined with a hedge. In the framework of this hedge portion, resourceful investors were betting on declining prices of stocks they perceived as overvalued by selling them short. In this manner, the overall return consists of the difference between the various stock price movements. The general market trend can be neutralized to some extent by this method, which is called a market-neutral strategy.

Speculating on declining stock prices is often questioned from an ethical perspective. From the Austrian School's perspective, they are not condemned if they are pursued to a healthy extent. Their economic significance consists of the fact that a necessary selection of productive and unproductive companies takes place. In a sound monetary system, which as a rule is characterized by interest rates well above the price inflation rate, speculation on declining stock prices involves significant opportunity costs. In order to sell stocks short, investors have to borrow securities, which they then sell in the market in order to buy them back at a later stage to return them to the lender. Borrowing securities naturally involves costs. An important part of the costs in securities lending are (implicit) interest costs, which are included in lending fees. Borrowing securities – similar to normal credit transactions – becomes increasingly unattractive the higher borrowing costs become. In times of structurally low real interest rates, such transactions can be done at excessively low costs, which results in an explosive increase in short-term speculation.

Hedge funds as an asset class developed rapidly in the 1970s. New strategies which speculate on macro-economic developments were springing up ("Global Macro"). A giant playground for this was created with the repudiation of the gold-exchange standard in the form of foreign exchange speculation. The foreign exchange market has become a huge market that employs a veritable army of traders and speculators today. George Soros became famous for his successful speculation against the British pound. Volatility in commodity markets has also increased strongly since the end of the gold exchange standard.

The structurally low level of real interest rates in recent decades had a major effect on the boom in hedge funds as an asset class. On the one hand, the interest rate backdrop practically forces people to invest in speculative asset classes in order to achieve returns. On the other hand, low financing costs for short sales and leveraged trades are creating the ideal preconditions for these asset classes. Speculation that would never pay off under normal circumstances becomes profitable. Such a surfeit of speculation is a typical symptom of an unsound monetary system.

The trend becomes especially conspicuous when a paper money system enters its terminal stage. Descriptions of the enormous growth in speculative activity during the Weimar Republic are well-known from numerous books and reports. A multitude of hedge fund strategies has come into being in the meantime:

- *Global macro*: this strategy attempts to exploit global macro-economic trends and their effects on stocks, bonds, currencies and commodities using a top-down approach.

- *Long/short equity*: this involves taking positions in stocks both on the long and short side. Success depends on the manager's stock picking ability.

- *Arbitrage*: this strategy aims to eliminate market risk by exploiting price differences (often tiny ones) between similar asset classes. Arbitrage funds often employ highly complex valuation models.

- *Event-driven*: the fund manager attempts to exploit important events such as mergers, restructurings, or spin-offs for successful trades.

- *CTA (commodity trading advisors)/managed futures*: these strategies, which are often also referred to as "trend following" strategies, aim to quickly recognize and exploit trends. These funds are active in commodities, foreign exchange and stock markets, primarily via derivatives (futures contracts).

- *Private equity*: an alternative to hedge funds: investments in non-listed companies, which are believed to have especially strong growth potential over a longer-term investment horizon (often 5 to 10 years). Investments in private equity are illiquid and in most cases less transparent than hedge funds or traditional investment funds.

Digital Currencies

The spectacular rise in the digital currency Bitcoin has the drawn the attention of investors to the opportunity offered by digital investments. No other investment category has exhibited similar speculative price increase potential in such a short period of time as digital currencies. Interestingly, modern-day "Austrians" are both among the first critics as well as the pioneers of the digital currency scene. What potential and what dangers do digital currencies entail?

On the one hand, the digital sphere is extremely well suited for all sorts of bubbles, as the dot-com bubble showed. After all, there are no physical limits and capital requirements are quite small, while there is enormous scope for promises of a bright future. This is why many start-ups, modern company formations of the bubble economy that are in most cases eager to quickly sell themselves in distorted markets, are often found in the digital realm. Digital offerings are especially compatible with mass-media hype mechanisms, which create short-term reinforcement in favor of supposedly new things. This is relevant for speculators, for whom this area is an excellent playground. A certain intuition for what is likely to go "viral" is probably a decisive ingredient of speculative success in this sector.

On the other hand, digital tools do provide real value creation. The biggest field of value creation, which is largely independent of hype, subsidies, contracts and loans is something modern-day "Austrians" are especially fond of: tools that can be employed in the race between citizens and financial repression. The digital realm still eludes the State's all-encompassing grasp. This race between surveillance and encryption is not decided yet. There are still great opportunities and commercial incentives in this area for private creativity. Should digital tools win the race and restrict the intervention of increasingly desperate States, a likely consequence will be the partial blocking, shutdown and nationalization of global data networks. However, even to this there potentially exist entrepreneurial ripostes.

The control of payment streams is one of the most crucial areas of this race. However, a controlled digitization of currencies is perfectly congruent with the interests of States and the banking cartel. This is probably one of the reasons why the authorities have not yet cracked down on Bitcoin with full force. Other private alternatives to government-controlled currencies, which contrary to Bitcoin did not allow for any tracking of payment streams and were not pure fiat monies, have found their end with expropriations and jail sentences. Only regional currencies, which as a rule use government scrip as their reference and are not useful for the broad masses are tolerated as hobbies. The value of such regional currencies is mainly in providing niches outside the grasp of government. Exchange in such networks is providing satisfaction mainly because the bulk of the value involved is not retained for taxes and levies in every act of exchange. While taxes instill government scrip with its value, they concurrently lower its usefulness as a medium of exchange. This effect is widely underestimated.

It is therefore no surprise that the platform Silk Road was the first large market-place for the use of Bitcoins – a kind of Ebay for proscribed goods. One could only access it by installing software for anonymous access through so-called Tor servers. On the virtual silk road, all kinds of drugs were available; however, offers of other goods (e.g. weapons) were rather meager. The weakness of this platform is of course the problem of trust, after all, one's counterparty whom one must provide one's delivery address can easily turn out to be an undercover agent.

Bitcoins are virtual credit entries, which are produced in a decentralized manner by means of a random algorithm, which stands in relation to the computing power employed. This computing power is partially used to perform and audit book entries. The more computing power one can make available for this purpose, the higher the probability that one finds a Bitcoin. The total number of Bitcoins is moreover limited. The more coins have already been "mined", the more difficult it becomes to find new ones, as that requires more and more computing power – an effect similar to a real resource becoming more scarce.

The problem consists of the fact that the computing power that would actually be required for the allocation and administration of Bitcoins is infinitesimally small compared to that one has to employ in reality (as otherwise too many Bitcoins would be produced). The computing power as such has actually no further value. In the meantime, the electricity cost of running the computers has in any case increased beyond the possible Bitcoin yield. In short: Bitcoins have in effect no commodity cover for which an industrial demand exists in addition to monetary demand.

This fact is key to both the critique and explanation of the Bitcoin phenomenon by the Austrian School. Bitcoins are a proto-fiat money. While there is a small industrial demand for Bitcoins based on curiosity and their novelty value, the majority of demand is of a speculative nature. There is nothing wrong with this, and as such it is not an argument against Bitcoins. Every good that has the potential to become money is demanded by early adopters precisely because of this speculative opportunity. Bitcoin without a doubt has monetary potential. It is important for this potential to be realized that demand be not solely based on speculation: either there is industrial demand or the two other aspects of monetary demand have to play a role. While industrial demand for Bitcoins is by now infinitesimally small, it was of great importance for initial demand. Thereafter, all three types of monetary demand emerged: Bitcoins offer to make exchanges easier (cost-free and practically instant international transfers), as well as provide access to new markets. This new market was initially mainly Silk Road, where Bitcoins had the greatest marketability due to their at the time assumed anonymity. This rise in marketability of course did not entail the full replacement of all other means of payment by Bitcoin, but consisted of Bitcoin's role as a supplement to them.

This explains the problem of digital currencies that are primarily fiat money: their sources of demand are relatively unstable, which increases volatility. Bear in mind that an increase in speculation lowers volatility (all other things remaining equal). Volatility is not, as is commonly assumed, a result of speculation, but of sudden changes in people's

9. Austrian Investment Practice

valuations (fashions, hypes), and especially of artificial intervention and political meddling. Silk Road was – as was to be expected – shut down by the FBI, and the facilitation of exchange is subject to massive political interference as well. The biggest Bitcoin rally to date began when Chinese citizens realized the currency was a means of payment which they could use to easily and cheaply circumvent China's capital controls. China's government tolerated this development for a while, as it was able to observe in the form of a limited "experiment" how open capital markets might affect the People's Republic. The experiment was limited, because the threshold for using Bitcoins is relatively high: initially, only a technology-affine minority could employ them. Once the experiment threatened to grow beyond its controllable limits, interventions became more forceful. Since industrial demand is essentially absent from Bitcoins, they are under greater threat of artificial volatility from an Austrian perspective. This could only be compensated for by massive speculative activity. A large price decline occurred when the then largest Bitcoin exchange Mt. Gox stopped payouts and came under suspicion of practicing fractional reserve banking (it later turned out that large-scale fraud had been committed).

Unfortunately, the incentives are not especially good; due to the great political risks involved, the entrepreneurs initially active in the market are often rather shady types with excessively high risk preferences, who lack a long-term perspective and seriousness. For "Austrian" investors, digital currencies are at best a small portfolio supplement as a speculative trade, but are not useful for savings. Investments in companies that offer payment services have of course considerable potential – after all, this is a sector that is dominated by a monopoly and a cartel, and the need for innovation is accordingly great. However, similar to all other investments, this requires one to know the market. An important aspect one needs to pay attention to: in the digital field, anti-cyclical conduct is even more difficult than elsewhere, as the amplification effects are so large. Someone who is familiar with the digital field to the extent that he can seriously ponder investments, is usually especially prone to being so deeply embedded in the digital muck that he is continually bombarded by often subconscious signals through his digital devices.

There is hardly another sector in which it is possible to lose money as fast as in the digital one: in the event malinvestment occurs, not even scrap value is left.

Regional Investment

In light of overly complex and abstract investment products, ever more investors wish for a more direct relationship to investments in the real economy. This yearning for understandable and thus "cleaner" investments is fostered by a certain civilization fatigue, post-modern ideological trends, apocalyptic fears and a lack of community and identity. As a result, it stands to reason that it may be better not to venture into the distance and participate in global financial flows, but look for possibilities closer to home.

A model for regional "investments" is the German firm Regionalwert AG (its first foreign offshoot is going to be created in Northeastern Austria shortly). This is a non-listed stock corporation, through which approximately 500 citizens with shareholdings valued at between 500 and 150,000 euro become co-owners of small companies in their region, especially in the agricultural sector. Currently, Regionalwert AG holds participatory interests in nearly 25 enterprises; most of the participation models are limited partnerships with a limited liability company as general partner and silent partnerships, partly as a minority, partly as a majority partner. Another type of participatory interest takes the form of purchasing land and farming estates and choosing leaseholders. Dividends have not been paid yet, the main motives for buying shares are of an idealistic nature; ecological, social and political criteria also play an important role.

Models such as this one can not as yet be regarded as investments in the strict sense. They rather serve as an inspiration for what "endowments" as we have described and recommended them above could actually look like. The greater the ambition, however, the more difficult it is to achieve it. The more intentions to save the world become the focus, through opinions reinforced by the spirit of the times and participation that not only wants to supervise but control, the greater the danger of capital destruction. However, even, or especially, in a long-term engagement that is primarily driven by idealistic motives, value creation without the risk of loss is unthinkable.

Apart from stocks, profit-sharing subordinated loans and silent partnerships can be chosen for idealistic investments, but in most cases the regulatory framework rather than economic intentions will be the decisive criterion for the most suitable legal structures. An interesting alternative are *de natura* investments, which in most cases correspond to participatory notes, a mixture between stocks and bonds. These involve the payment of non-cash dividends, depending on the company's success. An example for these are so-called "sheep shares". As of yet, these models are not investments in the narrower sense, as idealism plays too great a role – real equity participation is not created, it is in fact rather a kind of consumption subscription. From the perspective that severe economic upheaval could possibly lead to supply disruptions, one could tie purchase guarantees to delivery guarantees.

All these examples offer inspiration for further investment innovations that the market is calling for – but that politics and the banking cartel are often obstructing. Regionalwert AG that was mentioned above also has the ambition to achieve profitability and value creation with its investments in the long term. This is supposed to be achieved by covering the entire chain of value creation, from production to processing to retailing. This shows how close very long-term oriented investments and endowments are to each other. Investors can increase the value of their investments by buying the products of their operations; many are also motivated by the desire to increase the security of supplies in their region.

The lack of profitability of many regional and agricultural investments is largely a result of economic distortions. Due to the Cantillon effect, there is a continual redistribution of purchasing power, intelligence and creativity from outlying regions to urban centers – which are the centers of politics and the financial industry. As a result, no one is surprised to see a 25 year-old banker driving a Porsche, but the same would be quite surprising in a young farmer. This could change after a major crisis. Today, every year 2,500 farmers find no successor in Austria, because young farmers lack savings or financing possibilities. Subsidies essentially increase concentration and destroy the entrepreneurial spirit of farmers by making them into highly regulated government-paid bureaucrats. Political interventions, meant to prevent the dying out of farms, ultimately hasten the process – something Austrian economists have always predicted. Thus five large dairies dominate Austria's dairy sector today.

In spite of inflationism, small enterprises find it ever more difficult to obtain loans from banks. This suggests that it may make sense to circumvent banks as intermediaries of savings. Such ideas are of course greatly obstructed by regulations designed to protect the banking cartel from competition. A recent case that illustrates these challenges and provides a wealth of inspiration for designing creative forms of financing is the clash between Austrian shoe manufacturer GEA and the financial markets supervisory authority. Due to strong support from the population, the authorities have thus far refrained from intervening, and are trying almost desperately to persuade the entrepreneur Heinrich Staudinger to back down.

It seems likely that market differentiation between such types of investments will increase. These can cover a large range: from strongly idealistic forms, which correspond essentially to non-profit associations and endowments, to more risky, strongly profit-oriented venture funds, which are more akin to incubators for regional company start-ups. In the peak period of the bubble economy, the artificial boom, there exist political economies of scale, which are more favorable to large companies and multinational corporations than to their small, regional peers. In correction periods, however, small enterprises that are embedded in regional value creation chains are far more resilient. Start-ups are highly risky, which makes diversification necessary. This diversification often leads to investors biting off more than they can chew, ultimately making capital destruction inevitable (i.e., entrepreneurial errors of judgment end up destroying most of the value). The problem is the same that led to the insolvency of the credit cooperatives described above. Enterprises that are not artificially supported by the bubble economy require entrepreneurship after all, which is difficult, uncomfortable and rare. Entrepreneurship can only be delegated or bought in to a very limited degree. Max Wirth describes the problem in his *Geschichte der Handelskrisen* (*History of Business Crises*) as follows:

> It is already difficult to find diligent expert workers for individual industrial or trade branches, but it is entirely impossible to bring men aboard who are capable of overseeing and judging many or all branches of industry and trade, and are able to lead such different establishments in a profitable manner. This is however the task the credit cooperatives have set for themselves; they engage in stock market business, which one man cannot fully grasp in his entire lifetime; normal banking business; they establish artful cotton, cigar and machine factories; if they lead the latter enterprises themselves, they must necessarily suffer losses on the whole, because they cannot manage and oversee so many heterogeneous things; however, if they only establish these businesses in order to sell the shares again, they declare themselves the public's wardens in things they do not understand, whereby they can create vast losses for shareholders without even realizing it.[147]

Regional investments have an advantage in terms of this problem, if regional limitation is associated with a special concentration of regional knowledge. Since regional structures are almost always more traditional structures, which can be traced back to the age prior to the monetary revolution, they offer additional opportunities, but also additional risks (in entrepreneurship, these always go hand in hand). The opportunity consists in rediscovering knowledge that has been largely lost; the danger consists in doing something that fails to address the needs and conditions of today. Limiting oneself to regional activities is favorable from an entrepreneurial perspective in terms of knowledge and resources, but unfavorable in terms of sales and marketing. The biggest value creation potential is harbored by regional companies that cater to global needs: for instance Asia's awakening hunger for education, authenticity, nature, culture and quality of life. This is of course contrary to many an idealistic ambition, as in light of the current distortions, every attempt to address larger markets is always also an invitation for bubble finance and demand hype. It is therefore sensible to strictly differentiate between the aspects of investment (with the goal of value creation for strangers willing to pay) and endowment (with the goal of promoting what one deems just and important) and consider them separately. Otherwise, there is a risk that one engages in feel-good consumption for oneself, which ultimately is not worth the effort – i.e., which ends up being neither an investment nor a sustainable endowment.

Microcredit

Since receiving the Nobel Prize, Muhammad Yunus has become the figurehead of the micro-credit business. In 1974, he had the idea to extend loans instead of making donations. His homeland, Bangladesh, had just gone through a famine, and most people lacked even the basic necessities of life. Yunus helped 42 families with tiny amounts, insisted however that they be paid back. The debt thus created was intended to serve as an incentive to employ the funds productively. The simplest possibility was and continues to be the purchase of goods for resale. The economist succeeded in instilling great enthusiasm for this particular way of credit extension among influential friends in the government and after a few years received the privilege of a banking license and broad tax exemptions. Yunus calls credit a "human right" and opines:

> If we are looking for one single action which will enable the poor to overcome their poverty, I would go for credit.[148]

An "Austrian" economist would view this assertion with skepticism. Yunus provides indeed a bad example for the possibilities of micro-loans. He received a first big subsidy from the UN, which was followed by Bangladeshi taxpayer funds. In addition, his brainchild Grameen Bank now receives subsidies from US foundations and through cheap loans infused with government guarantees from all over the world. These loans are passed on by Grameen primarily to women at average interest rate charges of 20 percent. The criteria employed to determine creditworthiness are unusual and not unproblematic: only people who own less than 2,000 square meters (21,528 square feet) of land are "rewarded" for their poverty with a loan.

The preconditions for becoming a customer of Grameen go way beyond that though. The usually female debtors are combined into groups, which regularly engage in collective rituals. Among other things, they must recite the "16 decisions", a catalog of moral precepts, which is supposed to further the women's ethical education. In fact, this seems to represent Grameen's main recipe for success. Yunus has actually created a complex reeducation program, which merely employs loans as a means to create conditions of dependency and responsibility and to introduce a collective disciplining tool. While the educational programs tilt toward collectivism in terms of their content, it is definitely plausible that they are promoting the material welfare of the participants.

After Bangladesh, the trend spread to India, where more than 1,000 micro-credit organizations exist in the meantime, not counting the participating banks. The forms of organization vary however. The reeducation network of Yunus appears to have been rejected in India, more often the participants present themselves as "self-help groups". Professor Malcolm Harper attributes this to the fact that the people of Bangladesh are used to military dictatorships, while in India, more "democratic" forms of government are at least superficially preferred.[149]

The "self-help groups" on average operate at lower costs than Grameen Bank and as a result are able to charge lower interest rates. Nevertheless, opposition to micro-credit is far more pronounced in India. Between 2002 and 2006, 87,000 farmers committed suicide in the wake of crop failures as a result of over-indebtedness. When it became known in the Krishna district in 2006 that it was indeed micro-loans that drove women into overindebtedness and ultimately to suicide, the authorities temporarily shut down the branches of several micro-credit organizations and declared the debts invalid (*The Economist, 17 August 2006*).

Sudhirendar Sharma, a former World Bank analyst and director of the Ecological Foundation, regards the suicides as the "dark shadow" of the micro-credit movement, and warned in an article in the Indian *Financial Daily* (09/25/2002) that micro-credit could create a debt trap. Household savings would often be exhausted to pay back the loans – a paradoxical result, given that micro-loans are supposed to promote capital formation. It would be devastating if micro-loans were to prove detrimental to savings, especially in India: the country has one of the lowest savings rates in the world.

A bureaucratic problem makes things even worse: micro-credit organizations are in most cases legally prohibited from managing savings. While one of the most systematic studies on the effects of micro-loans performed to date arrives at a more positive conclusion, it nevertheless warns: micro-credit often ends up "imprisoning the poor in an ever deepening spiral of indebtedness and dependency".[150] According to this study, on the whole, micro-loans appear to help the poor far less than those who already possess assets. The study's authors David Hulme and Paul Mosley conclude that the more prosperous the borrower, the greater his income growth through a micro-loan employed in entrepreneurial activity. Borrowers who already possess wealth and qualifications can make better use of the loans. The poorest are less capable of shouldering risks or using the loans for growing their income. In fact, the situation of numerous of the poorest debtors got worse as a result of a micro-loan, as it burdened these people with more risk than they were able to bear.[151]

This seems actually obvious, unfortunately though, for ideological reasons many micro-lending programs are focused on the poorest people. Their "entrepreneurship" however has rarely anything to do with self-directed independence and a willingness to take risk. Most of these people would prefer to work for wages. We are therefore faced with a kind of paradox: the poorest are least able to productively employ micro-credit, and those who would be able to do so, actually do not need micro-loans, but larger amounts that are made available for the long term. However, even micro-loans to the poorest exhibit relatively high repayment ratios. Yet, often micro-loans are paid back by borrowing another micro-loan from a competing organization. In Bangladesh for instance, there exist now more than 10,000 organizations offering micro-credit in the wake of the hype surrounding Muhammad Yunus.

Nevertheless, micro-loans continue to offer astonishingly high and stable returns. These high returns may partially be returns from labor rather than capital.[152] Especially female workers are as a rule excluded from the work force in certain regions. As a result, it could be that they are only able to work in a self-employed capacity, which requires however a minimum of own funds. Micro-loans would in these cases make it possible to generate returns from labor that would otherwise not exist.

Micro-loans in most cases range between $40 and $1,200, the repayment rates stand at an impressive 98 percent on average. The terms tend to be relatively short: 6 to 36 months. Extension of a loan is conditional on a business idea. In order to prevent defaults, funds are primarily lent to groups. Additional loans are only made available if the first loan has been paid back in a timely fashion. Interest rates charges amount in most cases to around 20 percent, lenders earn returns ranging from 3 to 15 percent.

The largest micro-finance sector in the world is actually in Germany.[153] This may sound surprising, as micro-credit is mainly associated with the "third world". However, the "banking for the poor" movement has strong roots in Germany. Initially, savings associations were established, the first of which was founded in Hamburg in 1778. This was followed by the establishment of communal thrifts, with the first one founded in 1801. Two big names are associated with the spread and the firm anchoring of micro-finance in Germany: Raiffeisen and Schulze-Delitzsch.

Friedrich Wilhelm Raiffeisen focused on rural areas and developed so-called credit societies. Among other things, their goal was to make micro-loans available to farmers. These micro-loans were however not created by way of government-supported credit expansion (inflation), but were drawn from the savings of farmers themselves. The institutions which later came to be called Raiffeisen Banks, respectively "Kassen", helped channeling these savings into the most productive uses, so that the prosperity of the respective regions could grow in a slow, but sustainable manner. A debt spiral was ruled out, as the size of loan volumes was limited by the small amount of accumulated savings. Usurious interest rates were not necessary either, as demand for loans was not artificially pushed (by declaring credit a "human right") and administrative expenses remained modest due to the focus on self-help – Raiffeisen recommended an interest rate of five percent.

Hermann Schulze-Delitzsch was more active in urban areas. He established thrift and credit cooperatives for artisans and small entrepreneurs, which eventually became the so-called "Volksbanks" (people's banks). He always held the principles of self-help and personal responsibility dear. Similar to Raiffeisen, Schulze-Delitzsch knew that, to quote development economist Peter Bauer: "Having money is the result of economic development, not its precondition."[154]

Small entrepreneurs as a rule finance the expansion of their activities from their cash flow. Loans to the poor on the other hand, as a rule, serve to support consumption in periods of cyclical or unexpected emergencies. As Thomas Dichter emphasizes, economic growth came first, and the movement to make credit available to the masses only came thereafter.[155] However, this already contained the seeds of the inflationary business cycles of modern times: large companies in the consumer goods industries supported the political promotion of credit for the masses in order to encourage consumption.

In the meantime, the micro-credit movement has learned quite a bit from its experiences. Numerous professionally managed funds allow investment in micro-loans and offer surprisingly stable

9. Austrian Investment Practice

returns – unfortunately only very few private investors have been admitted so far. A big advantage of micro-finance is its low correlation to other asset classes. Micro-entrepreneurs are sufficiently far-removed from events in the financial world and on the stock exchanges. The "micro" aspect, the focus on smallness and small scale, harbors great potential for creating sustainable enterprises to improve the living standards of the poorest, namely with those undertakings that are able to put down local roots. In this respect, much could and should be learned from micro-credit projects. The greatest hope would be if the knowledge gained could be used for the accumulation of micro-capital. The micro-credit movement can provide us with important suggestions for more human, "micro-based" economic activity, if we do not allow wishful thinking and ideology to blind us.

Sensible investments through micro-loans are on the one hand direct "micro-participatory interests", such as those discussed in the context of regional investments. A certain geographical and cultural proximity is an advantage for choosing projects. Global investments via micro-loans on the other hand only make sense through investment funds, which allow for broad diversification. An investment through NGOs or smaller initiatives usually corresponds more to an endowment. The direct relationship between individual companies and creditors, such as that offered by some internet platforms, is in many cases a pure advertising ploy.

The stories presented are of individual cases that may well be touching, but they do not mean that it is really possible or sensible to invest in an individual company. So far the transaction costs are simply too high. With the success of crowd-funding platforms this may however change. Most platforms are based on price differentiation for prepaying consumers. Only very few of them offer real investments. One exception to this is the German platform seedmatch.de. The international extension of such concepts mainly fails due to differences in regulations, which are generally very restrictive so as to protect the respective banking cartels. Digital currencies could offer new opportunities in this respect.

In the best case, micro-loans are commensurate with the "Austrian" ideal: real savings flow into entrepreneurial projects with full responsibility for losses. As a result of the instability on account of currency debasement, civil wars and political madness subsidized by development aid, it is nigh impossible to accumulate savings in many parts of the world. International investments are often the only way to bring about the unfolding of people's entrepreneurial and creative potential through capital accumulation. The smaller the role played by ideology, "development aid", politics and banks, the greater an investment alternative micro-loans are likely to offer.

Conclusion

What do investors expect from economic theory? Firstly, clear statements about where things will go from here; secondly, clear recommendations on how one can do things better on one's own, in order to accumulate wealth and protect it. There are countless forecasts, and an even larger number of more or less clear words. We have attempted to adjust expectations a little bit. The Austrian School of Economics occupies a sober, realistic and modest position between the two remaining economic currents of modern times: the bastard of neo-classical economics, Keynesianism and Monetarism ("orthodox") and the bastard of Historicism and Marxism ("heterodox").

The former tradition regards the government-directed market as efficient, which leaves investors with nothing to do but to trust bankers and politicians: the future is already priced in, the economy is controllable and predictable. The latter tradition hopes for the end of the "system" and forecasts a historically predetermined systemic change and ultimately denies that economic laws exist. All that is allegedly needed is the primacy of the "correct politics". The Austrian School by contrast regards the future as uncertain, but not as arbitrary. Theory helps us recognize patterns and take responsibility based on these patterns, in the process shaping the future.

Due to the open nature of the future, we cannot deliver unambiguous forecasts. Anyone who is absolutely certain what is going to happen tomorrow is either a fool or a scammer. What we can do, however, is share our personal assessment. This is not the result of calculations based on a model, the secret formula of which is hidden away somewhere by economists, but a subjective consideration of the currently visible patterns, which economic theory allows us to recognize and interpret.

Conclusion

We have already indicated our assessment above: stagflation in the short term, on the thin line between hyperinflation and hyper-deflation, which is increasingly accompanied by financial repression; in the medium term, attempts at global coordination under a new leading currency, which should go hand in hand with global conflicts; in the long term, a massive correction of the economic structure, after which more sustainable development should once again become possible.

On a global scale it is of course quite possible for one thing to happen concurrently with another, the different scenarios are likely to overlap. The current "reflation" period has definitely nothing to do with a genuine recovery. Debt problems cannot be solved in the long term with additional debt, the fallout of bubbles cannot be fixed by creating new bubbles. An important reason for past and present problems is the command economy-like debt system, which almost no-one questions anymore today. Without a deeper understanding of the monetary system it is however impossible to understand current trends – which is why we have focused so much on monetary theory.

The paragraphs above perhaps appear couched in too general terms to be acceptable as a "forecast". If a disappointed reader chooses to lend an ear to more hip prophets and "experts", armed with reams of numbers, we cannot keep him from doing so. However, our assessment is surely concrete enough to use it as the basis of an investment strategy. The future is uncertain, but we are not powerless because of this – on the contrary!

Theory helps us to venture into practice, to learn from mistakes, to venture out again, perhaps to fail again, to move step by step ahead into the darkness of the future. Some may just stand still, or blindly follow what others are doing, what news presenters are recommending and what politicians are promising. Others may run just as blindly in one direction until they bump into a wall. No theory can give one more than a little courage, a little wisdom and caution, a little feeling for the proper balance of things – but that would already be quite a lot, since these are all considered cardinal virtues.

Conclusion

If we do not offer a precise forecast on the basis of which one can march off into the next betting shop, what does the concrete advice consist of? Those who have read this book carefully will have found abundant advice in it. However, even the best advice is no substitute for human action and cannot overcome the contradictions that are given by the differences between people and their framework conditions. Even if we had listed in detail what to buy at what price and when, who could then still advise the reader to actually believe it?

We have attempted to combine general advice with concrete examples of investment possibilities and strategies. Even a specific portfolio was presented, however, like any decision it is dependent on context. Investing in the permanent portfolio has been one of the best strategies over the past fifty years under the condition of an unknowable future. It participates in the bubble economy without fully surrendering to it. Things could of course be different in the next fifty years. It is always easy to present great strategies in retrospect. Thus making clear that the unknowable future is a precondition is good and realistic advice from the outset. However, we are not completely blind with respect to the future when all is said and done. As Hans-Hermann Hoppe put it:

> Thus, while economic forecasting will indeed always be a systematically unteachable art, it is at the same time true that all economic forecasts must be thought of as being constrained by the existence of a priori knowledge about actions as such. [...] someone who based his predictions on correct praxeological reasoning would necessarily have to be a better predictor of future economic events than someone who arrived at his predictions through logically flawed deliberations and chains of reasoning. It means that in the long run, the praxeologically enlightened forecaster would average better than the unenlightened ones.[...] To understand the logic of economic forecasting and the practical function of praxeological reasoning, then, is to view the a priori theorems of economics as acting as logical constraints on empirical predictions and as imposing logical limits on what can or cannot happen in the future.[156]

Conclusion

The theory of the Austrian School helps us to recognize long-term patterns. We can reject numerous portfolios and investment strategies on the basis of economic theory, such as for instance the "extremely conservative" portfolio that is highly vulnerable to a bursting of the bubble in bonds. The task of the Austrian School is to point us to additional options – especially those that are not immediately discerned nowadays. The further away the future and the more it differs from the present, the more important theory becomes; concrete factors and current practice diminish in value, while the value of general reflection increases. For this reason, we have apart from more concrete proposals also outlined a "philosophical portfolio", i.e., the most general advice on structure and strategy, which is as independent as possible of definite events.

We have attempted a difficult balancing act in this book: to present theory that will still be able to provide suggestions 50 years hence, but to consider practical contemporary aspects as well. Ultimately, these are two different pairs of shoes, accordingly the breaks in this book are at times sharp. The difference in these approaches is akin to the difference between speculator and economist, two callings that are both legitimate, but also have their own weaknesses. In this, we were neither able to focus solely on economic theory in its full historical breadth, which fills thick tomes with abstract sophistries, nor solely on the concrete speculative activity of modern times, which in its panic over devaluation is rushing to ever new buzz words, hypes and asset classes.

The speculator often pays for his good sense of timing by being shaped too strongly by the spirit of the times, while the economist can easily let time pass him by, ensconced in his ivory tower. The Austrian School therefore emphasizes the importance of the one actor who is able to combine theory and practice: the visionary entrepreneur. It is also this entrepreneur's "fault" that the future is neither certain nor destined to be negative. Capable entrepreneurs similar to capable theoreticians are often ahead of their time, they see the world as it should be, not only as it appears to be at the moment, and are taking cautious risks on the basis of critical reflection.

Conclusion

Studying the Austrian School is not a precondition for successful entrepreneurship, and not for investment acumen either. In its full depth as a theoretical tradition, it is only interesting to theoreticians – those who imagine and shape the world beyond tomorrow. For practical entrepreneurs, those who create the world of tomorrow, this tradition can provide a valuable way of setting things straight, and a necessary deliverance from deception. Not because it is "Austrian", but because economical thought has survived under this label throughout the turmoil of history, thought that has withstood the madness of the 20th century.

Mistakes have been and are committed in the tradition of the Austrian School as well. It is not even a uniform and closed tradition. The old Viennese economists and their successors have no secret knowledge, their methods are not the only correct ones and reading them will not straighten out all of today's problems overnight. Nevertheless, the best advice one can give someone today who is concerned about his savings is: take your eyes off the news ticker and direct them toward the books of this "Austrian" tradition – even if that is likely to initially increase your worries.

Our book is meant as an immunization against the comfortable heedlessness of our age, without simply slipping into impotent whining. In this, we had to answer one question: what can the Austrian School of Economics contribute toward improving the understanding of current economic events and to making better investment decisions? Perhaps the answer is disappointing: this little! In all modesty, we would however once again warn against those traditions, recipes, gurus and products, which promise more than this little bit. Ultimately, this is precisely the appeal of economics, which makes Austrian economics so suspenseful as well: the economy is as diverse, surprising, unforeseeable, full of doubts and contradictory as all human action.

In the best sense, economic theory is an invitation to reflect on our actions – this is to say, properly understood a part of philosophy. Ethics is reflection on our individual habits and principles, politics reflection on human community and conflict. Economics, as the third part of practical philosophy, is reflection on the structure of our households and companies. Since most human beings can only improve their own quality of life to a sufficiently high level by the indirect path of creating value for others, and can only recognize, develop and unfold their potential in exchanges with others, we are dependent on economics – in light of global interrelations, also on macroeconomics. This makes it necessary to look at the economy not only from an ethical or political perspective – i.e., not as we would like it to be - but from a realistic one, this is to say, in relation to the subject itself. In the limited scope of this book, we have presented general ordering principles and patterns, and explained and interpreted concrete events, opportunities and dangers.

If the reader now looks at day-to-day events from a slightly different perspective, gains a new thought, at some point notices something he would otherwise have overlooked, faces the uncertain future in a slightly more sober, steadfast and responsible manner, then we have already achieved a great deal.

Endnotes

1. Friedrich August von Hayek: Prices and Production. 2nd ed. New York: Augustus M. Kelley, 1967 (1935), p.2.
2. Mark Spitznagel: The Dao of Capital: Austrian Investing in a Distorted World. Hoboken, NJ: John Wiley & Sons, 2013.
3. Willem Buiter: "The unfortunate uselessness of most 'state of the art' academic monetary economics". In: Financial Times, 03/03/2009.
4. Ryan Grim: "Priceless: How the Federal Reserve Bought Off the Economics Profession". The Huffington Post. 10/23/2009. http://www.huffingtonpost.com/2009/09/07/priceless-how-the-federal_n_278805.html
5. https://en.wikipedia.org/wiki/Marginal_utility
6. Murray N. Rothbard: Man, Economy, and State with Power and Market. 2nd ed. Auburn, AL: Ludwig von Mises Institute, 2009 (1962/1970), pp. 73–74.
7. Paul Vreymans: "The Monetary Stimulus Myth – An Evidence-based Analysis. Can our Monetary System survive another Shock?" Workforall.net, 2012.
8. Erich Fromm: To Have or to Be? New York: Continuum, 2005 (1976), p. 8.
9. Antal Fekete: Monetary Economics 102: Gold and Interest. 2003.
10. Friedrich August von Hayek: Denationalisation of Money – The Argument Refined. 3rd ed. London: The Institute of Economic Affairs, 1990 (1976), p. 56.
11. Wilhelm Röpke: The Social Crisis of Our Time. Chicago: University of Chicago Press, 1950 (1942), p. 10.
12. Ludwig von Mises: Human Action – A Treatise on Economics. Auburn, Alabama: Ludwig von Mises Institute, 1998, p. 141.
13. Andrew Dickson White: Fiat Money Inflation in France. New York: The Foundation For Economic Education, 1959, pp. 108–109.
14. Friedrich August von Hayek: The Counter-Revolution of Science: Studies on the Abuse of Reason. London: The Free Press, 1955, p. 165.
15. Ludwig von Mises: Bureaucracy. New Haven: Yale University Press,

1944, pp. 91–92.

16 Stefan Zweig: The World of Yesterday – An Autobiography. Lincoln/London: University of Nebraska Press, 1964 (1943), pp. 1–2.

17 Jim Rogers: Street Smarts: Adventures on the Road and in the Markets. New York: Crown Business, 2013, p. 70.

18 Rosenzweig, Philip: The Halo Effect: ...and the Eight Other Business Delusions That Deceive Managers. New York: Free Press, 2007, pp. 107–112.

19 Own translation of original German quote from: Felix Somary: Erinnerungen eines politischen Meteorologen. München: Matthes & Seitz, 1994 (1955), p. 90.

20 Walter Meier: "In der besten aller Welten". Neue Zürcher Zeitung, no. 38, 02/15/2007, p. 16.

21 Ludwig von Mises: Memoirs. Auburn, Alabama: Ludwig von Mises Institute, [1978] 2009.

22 Own translation of original German quote from: Felix Somary: Erinnerungen eines politischen Meteorolgen. München: Matthes & Seitz, 1994 (1955), p. 15.

23 Own translation of original German quote from: Ibid., p. 238.

24 Own translation of original German quote from: Ibid., p. 239.

25 Wilhelm Röpke: Die Schweiz und die Integration des Westens. Zürich: Schweizer Spiegel, 1965.

26 http://www.forbes.com/sites/rickferri/2013/01/10/ts-official-gurus-cant-accurately-predict-markets/

27 Margit von Mises: My years with Ludwig von Mises. New Rochelle, NY: Arlington House, 1976, p. 31.

28 http://blogs.reuters.com/rolfe-winkler/2009/08/04/buffetts-betrayal/

29 Friedrich August von Hayek: "›On Being An Economist‹. Address to the Student's Union of the London School of Economics, February 23, 1944". In: The Trend of Economic Thinking: Essays on Political Economists and Economic History. Indianapolis: Liberty Fund, 2009.

30 Michael T. Kaufman: Soros: The Life and Times of a Messianic Billionaire. New York: Alfred A. Knopf, 2002, p. 140.

31 Own translation of original German quote from: Felix Somary: Erinnerungen eines politischen Meteorologen. München: Matthes & Seitz, [1955] 1994, p. 9.

32 Own translation of original German quote from: Ibid., p. 10.
33 Friedrich August von Hayek: The Counter-Revolution of Science: Studies on the Abuse of Reason. London: The Free Press, 1955, p. 84.
34 Mark Spitznagel: The Dao of Capital: Austrian Investing in a Distorted World. New Jersey: Wiley, 2013, p. 11.
35 Jim Rogers: Street Smarts: Adventures on the Road and in the Markets. New York: Crown Business, 2013, p. 46.
36 Nassim Nicholas Taleb: Fooled by Randomness. The Hidden Role of Chance in Life and in the Markets. New York: Random House, 2001.
37 David Hume: Treatise on Human Nature. David Fate Norton, Mary J. Norton (Pub.). Oxford: Oxford University Press, [1739] 2000.
38 Mark Spitznagel: The Dao of Capital: Austrian Investing in a Distorted World. Hoboken, NJ: John Wiley & Sons, 2013, p. 345.
39 James Grant – The Austrian Economics Newsletter, 1996, http://www.valueinvestingworld.com/2009/06/austrian-economics-newsletters-1996.html.
40 Carl Menger: Investigations into the Method of the Social Sciences with Special Reference to Economics. New York/London: New York University Press, 1985, p. 146.
41 Ibid., p.154.
42 Carl Menger: Principles of Economics. Auburn, Alabama: Ludwig von Mises Institute, 2007, pp. 261–262.
43 Friedrich von Wieser: Natural Value. London: Macmillan, 1893, p. 47.
44 Ludwig von Mises: The Theory of Money and Credit. New Haven: Yale University Press, 1953, pp. 109–110.
45 William Stanley Jevons: Money and the Mechanism of Exchange. New York: D. Appleton and Co., 1876, ch. 5.
46 Carl Menger: Principles of Economics. Auburn, Alabama: Ludwig von Mises Institute, 2007, p. 241.
47 Carl Menger: "Geld". Handwörterbuch der Staatswissenschaften.3rd ed., Jena 1909 (1892), vol. 4, p. 55.
48 Ibid., p.56.
49 Xenophon: On Revenues. Project Gutenberg, http://www.gutenberg.org/files/1179/1179-h/1179-h.htm.
50 William Stanley Jevons: Money and the Mechanism of Exchange. New York: D. Appleton and Co., 1876.

Endnotes

51 Antal Fekete: "Whither Gold?" Memorial University of Newfoundland, St. John's, Canada 1996.
52 Ludwig von Mises: The Theory of Money and Credit. New Haven: Yale University Press, 1953, p. 61.
53 Ibid., pp. 91–92.
54 Georg Holzbauer: Barzahlung und Zahlungsmittelversorgung in militärisch besetzten Gebieten. Jena: Fischer, 1939, pp. 85–87.
55 Carl Menger: Principles of Economics. Auburn, Alabama: Ludwig von Mises Institute, 2007, pp. 282–283.
56 Ludwig von Mises: Human Action. A Treatise on Economics. Auburn, Alabama: Ludwig von Mises Institute, 1998, p. 395.
57 http://goldsilverworlds.com/gold-silver-insights/research-shows-all-paper-money-systems-failed/
58 http://www.incrementum.li/en/austrian-school-of-economics/august-1971-the-beginning-of-a-global-fiat-monetary-regime/#footnotes
59 Murray N. Rothbard: "Austrian Definitions of the Supply of Money". In: New Directions in Austrian Economics. Louis M. Spadaro (Pub.). Kansas City: Sheed Andrews and McMeel, 1978, pp. 143–156.
60 Der große Herder. Freiburg/Br.: Herder Verlagsbuchhandlung, 1933, Bd. 6, p. 522.
61 Jörg Guido Hülsmann: The Ethics of Money Production. Auburn, Alabama: Ludwig von Mises Institute, 2008, pp. 65–66.
62 Alan S. Blinder: "The Fed Plan to Revive High-Powered Money". In: Wall Street Journal, 12/10/2013.
63 Ludwig von Mises: Liberalism – In the Classical Tradition. New York: Foundation for Economic Education, 1985, p. 8.
64 Roger W. Garrison: Time and Money – The Macroeconomics of Capital Structure. London/New York: Routledge, 2001.
65 Ludwig M. Lachmann: Capital and Its Structure. Kansas City: Sheed Andrews and McMeel, 1978 (1956), p. 12.
66 Knut Wicksell: Interest and Prices. New York: Sentra Press, 1898, p. 102.
67 Friedrich A. von Hayek: Prices and Production. New York: Augustus M. Kelly, 1931.
68 Ludwig von Mises: Human Action – A Treatise on Economics. Auburn, Alabama: Ludwig von Mises Institute, 1998, p. 550.

69 Ludwig von Mises: Human Action – A Treatise on Economics. Auburn, Alabama: Ludwig von Mises Institute, 1998, p. 557.
70 Roland Baader: "Ozeane aus Scheingeld". In: Smart Investor, Nr. 8/2010, pp. 26–29.
71 Jesús Huerta de Soto: "Rezessionen, Reformen der Finanzindustrie und die Zukunft des Kapitalismus". Liberales Institut, Dezember 2010.
72 Friedrich A. von Hayek: "Preface to the German Edition ›Geldtheorie und Konjunkturtheorie‹ (1929)". In: The Collected Works of F. A. Hayek. Chicago: The University of Chicago Press, 2012, p. 55.
73 Murray N. Rothbard: America's Great Depression. Auburn. 2000, p. 13.
74 Ludwig von Mises: Human Action – A Treatise on Economics. Auburn, Alabama: Ludwig von Mises Institute, 1998, p. 570.
75 Robert E. Lucas: "Monetary Neutrality". In: Journal of Political Economy, vol. 104, no. 4, 1995.
76 John Maynard Keynes: The Economic Consequences of the Peace. 1919, ch. 6, p. 235.
77 Andrew Lawrence: "The Skyscraper Index: Faulty Towers". Property Report. Dresdner Kleinwort Wasserstein Research, 1/15/1999.
78 Mark Thornton: "Skyscrapers and Business Cycles". In: The Quarterly Journal of Austrian Economics, vol. 8, no. 1, 2005, pp. 51–74.
79 Ibid.
80 "Hybris lässt grüßen". In: Institutional Money Online, 1/2010.
81 "Abu Dhabi stützt Dubai in letzter Minute". In: Frankfurter Allgemeine Zeitung, 14/12/2009.
82 Inocencio, Rami. 2013. "Could world's tallest building bring China to its knees?", CNN, 08/06/2013, accessed 04/15/2015, http://edition.cnn.com/2013/08/05/business/china-sky-city-skyscraper-index/
83 Ludwig von Mises: "Die Goldwährung und ihre Gegner". Part 1. In: Neue Freie Presse, 12/25/1931.
84 Felix Somary: Erinnerungen eines politischen Meteorologen. München: Matthes & Seitz, 1994 (1955), p. 145.
85 Nicolaus Copernicus: Monete cudende ratio – Essay on the Coinage of Money, 1526.
86 Peter Bernholz: Monetary Regimes and Inflation. History, Economic and Political Relationships. Aldershot: Edward Elgar, 2006.
87 Antal Fekete: "Monetary Economics 101: The Real Bills Doctrine of

Endnotes

       Adam Smith. Lecture 10: The Revolt of Quality", Memorial University of Newfoundland, St. John's, Canada 2002.
88   International Monetary Fund: Fiscal Monitor. Taxing Times. October 2013, p. 49.
89   Deutsche Bundesbank: Monthly report. January 2014.
90   Radio interview with Daniel Selter (BCG), interviewer: André Hatting. Deutschlandradio Kultur, 04.20.2013.
91   Interview article with Jean-Claude Juncker. In: Der Spiegel, 52/1999, 12/27/1999. p. 136.
92   Jim Rickards: Interview with Peak Prosperity, 09/21/2013.
93   See China Daily: "China eyes SDR as global currency", March 2009.
94   See The Telegraph: "Russia backs return to Gold Standard to solve financial crisis", March 2009.
95   Carl Menger, Erich W. Streissler (pub.) und Monika Streissler (transl.): Carl Menger's Lectures to Crown Prince Rudolf of Austria. Aldershot: Edward Elgar, 1994, p. 104.
96   Giovanni Boccaccio: Decameron. Prima giornata (la peste a Firenze).
97   Matteo Villani: Cronica di Matteo Villani, vol. 1, ch. 4.
98   Roland Baader: Money-Socialism – The Real Cause of the New Global Depression. Bern: Johannes Müller, 2010, p. 36.
99   Stefan Zweig: The World of Yesterday – An Autobiography. Lincoln/London: University of Nebraska Press, 1964 (1943), p. 301.
100   Walter Bagehot: Lombard Street. A Description of the Money Market. 1873, p. 47.
101   Alastair Crooke: Resistance – The Essence of the Islamist Revolution. London: Pluto Press, 2009, p. 127.
102   Carl Menger: Principles of Economics. Auburn, Alabama: Ludwig von Mises Institute, 2007, p. 242.
103   Antal Fekete: "Monetary Economics 102: Gold and Interest", 2003.
104   Roland Baader: Gold: Letzte Rettung oder Katastrophe? Ebmatingen/Zürich: Fortuna Finanz-Verlag, 1988, p. 212.
105   http://www.theregister.co.uk/2013/01/16/developer_oursources_job_china/
106   B. und W. Bonner: Family Fortunes – How to Build Family Wealth and Hold on to It for 100 Years. Hoboken, NJ: John Wiley & Sons, p. 96.
107   Thorstein Veblen: The Theory of the Leisure Class. Oxford: Oxford

University Press, 2007 (1899), p. 59.
108 Alexander von Schönburg: Die Kunst des stilvollen Verarmens. Wie man ohne Geld reich wird. Reinbek: Rowohlt Taschenbuchverlag, 2007, p. 172.
109 Erich Fromm: To Have or to Be? New York: Continuum, 2005 (1976), p. 95.
110 Victor Mataja: Die Reklame. Eine Untersuchung über Ankündigungswesen und Werbetätigkeit im Geschäftsleben. München/Leipzig: Duncker & Humblot, 1916, p. 12.
111 Ludwig von Mises: Socialism – An Economic and Sociological Analysis. New Haven: Yale University Press, 1951, p. 446.
112 Frank A. Fetter: The Principles of Economics. 3rd ed., New York, 1913, p. 394.
113 Etienne de la Boétie: The Politics of Obedience – The Discourse of Voluntary Servitude. Auburn, Alabama: The Mises Institute, 1975 (1548), pp. 48, 71–72.
114 William L. Anderson: "New Economy, Old Delusion". In: The Free Market. The Mises Institute Monthly, Vol. 18, 08.01.2000.
115 Mark Thornton: "Housing: Too Good to Be True". In: Mises Daily, 06.04.2004.
116 John Stuart Mill: "An Article read before the Manchester Statistical Society in December 11, 1867, on Credit Cycles and the Origin of Commercial Panics". In: Financial crises and periods of industrial and commercial depression, T. E. Burton (pub.). New York-London: D. Appleton & Co., 1931 (1902).
117 Harry Browne: Fail-Safe Investing. Lifelong Financial Security in 30 Minutes. New York: St. Martin's Griffin, 2001. In this context, the book of Craig Rowland and J.M. Lawson (The Permanent Portfolio: Harry Browne's Long-Term Investment Strategy. Hoboken, NJ: John Wiley & Sons, 2012) can be recommended. The authors focus on innovations which are relevant for the concept of the Permanent Portfolio (e.g. ETFs as economical building blocks).
118 Antony Sutton: The War On Gold. How To Profit From the Gold Crisis. Self-Counsel Press, 1979, ch. 4.
119 Ronald Stöferle, Mark J. Valek: In Gold we Trust, Report 2013.
120 Richard Michaud, Robert Michaud, and Katharine Pulvermacher: Gold

as a Strategic Asset. London: World Gold Council, 2006.
121 Barton, Philipp [Forthcoming]. The Dawn of Gold.
122 Israel M. Kirzner: The Driving Force of the Market. Essays in Austrian economics. London: Routledge, 2000.
123 Chris Leithner: "Ludwig von Mises, Meet Benjamin Graham: Value Investing from an Austrian Point of View", Paper prepared for "Austrian Economics and Financial Markets", Las Vegas, 2005.
124 Benjamin Graham: Security Analysis: The Classic 1940 Edition. McGraw-Hill Professional Publishing, 2002, ch. 50 and 51; Graham: The Intelligent Investor, 1949/2003.
125 Thomas Braun, Georg von Wyss: "Geduld ist das Rezept der Value-Investoren". In: INVEST "Portfolio 2000" der "Finanz und Wirtschaft", 12/11/1999.
126 Linda Grant: "Striking Out at Wall Street". In: U. S. News & World Report, 06/20/1994, p. 58; Janet Lowe. Warren Buffet Speaks: Wit and Wisdom from the World's Greatest Investor. New Jersey: Wiley, 2007, p. 149.
127 Especially the American Federal Reserve System should be named here, which has expanded its balance from USD 820 bn in 2008 to USD 3.600 bn in 2013.
128 See for example: Massimo Guidolin; Elizabeth A. La Jeunesse: "The decline in the U. S. personal saving rate: is it real and is it a puzzle?" Federal Reserve Bank of St. Louis, Issue nov. 2007.
129 Philipp Sieger, Thomas Zellweger: "Entrepreneurial Families. Vom Familienunternehmen zur Unternehmerfamilie. Generationenübergreifende Wertgenerierung in Unternehmerfamilien". Center for Family Business, University of St. Gallen, March 2013.
130 Christoph Kaserer, Benjamin Moldenhauer: "Insider ownership and corporate performance: evidence from Germany". In: Review of Managerial Science, 2/1, March 2008, pp. 1–35.
131 Ronald C. Anderson, David M. Reeb: "Founding-Family Ownership and Firm Performance: Evidence from the S&P 500". In: The Journal of Finance, 58/3, June 2003, pp. 1301–1327.
132 Belen Villalonga, Raphael Amit: "How do family ownership, control and management affect firm value?« In: Journal of Financial Economics, 80 (2006), pp. 385–417.

133 James Tobin: "A General Equilibrium Approach To Monetary Theory". In: Journal of Money, Credit and Banking, February 1969.
134 Mark Spitznagel: The Dao of Capital: Austrian Investing in a Distorted World. Hoboken, NJ: John Wiley & Sons, pp. 179.
135 Mark Spitznagel: "The Austrians and the Swan: Birds of a Different Feather". Universa Working White Paper, 2012.
136 Mark Spitznagel: "The Dao of Corporate Finance, Q Ratios, and Stock Market Crashes". Universa Working White Paper, 2011.
137 Paul Francis Cwik: An Investigation of Inverted Yield Curves and Economic Downturns. Dissertation, Auburn: Auburn University, 2004, p. 157.
138 Gary North: The Yield Curve. The Best Recession Forecasting Tool, http://www.garynorth.com/public/department81.cfm
139 See Mark Thornton: "The Dao of the Austrian Investor". Ludwig von Mises Institute, 12/20/2013.
140 Thomas Aubrey: Profiting from Monetary Policy: Investing Through the Business Cycle. Basingstoke: Palgrave Macmillan, 2013.
141 Ansgar Belke: A More Effective Euro Area Monetary Policy than OMTs – Gold-Backed Sovereign Debt, 2012.
142 Antal Fekete: "Cut the Gordian Knot: Resurrect the Latin Monetary Union", 2011.
143 Antal Fekete: "Whither Gold?" Memorial University of Newfoundland, St. John's, Canada 1996.
144 "Net sales of long-term UCITS jumped to EUR 31 billion in December and reached EUR 320 billion in 2013". Pressemitteilung European Fund and Asset Management Association, 02/13/2014.
145 Jim Rogers: Street Smarts. Adventures on the Road and in the Markets. New York: Crown Business, 2013, pp. 184–185.
146 Hortense Bioy: "Und was ist mit physisch replizierenden ETFs?" In: Morningstar, 10/20/2011.
147 Max Wirth: Geschichte der Handelskrisen. Frankfurt/M.: J. D. Sauerländer, 1858, p. 320.
148 Mohammed Yunus: "Does the Capital System Have to Be the Handmaiden of the Rich?" Keynote address at the 85th Rotary International Convention in Taipei, June 12–15, 1994.
149 Thomas Fisher, M. S. Sriram, Malcolm Harper: Beyond micro-credit:

putting development back into micro-finance. New Delhi: Vistaar Publications, 2002.
150 David Hulme, Paul Mosley: Finance against poverty, vol. 1. London: Routledge, 1996. p. 206.
151 Ibid., p. 120.
152 M. Shahe Emran, A. K. M. Mahbub Morshed, Joseph E. Stiglitz: "Microfinance and Missing Markets". SSRN Working Paper, March 2007.
153 Hans Dieter Seibel: "Does History Matter? The Old and the New World of Microfinance in Europe and Asia". Working Paper, Development Research Center (University of Cologne), 2005.
154 Peter T. Bauer: From Subsistence to Exchange and Other Essays. Princeton, NJ: Princeton University Press, 2000. p. 6.
155 Thomas Dichter: "A Second Look at Microfinance. The Sequence of Growth and Credit in Economic History." Development Policy Briefing Paper. Washington DC: Cato Institute, 02/15/2007.
156 Hans-Hermann Hoppe: Economic Science and the Austrian Method. Auburn, Alabama: Ludwig von Mises Institute, 1995, pp. 44–48.

Authors

RAHIM TAGHIZADEGAN is an economic philosopher and founder and director of the learning enterprise *scholarium* (scholarium.at) in Vienna, Austria. He taught at the *University of Liechtenstein*, *Vienna University of Economics* and the *University of Halle* and currently holds teaching positions at the *International Academy for Philosophy* (Liechtenstein) and the *IMC University* (Krems).

RONALD STÖFERLE is managing partner at *Incrementum AG*. In 2006, he joined Vienna-based *Erste Group Bank*, covering International Equities and began writing reports on gold. His six benchmark reports called 'In GOLD we TRUST' drew international coverage on *CNBC, Bloomberg, the Wall Street Journal* and the *Financial Times*. He was awarded 2nd most accurate gold analyst by *Bloomberg* in 2011. Ronald managed two gold-mining baskets as well as one silver-mining basket for *Erste Group*, which outperformed their benchmarks from their inception.

MARK VALEK is partner and investment manager at *Incrementum AG*. In 2002, Mark joined *Raiffeisen Capital Management*. He was ultimately part of the multi-asset strategies team, with total assets under management of more than EUR 5 bn. His responsibilities included fund selection of alternative investments and as well as inflation protection strategies. In this role, he was fund manager of an Inflation Protection Fund as well as fund manager of various alternative investment funds of funds.

HEINZ BLASNIK is an independent trader and market analyst for the consulting firm *Hedgefund Consultants Ltd*, as well as a consultant to *Seasonax*, a financial app developer. He also writes on Austrian economic theory for the *Independent Research House Asianomics* in Hong Kong on a regular basis. Heinz is the publisher of the blog *www.acting-man.com*, which offers analyses on financial markets, the economy and economic history from an Austrian perspective.